Bloom's Modern Critical Views

Bloom's Modern Critical Views

AMERICAN WOMEN POETS
New Edition

Edited and with an introduction by
Harold Bloom
Sterling Professor of the Humanities
Yale University

BLOOM'S
LITERARY CRITICISM
An Infobase Learning Company

Bloom's Modern Critical Views: American Women Poets—New Edition
Copyright © 2011 by Infobase Learning
Introduction © 2011 by Harold Bloom

Bloom's Literary Criticism
An imprint of Infobase Learning
132 West 31st Street
New York NY 10001

Library of Congress Cataloging-in-Publication Data
  American women poets / edited and with an introduction by Harold Bloom.
— New ed.
    p. cm. — (Bloom's modern critical views)
  Includes bibliographical references and index.
  ISBN 978-1-60413-991-4
  1. American poetry—Women authors—History and criticism. 2. Women and literature—United States—History—20th century. 3. American poetry—20th century—History and criticism. 4. Women in literature.   I. Bloom, Harold.
  PS151.A44 2011
  811.009'9287—dc23
                                    2011025761

Bloom's Literary Criticism books are available at special discounts when purchased in bulk quantities for businesses, associations, institutions, or sales promotions. Please call our Special Sales Department in New York at (212) 967-8800 or (800) 322-8755.

You can find Bloom's Literary Criticism on the World Wide Web at
http://www.infobaselearning.com

Contributing editor: Pamela Loos
Cover designed by Alicia Post
Composition by IBT Global, Troy NY
Cover printed by Yurchak Printing, Landisville PA
Book printed and bound by Yurchak Printing, Landisville PA
Date printed: March 2011
Printed in the United States of America

10 9 8 7 6 5 4 3 2 1

Contents

Editor's Note

My introduction cites some of the defining women poets leading up to our current time, and I rely on the authors assembled here to fill in and extend that legacy. Henry Taylor astutely walks us through the world of Gwendolyn Brooks's poetry, followed by Brian Dillon's appraisal of one of Sharon Olds's central preoccupations, the father-daughter relationship.

Helen Vendler richly explores Rita Dove's rethinking of the lyric poem in relation to American black history. Jeanne Perreault then sheds some light on a trio of Native American poets.

The poet James Longenbach discusses Louise Glück's welding form of and experience in a search for lyrical transformation, after which Virginia C. Fowler embraces the contrarieties in Nikki Giovanni's work.

Zofia Burr visits Maya Angelou on the inaugural stage, followed by Hilary Holladay's extensive elucidation of the late Lucille Clifton's southern-infused poems.

Gale Swiontkowski revisits the incest fantasies haunting the work of Sylvia Plath and Anne Sexton, followed by Rose Lucas's assessment of Mary Oliver's immeasurable poetics. The volume concludes with Jane Hedley's interrogation of the confessionalist tensions informing the writings of Adrienne Rich.

Introduction

A tradition of poets that includes Emily Dickinson, Marianne Moore, and Elizabeth Bishop has a palpable distinction, but it may be too soon to speak or write of a canon of "American women poets." The poets studied in this volume are not chosen arbitrarily, yet consideration of the book's length as well as the poets' canonical probability have entered into my selection. But the poets studied here do seem a central grouping, and the canonical process is always an ongoing one anyway. Future editions of this volume may be relied on to correct emphases and clarify choices.

Two distinguished critics of literature by women, Sandra M. Gilbert and Susan Gubar, have taught us to speak of "the tradition in English," yet with characteristic fairness they quote the great poet Elizabeth Bishop's denial of such a tradition:

> Undoubtedly gender does play an important part in the making of any art, but art is art, and to separate writings, paintings, musical compositions, etc., into two sexes is to emphasize values in them that are *not* art.

Bishop, a subtle intellect, makes clear that gender is a source of *values* in the genesis of art but asserts that such values are not in themselves aesthetic. Though my inclination is to agree with her, I am wary of arguing against the tendency of origins to turn into ends or aims in the genealogy of imagination. Since I myself am frequently misunderstood on this point by feminist critics (though never, I am happy to say, by Gilbert and Gubar), I have a certain desire to illuminate the matter. Most Western poetry has been what Gertrude

Stein called "patriarchal poetry," and most Western criticism necessarily has been patriarchal also. If Dr. Samuel Johnson, William Hazlitt, Ralph Waldo Emerson, and Dr. Sigmund Freud are to be considered patriarchal, then I as their ephebe presumably must be patriarchal also. So be it. But such a coloring or troping of critical stance is descriptive rather than prescriptive. Most strong Western poets, for whatever reasons, have been male: Homer and the Yahwist, presumably, and certainly Virgil, Lucretius, Horace, on through Dante, Petrarch, and Chaucer to Shakespeare, Spenser, Milton, Pope, Wordsworth, Goethe, Shelley, Leopardi, Hugo, Whitman, Baudelaire, Browning, Yeats, Rilke, Stevens, and so many more. To this day, the only woman poet in English of that stature is Dickinson. Not every poet studied in this volume seems to me of proven achievement; I have grave reservations about Plath and one or two others. However, there are values also, in nearly all the others, that seem to me rather different from the qualities of their strongest male contemporaries, and some of those differences do ensue from a vision, an experiential and rhetorical stance, that has its origin in sexual difference. To locate the differences in stance seems to me the admirable enterprise of the best feminist literary criticism. That polemic and ideology should be so overt in much feminist literary criticism is understandable, and unfortunately aesthetic considerations sometimes are submerged in political and programmatic designs, but nothing is got for nothing, and I foresee that the emphases of feminist criticism will be modified by the success of that criticism. Though I attempt to isolate differences in vision from male precursors in regarding the poets included in this volume, I am aware that I am a patriarchal critic, and I cannot attempt to mask my own sense of the dilemmas confronted by women poets and poetry.

HENRY TAYLOR

Gwendolyn Brooks: An Essential Sanity

Gwendolyn Brooks's emergence as an important poet has been less sche-
matic, but not less impressive, than commentary upon it has suggested. It is
difficult to isolate the poems themselves from the variety of reactions to them;
these have been governed as much by prevailing or individual attitudes toward
issues of race, class, and gender, as by serious attempts at dispassionate examination and evaluation. Furthermore, Brooks's activities in behalf of younger
writers have demonstrated her generosity and largeness of spirit, and wide
recognition of these qualities has led some critics away from the controlled
but genuine anger in many of the poems. Brooks has contributed to this process; in interviews, and in her autobiographical *Report from Part One* (1972),
she speaks engagingly and with apparent authority about her own work, and
many of her judgments have become part of the majority view of her career.
Nevertheless, it is worthwhile to consider whether there might be more unity
in the body of her work than conventional divisions of her career suggest.

Brooks herself, as William H. Hansell has noted, indicated the divisions when, "in a 1976 interview at the University of Wisconsin–La Crosse,
[she] said that her work falls into three periods that correspond to 'changes'
in her perspective." Hansell's note: "Works of the first period are *A Street
in Bronzeville* (1945), *Annie Allen* (1949) and *The Bean Eaters* (1960). The
second period is represented by the "New Poems" section of *Selected Poems*

From *The Kenyon Review* 13, no. 4 (Fall 1991): 115–31. Copyright © 1991 by Henry Taylor.

(1963) and by two uncollected poems, 'The Sight of the Horizon' (1963) and 'In the Time of Detachment, in the Time of Cold' (1965). The third phase of her development is marked by her most recent collections: *In the Mecca* (1969) [1968], *Riot* (1969), *Family Pictures* (1970) and *Beckonings* (1975)."[1]

Whether a writer's development involves improvement is highly questionable, but writers often think they are improving, because they are usually more interested in work in progress than they are in work long since completed. Since the mid-1960s, Brooks has revealed these attitudes in numerous comments on her awakening to the situation of the Black writer in America. On the other hand, when she ended her association with Harper & Row, and began to place her work with Black publishers, she retained the rights in her early work, and reprinted the bulk of it in a collected volume entitled *Blacks*.[2] The stark inclusiveness of that one-word title suggests that Brooks perceives unity as well as variety in the range of her concerns and voices.

Report from Part One and, more recently, the late George Kent's *A Life of Gwendolyn Brooks*,[3] provide generous insight into the origins of Brooks's art. Her own work provides a livelier evocation of her early years than Kent manages in his first two chapters, but he has made a thorough examination of the young girl's notebooks, which she kept industriously. The child appears to have taken seriously her mother's prediction that she would grow up to be the "lady Paul Laurence Dunbar." Kent finds that she was a victim of an intraracial prejudice which put very dark girls at a social disadvantage among Black people of her age. (This theme recurs in Brooks's poetry through *In the Mecca*.) The energy which might have gone into a more active social life was instead poured into poems and stories which show promise more in their profusion than in their accomplishment.

Though she had been publishing poems in the *Chicago Defender* since her high school days, she was twenty-eight when *A Street in Bronzeville* (poems, 1945) appeared. Concerning what was "new" about it, Kent writes:

> The poet had rejected the exotic vein of the Harlem Renaissance—
> the celebration of unique racial values, such as defiance of social
> proscription through emphasis upon joy and soul. A few poems in
> *A Street* work close to this vein, allowing the reader the enjoyment
> of the old colorful images, but use one device or another to bring
> them to the court of critical intelligence. Thus "patent leather" and
> other poems devalue the "hipness" that the Harlem Renaissance
> would have celebrated.[4]

As have all American poets, Brooks inherited the old problem of language, which in the nineteenth century divided poets into rebels and

loyalists—those who knew that the central problem was to establish independence in the language of the colonizing country, and those who were
content with the poetic tradition of the colonizers. This dilemma is exponen-
tially more difficult for a Black woman; a term like "the lady Paul Laurence
Dunbar" hardly needs comment on the forms of oppression it implies and,
implicitly, accepts.

Still, Brooks had applied herself assiduously to the absorption of a largely
white male tradition, in the apparent belief that all great poetry in English
had something of value to teach her. *A Street in Bronzeville* introduced a poet
of more technical accomplishment than was usual even in the mid-1940s.
Forty-five years later, the variety of forms and tones in the collection remains
impressive; Donne, Robinson, Frost, Dickinson, and even Ogden Nash seem
to have left occasional marks, as well as Hughes and the blues.

But what strikes most forcibly now is the sophistication, and the Dickin-
sonian way in which sophistication sometimes becomes a shield, from behind
which almost invisible darts fly often and accurately. Throughout Brooks's
poetry, delicate satire regularly breaks through a surface which is pretending
in some way to be well-behaved.

In twelve lines, for example, "the vacant lot" provides a richly populated
scene, in tones modulating from apparent nostalgia and regret through sarcasm to controlled, satiric flatness:

> Mrs. Coley's three-flat brick
> Isn't here any more.
> All done with seeing her fat little form
> Burst out of the basement door;
> And with seeing her African son-in-law
> (Rightful heir to the throne)
> With his great white strong cold squares of teeth
> And his little eyes of stone;
> And with seeing the squat fat daughter
> Letting in the men
> When majesty has gone for the day—
> And letting them out again.
>   (41)

Throughout *A Street*, individual poems have lowercase titles when they
are grouped under a larger heading. Despite this consistency, however, the
device occasionally creates a local effect; here the suggested insignificance
of the lot is emphasized by an immediate and energetic portrayal of what
is not there. Among the departures is the mysterious African son-in-law,

who briefly dominates the poem, his teeth packing the seventh line with
stressed monosyllables, but whose "majesty," by the end of the poem, is cru-
elly diminished.

The gulf between imagined majesty and hard reality is a frequent
theme in *A Street*. Its most ambitious treatment is "The Sundays of Satin-
Legs Smith," a narrative of just over 150 lines in which satire is deepened by
compassion. The ironic contrasts begin with the title; the protagonist's name
yokes the exotic and the ordinary. The polysyllabic opening introduces a narrator whose self-consciously elegant language is mock-heroic:

> Inamoratas, with an approbation,
> Bestowed his title. Blessed his inclination.
>
> He wakes, unwinds, elaborately: a cat
> Tawny, reluctant, royal. He is fat
> And fine this morning. Definite. Reimbursed.
>   (42)

As Satin-Legs commences his morning ablutions, the speaker becomes
an ironically patient lecturer, addressing a "you" who is presumed innocent
of the life being unfolded here, and who may therefore be taken as white. In
the following excerpt, the sentence "Maybe so" ends a passage of fourteen
lines, concerning the appropriateness of Satin-Legs's choice of scents and
oils, which both recalls and quietly subverts the sonnet tradition:

> ... might his happiest
> Alternative (you muse) be, after all,
> A bit of gentle garden in the best
> Of taste and straight tradition? Maybe so.
> But you forget, or did you ever know,
> His heritage of cabbage and pigtails,
> Old intimacy with alleys, garbage pails,
> Down in the deep (but always beautiful) South
> Where roses blush their blithest (it is said)
> And sweet magnolias put Chanel to shame.
>   (42–43)

Satin-Legs has only an artificial flower, made of feathers, for his lapel; in
the first of two brief asides, the speaker says, "Ah, there is little hope." Satin-
Legs will have "his lotion, lavender, and oil."

Unless you care to set the world a-boil
And do a lot of equalizing things,
Remove a little ermine, say, from kings,
Shake hands with paupers and appoint them men. . . .
   (43)

But the speaker decisively returns to an inspection of "The innards of this closet." More strongly than "Maybe so" above, "innards" underscores the speaker's dualistic sense of language and class; if Satin-Legs is being satirized, so is the addressee, whose ignorance is more broadly satirized in such later poems as "I love those little booths at Benvenuti's," "The Lovers of the Poor," and "Bronzeville Woman in a Red Hat."

The closet contains the gaudy accoutrements of such a dandy as Satin-Legs is, or aspires to be; colors are "sarcastic," tailoring is "cocky," ties are "hysterical." Following this exposition of his tastes, two lines in a second brief aside hover between solemnity and humor:

People are so in need, in need of help.
People want so much that they do not know.
   (44)

True enough; but the idea is complicated by its placement, which suggests that Satin-Legs needs advice from a refined haberdasher. Creating himself "is all his sculpture and his art." However, after he enters the street, halfway through the poem, there is no further description of his appearance; instead, we see how things appear to him. Through the narrator, we experience his surroundings more vividly than he does. "He hears and does not hear" an alarm clock, children, a plane, voices, and the elevated train. "He sees and does not see" broken windows patched with newspaper, children in worn but decently patched clothes, and

                      men estranged
From music and from wonder and from joy
But far familiar with the guiding awe
Of foodlessness.
   (45)

The music he hears is popular blues; the narrator notes the absence of strains by Saint-Saëns, Grieg, Tschaikovsky, Brahms, and questions whether he could love them if they were audible; one brings to music what one is:

The pasts of his ancestors lean against
Him. Crowd him. Fog out his identity.
Hundreds of hungers mingle with his own. . . .
    (46)

From a movie, where he is reminded that "it is sin for his eye to eat of" the heroine's "ivory and yellow," he proceeds toward the goal of all his efforts. In a line that tumbles anticlimactically from faint echoes of the courtly tradition to a place where main courses are served on meat platters, he "Squires his lady to dinner at Joe's Eats" (46). The "lady" is different every Sunday, but there are constant characteristics, most of them supplied by the overstated dress and makeup that Satin-Legs could be expected to admire. The ending of the poem subtly suggests that this is a kind of death-in-life. Remarking that the food is plentiful at Joe's Eats, the narrator interjects: "(The end is—isn't it?—all that really matters.)" The poem concludes with the achievement of Satin-Legs's objective:

Her body is like new brown bread
Under the Woolworth mignonette.
Her body is a honey bowl
Whose waiting honey is deep and hot.
Her body is like summer earth,
Receptive, soft, and absolute . . .
    (47)

The slant rhymes undercut the directness of the statements, and draw attention to the "absolute" nature of receptive earth, where, in the old courtly usage, Satin-Legs Smith is about to die. Unlike the pool players in "We Real Cool," who "die soon" in many senses, Satin-Legs will survive; this Don Juan's version of Hell is to repeat this cycle indefinitely, with "little hope" of redemption. The ignorant white observer is presumed to accept this ending as all that really matters.

Brooks wrote this accomplished poem toward the end of her work on *A Street*, probably in response to Richard Wright's evaluation of the manuscript she had sent to Harper & Brothers; he praised her skill and genuineness, but added that "most volumes of poems usually have one really long fine poem around which shorter ones are added or grouped."[5]

A Street concludes with a sequence of twelve sonnets, "Gay Chaps at the Bar," which is close enough to what Wright was asking for. "Gay Chaps" is among the stronger poetic responses we have to World War II, and deserves inclusion in anthologies devoted to that subject, along with "Negro Hero," the monologue of a Black mess attendant who took up a machine gun and used it effectively when his ship was attacked at Pearl Harbor, despite regulations of the strictly segregated Navy of that era, in which Black personnel did not handle firearms.

Brooks adopts several points of view throughout "Gay Chaps at the Bar"—omniscient, first person singular, first person plural—and her speakers demonstrate that Black soldiers suffered the same terrors and hopes as any other soldiers. But she is equally concerned to present the injustices of the Black warriors' situation, and reasonable doubts about what they might have been fighting for. The sonnets submit to convention in several ways, but Brooks uses slant rhyme in them more often than she had earlier; they extend the range of sonic choices, and help to emphasize the paradox that these men were fighting for a country which in many ways refused to claim them.

*   *   *

Brooks's interest in traditional technical virtuosity reaches an apex in *Annie Allen*, the collection for which she received the 1950 Pulitzer Prize. The book is arranged in three sections: "Notes from the Childhood and the Girlhood," "The Anniad" (which includes the long poem of that title and two short pieces as "Appendix to The Anniad"), and "The Womanhood." The eleven short poems in the first section establish Annie as a daydreamer, resentful of restrictions imposed by her parents and society, hopeful of some idealized rescuer.

"The Anniad" is a technical tour de force: 301 lines in forty-three seven-line stanzas, employing thirty different rhyme schemes, a compelling meter (trochaic tetrameter catalectic), and a diction that is elaborate, dense, and compressed. Paraphrase is often difficult, and it is also difficult to resist being carried along on the sound waves, heedless of incomprehension. There is a definite narrative; some of the details are obscure, though the poems in the first section of *Annie Allen* provide background for the entrance to the poem:

> Think of sweet and chocolate,
> Left to folly or to fate,
> Whom the higher gods forgot,
> Whom the lower gods berate;
> Physical and underfed
> Fancying on the featherbed
> What was never and is not.

What is ever and is not.
Pretty tatters blue and red,
Buxom berries beyond rot,
Western clouds and quarter-stars,
Fairy-sweet of old guitars
Littering the little head
Light upon the featherbed.

. . . .

Watching for the paladin
Which no woman ever had,
Paradisiacal and sad
With a dimple in his chin
And the mountains in the mind;
Ruralist and rather bad,
Cosmopolitan and kind.
   (99–100)

The imperative of the first line, repeated six more times throughout the poem, implies a reader or listener. This strategy, not as fully developed as in "The Sundays of Satin-Legs Smith," still gives the speaker awareness of an audience, and an inclination to perform. In various tones—affectionate tolerance, adult amusement, or sadness and anger—the speaker shows us the impossible romantic aspirations that fill Annie's "light" and "little" head. The paladin's virtues are impossibly contradictory; that he is not a person, but an imaginary being, is obvious enough, but emphasis is provided in the relative pronoun: "Which no woman ever had."

As she grows older, a "man of tan" courts Annie, and his qualities and her predilections arouse her:

What a hot theopathy
Roisters through her, gnaws the walls,
And consumes her where she falls
In her gilt humility.
   (100)

They move to a "lowly room" which she tries to transform into a lovely love nest. There follows a passage which has been subject to more than one critical bias:

Doomer, though, crescendo-comes
Prophesying hecatombs.
Surrealist and cynical.
Garrulous and guttural.
Spits upon the silver leaves.
Denigrates the dainty eves
Dear dexterity achieves.

Names him. Tames him. Takes him off,
Throws to columns row on row.
Where he makes the rifles cough,
Stutter. Where the reveille
Is staccato majesty.
Then to marches. Then to know
The hunched hells across the sea.

Vaunting hands are now devoid.
Hieroglyphics of her eyes
Blink upon a paradise
Paralyzed and paranoid.
But idea and body too
Clamor "Skirmishes can do.
Then he will come back to you."
      (101–102)

To the reader biased toward a belief in the occasional usefulness of paraphrase, "Doomer" presents difficulties; but the second of these three stanzas helps to identify it as a power suggestive of Uncle Sam, the draft, and the intrusion of war. Noisily, prophesying slaughter, speaking almost bestially, it attacks the little home life Annie has with difficulty achieved. It calls "tan man's" name, inducts him into armed service, sets him to drill with guns, reveille, and marches, and ships him overseas. Annie, bereft, looks blankly on her altered life, but wants to believe he will not be killed.

Hortense J. Spillers, on the other hand, offers a feminist reading of the passage in "Gwendolyn the Terrible: Propositions on Eleven Poems": "As it turns out, he is not the hot lover 'theopathy' would make him out to be, but Annie denies it, fearing that to say so would be to evoke an already imminent betrayal: [quotes first and third of above stanzas]. This scene of 'ruin,' brought on by sexual impotence, gains a dimension of pathos because it anticipates the woman's ultimate loneliness, but this judgment is undercut by the caricature of the male."[6]

This may constitute misreading for the sake of an overriding theme, but Spillers characterizes, with justice and unintended irony, the poem's "specific end: to expose the sadness and comedy of self-delusion in an equally deluded world."[7]

Upon his return, troubled by conflicting recollections of horror and of power, and by predilections imposed on him in a white-dominated society, "tan man" finds a mistress whose color is more honey than chocolate. The twenty-third stanza begins by repeating the first line of the poem, and launches an account of Annie's life alone, from winter through the following fall; she attempts social gaiety, esoteric learning, the high life, and then tries to settle toward her husband's return. The speaker turns to "tan man" and chastises him:

> Hence from scenic bacchanal,
> Preshrunk and droll prodigal!
> Smallness that you had to spend,
> Spent. Wench, whiskey and tail-end
> Of your overseas disease
> Rot and rout you by degrees.
>   (107)

At home again, he wastes away, and at last leaves the world, and the two women, who are contrasted harshly in successive stanzas:

> Leaves his mistress to dismiss
> Memories of his kick and kiss,
> Grant her lips another smear,
> Adjust the posies at her ear,
> Quaff an extra pint of beer,
> Cross her legs upon the stool,
> Slit her eyes and find her fool.

> Leaves his devotee to bear
> Weight of passing by his chair
> And his tavern. Telephone
> Hoists her stomach to the air.
> Who is starch or who is stone
> Washes coffee-cups and hair,
> Sweeps, determines what to wear.
>   (108–109)

The second of these stanzas, the fortieth in the poem, reflects Annie's static helplessness; it is the only one with two rhymes instead of three. She becomes the victim of nightmares and a harried resignation, but the final stanza mutes the verbal flash:

> Think of almost thoroughly
> Derelict and dim and done.
> Stroking swallows from the sweat.
> Fingering faint violet.
> Hugging old and Sunday sun.
> Kissing in her kitchenette
> The minuets of memory.
>   (109)

Though much of the satire in this poem seems to be directed at Annie's innocent romanticism, and at the circumstances which have nourished it, the tone of the last stanza turns toward sympathy. Annie's pathetic stillness, the amatory participles describing small aimless gestures, are mitigated by the "almost" in the first line, and by the iambic fullness of the last. Annie is now twenty-four, and has endured a series of disillusionments and bereavements. If she is to blame for some of them, so is the world.

Whereas the poems of the first two sections of *Annie Allen* speak of Annie in the third person, the third section opens with a sequence of five sonnets, "the children of the poor," in which the mother speaks in the first person. The sequence quickly ranges over several questions arising from the profoundly mixed blessings and curses of disadvantaged parenthood—how to protect children, teach them, prepare them for the fact of death. The fourth sonnet is a complex variation on the persistent American theme that art could not flourish in the period when people of ability were occupied with settling the country. Its punctilious adherence to Petrarchan conventions of structure momentarily withholds the sarcasm that bursts through in the sestet. It begins with two short sentences occupying exactly half a line: "First flight. Then fiddle." The remainder of the octave describes the fiddling, fraught with "feathery sorcery" and "silks and honey," yet covertly rebellious:

> muzzle the note
> With hurting love; the music that they wrote
> Bewitch, bewilder.

The sestet returns to the fighting:

But first to arms, to armor. Carry hate
In front of you and harmony behind.
Be deaf to music and to beauty blind.
Win war. Rise bloody, maybe not too late
For having first to civilize a space
Wherein to play your violin with grace.
   (118)

Enjambment and shifting caesuras lend energy to much of the poem,
but in the final couplet the energy is "civilized" to excessive tameness, reinforcing the "maybe" in the preceding line. The poem hovers between satire
and direct polemic, both attacking and appropriating the notion behind it.

The inclusive vision that results in such a poem finds a variety of more
single-minded expressions in the remainder of the book; this section of *Annie
Allen* contains a few underachieved poems, but on the whole it is a sustained
illustration of Brooks's many virtues. There are straightforwardly affectionate sketches, satiric portrayals of Black characters and of ignorant or shel-
tered whites, seized moments in the manner of Emily Dickinson, love poems,
polemical addresses. The book concludes with an untitled poem of considerable power, addressing "Men of careful turns, haters of forks in the road," and
declaring the speaker's full humanity. Its characterization of establishment
caution is icily exact:

      "What
We are to hope is that intelligence
Can sugar up our prejudice with politeness.
Politeness will take care of what needs caring.
For the line is there.
And has a meaning. So our fathers said—
And they were wise—we think—at any rate,
They were older than ourselves. And the report is
What's old is wise. At any rate, the line is
Long and electric. Lean beyond and nod.
Be sprightly. Wave. Extend your hand and teeth.
But never forget it stretches there beneath."
   (140)

The poem ends with a chilling recognition that things will not soon
change, especially if polite requests are depended on. The last line memorably
combines determination and pessimism:

Let us combine. There are no magics or elves
Or timely godmothers to guide us. We are lost, must
Wizard a track through our own screaming weed.
   (140)

If there are sharp divisions in Brooks's career, one of them comes at this point. As George Kent puts it, "For both whites and Blacks, Gwendolyn would from now on be tagged 'the first Negro to win a Pulitzer Prize,' and with that label would come the roles of spokeswoman and arbiter in the upper realms of her city's and her nation's cultural affairs" (Kent 102). We may be able to see whether Brooks's work changed noticeably after this, but the question is obfuscated by the churning assortment of critical responses to her new status. The problem of Brooks's place in a white literary establishment had in fact been thrown into relief by Paul Engle's August 26, 1945, review in the *Chicago Tribune*, of *A Street in Bronzeville*. Especially in the 1940s, trying to declare Brooks's transcendence of racial differences was to fall into the nearly inescapable trap of simultaneously affirming and denying the importance of race in her work: "Miss Brooks is the first Negro poet to write wholly out of a deep and imaginative talent, without relying on the fact of color to draw sympathy and interest.... The finest praise that can be given to the book is that it would be a superb volume of poetry in any year by a person of any color."[8]

There is no reason to doubt Engle's sincere admiration of Brooks's work, or the honesty of his conviction that race should not be the issue that it is; but it is hard to get away from the hint of exclusiveness, the suggestion that Brooks is a fine poet, not regardless of her color, but despite it. In later years, increasing numbers of Black writers would question the extent of Brooks's commitment to Blackness; but there were confusing earlier questions by less militant writers. J. Saunders Redding, for example, in a generally favorable review of *Annie Allen* in the *Saturday Review*, found references to intraracial color preferences too esoteric: "Who but another Negro can get the intimate feeling, the racially-particular acceptance and rejection, and the oblique bitterness of this? ... The question is ... whether it is not this penchant for coterie stuff—the special allusions, the highly special feeling derived from an even more special experience—that has brought poetry from the most highly regarded form of communication to the least regarded."[9]

Redding and Engle were saying remarkably similar things, and missing an important element of Brooks's art. She sought to make her Black characters as rounded as poetry permits; this necessarily involved treating aspects of the Black experience which are imposed by white society. Through her first two books, her anger at injustice is comparatively restrained, but several poems in *The Bean Eaters* greatly increase the pressure of rage against the control of mature technique.

In one or two instances, the pressure overcomes control. "A Bronzeville Mother Loiters in Mississippi. Meanwhile, a Mississippi Mother Burns Bacon" is a daring response to the murder of Emmett Till, a Chicago teenager who was beaten and killed in 1955, during a visit to Mississippi. Brooks adopts the point of view of the young white woman who accused the youth of making sexual advances toward her. The sympathetic portrayal of the woman is striking; the husband, however, is a flat symbol of murderous white male oppression. He deserves that status, but in the poem he fails to earn it; instead of a plausible and therefore frightening and disgusting human, we have something too much like a cartoonist's drawing of Bull Connor. On the other hand, the woman's romantic vision of southern womanhood collapses convincingly before her growing knowledge of the Dark Villain's innocent youth:

> Had *she* been worth the blood, the cramped cries, the little
>   stuttering bravado,
> The gradual dulling of those Negro eyes,
> The sudden, overwhelming *little-boyness* in that barn?
> (336)

Flat portrayal of white characters is more effective in such satirical poems as "The Lovers of the Poor" and "Bronzeville Woman in a Red Hat," where reduction of characters to cartoons serves a dual function: it permits broad sarcasm and indulgence in playful diction, and it invites the white reader to feel excluded from the portrait until it is too late to escape inclusion in it. Both poems portray whites in the act of dehumanizing Blacks, though "Bronzeville Woman" is heavy-handed in this respect. A rich and overbearing woman has had to replace her Irish housemaid, and the agency has sent a Black woman, whom the employer calls "it" throughout the poem. The portrayal becomes more effective, if nearly sentimental, in contrasting the reactions of the employer and the employer's child, "Not wise enough to freeze or be afraid" (370).

The other major treatment of racial violence is "The Ballad of Rudolph Reed," a fiercely ironic narrative of the violence that follows a Black family's purchase of a house in a white neighborhood. Traditional ballad meter and language give the poem a strange atmosphere of remoteness:

> Rudolph Reed was oaken.
> His wife was oaken too.

And his two good girls and his good little man
Oakened as they grew.
   (376)

Contemporary racist brutality breaks with great force into such a setting, but the poem is strong enough to contain the atrocity of Reed's death, which comes as he is defending his house against rock-throwers who have wounded one of his daughters. The end of the poem is a powerful tableau of grief and strength:

By the time he had hurt his fourth white man
Rudolph Reed was dead.
His neighbors gathered and kicked his corpse.
"Nigger—" his neighbors said.

Small Mabel whimpered all night long,
For calling herself the cause.
Her oak-eyed mother did no thing
But change the bloody gauze.
   (378)

These somewhat extended poems concerned with racial injustice, white insensitivity, and violence, are scattered through an unusually varied collection of shorter poems, from the brilliant miniature "We Real Cool" to such humorous pieces as "On the Occasion of the Open-Air Formation of the Olde Tymer's Walking and Nature Club." It is this mixture, perhaps, more than the presence of the longer poems, which led some readers to regret the increased emphasis on social issues in *The Bean Eaters*—as if social issues were making their first appearance in Brooks's work. It is true that these longer poems are more explicit, and reveal anger more openly, than do most of Brooks's earlier poems; but most of the shorter poems aroused regret that Brooks could not be consistently polite.

The new poems in *Selected Poems* (1963) did little to change these impressions; "Riders to the Blood-Red Wrath," with its evocations of African majesty, the squalor of slave ships, and the commitment of Freedom Riders, both extends and rejects the polemical manner. Its content is occasion for celebration and exhortation, but in style it reverts to a density Brooks had not used at length since "The Anniad." It crams a racial history into a single consciousness, which ranges without transition between individual and collective recollection, and gathers momentum toward the polemical ending: "To fail, to flourish, to wither or to win. / We lurch, distribute, we extend, begin" (392).

On the other hand, a number of the new poems are brief character sketches; these presage the ambitious and thickly populated *In the Mecca* (1968), the book which has been said to initiate the third period in Brooks's career. If it does mark a significant shift in Brooks's way of writing and of thinking about what she is doing, this is more evident in the shorter poems that follow the title poem. "In the Mecca" is, at just over 800 lines, Brooks's most ambitious single poem; but in strategy and style it is an extension, not a repudiation, of her earlier excellences.

Epigraphs provide the information that the Mecca building, an extravagant apartment complex erected in Chicago in 1891, degenerated into an overcrowded tenement. Kenny J. Williams adds the important fact that the building was razed in 1952.[10]

In bare outline, the narrative is grim: Mrs. Sallie Smith returns to her apartment from hard domestic labor, and begins to prepare dinner for her family of nine children; she notices suddenly that the youngest, Pepita, is missing. There is a fruitless search, police are called, and at last the child is found murdered.

The poem begins with a single line on a page by itself: "Now the way of the Mecca was on this wise." It remains for the poem to unfold the wrathful irony in this echo of Matthew 1:18 ("Now the birth of Jesus Christ was on this wise"). The rest of the poem is based in the present tense; Mrs. Smith encounters four neighbors on the way to her apartment, and each is sketched briefly; Alfred, an English teacher and untalented would-be writer, comes to act as a choral commentator as the poem develops. The children have their distinctive ways of trying to defend themselves against the reality of their lives; Melodie Mary, for example, "likes roaches, / and pities the gray rat." She is dimly aware of headlines announcing strife and suffering in China, but

> What if they drop like the tumbling tears
> of the old and intelligent sky?
> Where are the frantic bulletins
> when other importances die?
> Trapped in his privacy of pain
> the worried rat expires,
> and smashed in the grind of a rapid heel
> last night's roaches lie.
>   (412)

When the family goes in search of Pepita, they inquire of several neighbors, each of whom is given several lines of characterization. Great-great Gram, who recalls her childhood in slavery, reverts to childhood as she recalls popping little creatures that "creebled" in the dirt of the cabin floor, thus inverting Melodie Mary's treatment of the same subject. Aunt Dill, reveling in her report of a child's rape and murder the previous week, is a gruesome parody of unfeeling self-satisfaction.

Toward the end of this section, there are three portraits without reference to Pepita or her whereabouts. The first, concerning Don Lee, is similar to several other poems Brooks has written about notable Blacks; even in the context of this poem, it appears to portray the poet and activist now named Haki R. Madhubuti. Along with Alfred's references to Léopold Sédar Senghor, "Poet, muller, President of Senegal," this constitutes unobtrusive anachronism. "In the Mecca" contains few references which can be dated precisely, but some of them, such as Senghor's presidency of Senegal (1960–1980), convey the impression that the Mecca existed in the 1960s. This effect is only slightly complicated for the reader in possession of such arcana as the year of its demolition; the building itself may have been infamous, but its destruction did not significantly change the lives with which the poem is concerned. Brooks's Mecca outlives its namesake, and becomes a perceptible metaphor as well as a symbol.

The increasing desperation of the search for Pepita is reflected in the rapidity with which new characters are introduced from this point on. In the whole poem, over fifty people are mentioned by name or characteristic label; more than half of them appear in the last 200 lines. Because this large cast moves in quickly, sometimes at the rate of four people per line, there is room near the end of the poem for four strophes of between a dozen and two dozen lines each, the first two introducing new characters, the third and fourth returning to Aunt Dill and Alfred, respectively. The two new characters reinforce the balanced vision of the whole poem: Way-Out Morgan is collecting guns, imagining "Death-to-the-Hordes-of-the-White-Men!" (430); Marian is ironing, wishing for some disaster to befall her so she may be noticeable. Absorbed in their visions, they have no time to wonder where Pepita is. Aunt Dill reappears in a gooey cloud of self-satisfaction; the narrator calls her

> the kind of woman you
> peek at in passing and thank your God or zodiac you
> may never have to know
>   (432)

In this welter of selfishness, Alfred makes a final appearance, allowing Brooks a sly reference to the temporal limbo in which she has erected this cosmos:

I hate it.
    Yet, murmurs Alfred—
who is lean at the balcony, leaning—
something, something in Mecca
continues to call! Substanceless; yet like mountains,
like rivers and oceans too; and like trees
with wind whistling through them. And steadily
an essential sanity, black and electric,
builds to a reportage and redemption.
    A hot estrangement
    A material collapse
that is Construction.
    (433)

The next strophe begins with two lines that look back toward this rev-
erie, and forward to the discovery of Pepita's body:

Hateful things sometimes befall the hateful
but the hateful are not rendered lovable thereby.
The murderer of Pepita
looks at the Law unlovably.
    (433)

Beneath Jamaican Edward's bed lies the body of Pepita, who "never learned
that Black is not beloved." Remembering a rhyme the child once made with
"rose," her mother decides to "try for roses." The final four lines of the poem
revert to what only Jamaican Edward could have seen, but the powerful
image of horror is rendered in a style that can only be the narrator's:

She whose little stomach fought the world had
wriggled, like a robin!
Odd were the little wrigglings
and the chopped chirpings oddly rising.
    (433)

"In the Mecca" is a large and largely successful poem, a benchmark in
Brooks's career. The poem draws its strength both from her increasing interest
in the possibilities for polemic in poetry, and from her broad and deep familiarity with poetry's technical resources. Except in scope and achievement, it
is not a radical departure from the work which preceded it. However, it was
completed during a time of upheaval in Brooks's sense of herself as a poet,

and the shorter poems collected with it are evidence of a major division in Brooks's career.

Much has already been made of the external forces that wrought important changes in Brooks's thinking about her life and work. At the Fisk University Writers' Conference in 1967, she encountered, more forcibly than she had before, the power of young Black writers committed to making a literature for Black people, and to liberating themselves and their people from white oppression. The experience energized her in new ways. She also worked briefly with the Blackstone Rangers, a street gang whose younger mentors, especially Walter Bradford and Don L. Lee, provided encouragement as she sought her "newish voice."[11]

"After Mecca" is a coherent sequence of separate poems; it gathers force by proceeding from individual portraits, through two "public occasion" poems and the three-part "Blackstone Rangers," to "The Sermon on the Warpland" and "The Second Sermon on the Warpland." As the field of vision expands from one poem to the next, the formal scope extends from brief and nearly metrical to more widely various free-verse lines. The diction, however, remains characteristically Brooksian, as in this conclusion to "The Leaders," the second part of "The Blackstone Rangers":

The Blackstone bitter bureaus
(bureaucracy is footloose) edit, fuse
unfashionable damnations and descent;
and exulting, monstrous hand on monstrous hand,
construct, strangely, a monstrous pearl or grace.
   (448)

But along with certainty that she had much to learn from younger Black writers, there came a desire to reach audiences unaccustomed to hearing or reading poetry. This arose partly from increasing doubt about dependence on the Eurocentric tradition she had so thoroughly commanded for most of her career; at this point, the language problem referred to early in this essay becomes extremely difficult, despite Anglo-American's flexibility and relative openness to other traditions. With a few notable exceptions such as "We Real Cool," Brooks's poetry has depended not only on fresh and unusual language, but on the varying degrees of surface difficulty that such wordplay often creates. Her attempts at a more accessible style have sometimes resulted in oversimplified moralizing, and in indecision about which poems or versions of poems to reprint.

Of the roughly fifty poems Brooks published between 1968 and 1987, a few have appeared only in periodicals, and only nineteen are collected in *Blacks*.

A white reader might be tempted to think that some of this indecision arises from Brooks's having accepted, in 1985, her second major accolade from the literary establishment, when she became Poetry Consultant to the Library of Congress; but in interviews over the past twenty years, and in her tireless work for Black writers during her tenure at the Library, she has demonstrated unwavering commitment to the cause of freedom for oppressed people.

Brooks's wavering over certain poems is evidence of crisis, but it is important to remember that crisis is usually much more rewarding for artists than for politicians. In adjusting her accustomed tools to her new tasks, she has taken some directions which she seems later to have reconsidered, but occasional frustrations have not sent her back to techniques in which she has long been adept. Her most recent collection, *Gottschalk and the Grande Tarantelle* (Chicago: The David Company, 1988), is cause for gratitude that she has not retreated from trying to perfect her new ways of working.

This handsome chapbook contains only four poems, but one of them is "Winnie," some 375 lines spoken by Winnie Mandela. The character is of course a literary creation, partaking of what Brooks knows of Mrs. Mandela, and of what she knows of herself and the world. There are passages where one might wish that more memorable language had been found for the urgent messages:

> we are all vulnerable—
> the midget, the Mighty,
> the richest, the poor.
>   (18)

But Brooks has hold of something here. In her early work, personal history (not necessarily her own) was a dependable provider of material. She began to merge social and political history with that strain in poems like "The Ballad of Rudolph Reed" and "A Bronzeville Mother Loiters," and perfected that merging in "In the Mecca." Now, she is after larger historical scope, and appears to be on the brink of finding the means to achieve it without surrendering particularity. As she has Winnie Mandela say,

> This is the time for Big Poems,
> roaring up out of sleaze,
> poems from ice, from vomit, and from tainted blood.
>   (19)

Notes

1. "The Poet-Militant and Foreshadowings of a Black Mystique: Poems in the Second Period of Gwendolyn Brooks." Maria K. Mootry and Gary Smith, *A Life*

Distilled: Gwendolyn Brooks, Her Poetry and Fiction (U of Illinois P, 1987; hereafter referred to as "Mootry and Smith"), 71 and note, 80.

2. *Blacks* (Chicago: The David Company, 1987; page references following quotations are to this volume unless otherwise specified).

3. George Kent, *A Life of Gwendolyn Brooks* (University Press of Kentucky, 1990). Hereafter referred to as "Kent."

4. Kent, p. 66.

5. Kent, p. 63.

6. Mootry and Smith, p. 230.

7. Ibid., p. 231.

8. Quoted in Kent, pp. 74–75.

9. Ibid., p. 79.

10. Mootry and Smith, p. 60.

11. Kent, pg. 180ff.

BRIAN DILLON

"Never Having Had You, I Cannot Let You Go": Sharon Olds's Poems of a Father–Daughter Relationship

In her first three books of poetry—*Satan Says* (1980), *The Dead and the Living* (1984), *The Gold Cell* (1989)—as well as recently published poems not collected into book form, Sharon Olds describes a dysfunctional family misruled by a father whose abuse of power the poems' speaker responds to both as a child and an adult.[1] Rather than one full-length *Prelude*-like account, Olds offers snapshots, literally dozens of short poems, a few which metaphorically delineate the father damaging the family structure, and others which narrate in specific detail the father's brutal presence. One anthology of literature commonly used in introductory level classes features three poems highlighting the speaker's relationship with her father.[2] In "The Chute" (included in *GC*) the father selects a child to suspend by the ankles inside the laundry chute, threatening to drop the helpless one: "he loved to hear / passionate screaming in a narrow space." In "The Victims" (included in *DL*), an abusive father is kicked out of the house, divorced by his wife, and fired from his job. And in "The Race" the adult speaker narrates a wild—nearly out of breath—dash through an airport to board a plane in order to cross the continent and arrive at her dying father's bedside. Whether deliberate or not, the anthology selection of Olds's poems allows readers to construct a plot, a linear progression from abuse to expulsion of the abuser to the apparent death of the abuser, with (perhaps) the speaker's

---

From *Literary Review* 37, no. 1 (Fall 1993): 108–18. Copyright © 1993 by *Literary Review*.

achievement of a peace with her past in "The Race." This last poem is included in *The Father*, Olds's most recent publication, and is just one of 52 poems in this book detailing the speaker's response to her father's dying and death.

To what extent, in looking at the entire Olds canon, can a plot about the father be discerned? The title poem for *Satan Says*, which opens Olds's first book, establishes a concern the poet returns to in her next two books and in poetry published since *The Gold Cell*. In circumstances more terrifying than Alice's wonderland dreamworld, the speaker is locked in "a little cedar box," apparently a small jewelry box. The voice of Satan promises her freedom if she repeats his vulgarities: "Say shit, say death, say fuck the father." The speaker complies, but her conflicted response about her parents highlights an emotion foreign to Satan: "I love them but / I'm trying to say what happened to us / in the lost past." Her expression of love prevents her escape from the cedar box. "*It's your coffin now*, Satan says." Though burdened by familial circumstances, the "pain of the locked past," the speaker's freedom lies in "trying to say what happened," as well as, the poem concludes, "the suddenly discovered knowledge of love" (*Satan Says*).

The voice of the speaker in "Satan Says" certainly seems to be the same voice we hear in numerous poems published over the next decade or more. In "The Chute," Olds's speaker details the chilling effect her father's behavior had on her and her two siblings. For whatever odd reason, the wiring for the doorbell was located partway down the laundry chute, and one child would be chosen by the father to be dangled down it to tape two wires together. Two features stand out. Early in the poem the description of the setting is interrupted. The speaker jumps to a later time and provides the reader with a glimpse of her father that is never explained and which seems to lie outside the concerns of "The Chute":

> . . . And halfway
> down there was an electric fixture for the
> doorbell—that bell my father would ring and
> ring years later when he stood at the door with that
> blood on him, like a newborn's caul,
> ringing ringing to enter. (*GC*)

Why does he have blood on him? Why is his ringing so persistent? Olds is not forthcoming with an explanation in this or other poems that appear to refer to the same incident. Consider the opening lines to "History: 13" (the number referring to the speaker's age at the time of the unsettling event):

When I found my father that night, the blood
smeared on his head and face, I did not
know who had done it. I had loved his body
whole, his head, his face, untouched,
and now he floated on the couch, his arms
up, like Mussolini hanging
upside down in the air, his head
dangling where they could reach him with boards and their
fingernails, those who had lived
under his tyranny. (*GC*)

As in "The Chute," the speaker fails to account for her father's bloodied appearance; instead, she focuses on her own initially confused and finally ambivalent response to him. She questions whether she or anyone in her family was responsible for his disturbing presence. And though she concludes with a label that damns the father, her sentiment is one of empathy: " . . . I turned my back / on happiness, at 13 I entered / a life of mourning, of mourning for the Fascist." It seems worth noting that this poem is placed seven poems prior to "The Chute," with a variety of poems about her parents viewed from both the child's and adult's perspective in between, suggesting that Olds refuses to make narrative continuity easy. Nine years earlier Olds began "That Year" with what appears to be the earliest reference to this minimally detailed incident. The poem is worth reading in full to get a sense of the genuine anguish the father caused, Olds's tendency to place family experiences within an easily recognizable historical context, and the speaker's attempts to assess her past from the perspective of an adult.

The year of the mask of blood, my father
hammering on the glass door to get in

was the year they found her body in the hills,
in a shallow grave, naked, white as
mushroom, partially decomposed,
raped, murdered, the girl from my class.

That was the year my mother took us and
hid us so he could not get at us
when she told him to leave; so there were no more
tyings by the wrist to the chair,
no more denial of food

or the forcing of foods, the head held back,
down the throat at the restaurant,
the shame of vomited buttermilk
down the sweater with its shame of new breasts.

That was the year
I started to bleed,
crossing over that border in the night,
and in Social Studies, we came at last
to Auschwitz. I recognized it
like my father's face, the face of the guard
turning away—or worse yet
turning toward me. (*SS*)

The loathing for the man depicted as Fascist and Nazi in these poems does not prepare the reader in search of narrative coherence for the adult, distanced perspective on the father the speaker offers in "The Chute." The reader who hopes Olds will reproduce experience will be disappointed in the elliptical quality of many of the poems about the father. The reader who hopes Olds will emphasize the speaker's evaluation of her experience will be intrigued. The child living through the experience asks, "how could you trust him?" But the adult speaker excuses the father's actions as she interprets the poem in the final lines.

> . . . We hung there in the dark,
> and yet, you know, he never dropped us
> or meant to, he only liked to say he would,
> so although it's a story with some cruelty in it,
> finally it's a story of love
> and release, the way the father pulls you out of nothing
> and stands there foolishly grinning. (*GC*)

The conclusion appears to be at cross purposes with the rest of the poem: the dramatic tension of the preceding narrative, the reader is informed, should not be understood as an implied criticism of the father's threatening behavior. The child's perspective of fear gets erased with this conclusion. The father analogously presented elsewhere as a Mussolini or a Nazi has not changed. Instead, the speaker makes a grand effort to understand him and to contemplate how he has penetrated the core of her being: "if you were / his, half him, your left hand maybe and your / left foot dipped in the gleaming / murky liquor of his nature, how could you / trust yourself?" The tension between the speaker's response to her father as a child and as an adult is left unresolved here (and in other poems treating the father–daughter relationship), which upsets efforts at reading for the plot.

The ending of "The Chute" admits the desire to explain, to provide mature, distanced explanation, however unsatisfying this might be for the reader. As one commentator on Olds has remarked, "As readers and as human beings, we may not agree with her; we may have other, happier versions of 'love / and release.' But Olds allows no room for such defection. The stories are hers, and they must be understood in her terms only" (McEwen 473). Yet the lines about her father ringing the doorbell are not fleshed out, justification for his appearance and action is left unstated, and an intratextual reading (one created by reading it in the context of other Olds's poems) merely restates the reference to the incident without illuminating it. Olds's 1990 poem "The Prepositions" (which is not included in *The Father*) is worth noting here: it recalls the speaker's seventh grade assignment to memorize a list of 45 prepositions, her school environment, and other associations prompted by memory of this task—"fourteen, the breaking of childhood, beginning of memory." Halfway through this poem Olds interjects the following lines:

> *Over, past, since, through,*
> that was the year my father came home in the
> middle of the night with those heavy worms of
> blood on his face, trilobites of
> elegant gore, cornice and crisp
> waist of the extinct form. . . .

These lines can only be understood intratextually, but even with such a reading, the father's experience and the speaker's response to it remain ambiguous. While the lines describing the father's appearance strain under the weight of lexical complexity, with the odd word "trilobites" drawing excessive attention to itself and away from what actually occurred, how this incident affected the speaker, and any account justifying reference to it in this poem, is unexplained. And Olds's characteristic avoidance of enjambment with the vertical drop induced by ending lines on weak words—the, of—forces the reader to plunge through her account of a painful experience. Again, Olds leaves the reader with hints and indirections, with the outlines of a plot.

Olds forces her reader to move from book to book and occasionally from section to section within the same book to piece together a portrait of this father. In *The Dead and the Living*, the speaker avenges the father who delighted in intimidating his children. The pronoun "it" carries much ambiguous weight in "The Victims": the abuse "it" suggests remains nonspe-cific. "When Mother divorced you, we were glad. She took it and / took it, in silence, all those years and then / kicked you out, suddenly, and her / kids loved it. . . . She had taught us to take it, to hate you and take it . . ." (*DL*). The father's loss of his job follows upon the divorce; the speaker's adult perspec-tive, asserted in the final lengthy sentence that begins with an overt marker of the temporal shift—"Now I / pass the bums in the doorways . . ."—expresses no empathy for the father, no attempt to shrug off the pains of the past as the final lines of "The Chute" attempt to do. The lack of sympathy evident in these lines, the assumption that these "bums" earned their misery, is a rare example of Olds venting spleen but without offering any conflicting response to suggest tension in her feelings toward the father. The reader's empathy with the speaker apparently is assumed. "The Departure" poses questions in an accusatory tone and equates the father with the Shah of Iran: both are guilty of engaging in impersonal acts of brutality. "Did you forget / the way you had had me tied to a chair, as / he forgot the ones strapped to the grille / in his name?" But even this poem demonstrates the speaker's effort to penetrate an emotional depth of the father, one that the speaker can literally identify with. While "The Victims" asserts that the speaker and her siblings "grinned inside" when the father was "kicked" out of the house, "The Departure" presents the father's leave-taking as deserving a serious rather than giddy reaction:

> . . . Did you weep as you left
> as Reza Pahlevi wept when he rose
> over the gold plain of Iran, did you
> suddenly want to hear our voices, did you
> start to rethink the darkness of our hair,
> did you wonder if perhaps we had deserved to live,
> did you love us, then? (*DL*)

The father has no voice in any of these poems. Yet with "The Departure," the speaker appears to be provoking a dialogue, and the reader is forced to imagine what the father would say were he allowed to speak. Since the father is a dominant presence in so many poems in Olds's first three books and the central subject in her fourth, why does she choose to keep him silent? To silence the abuser, the oppressor figure grants the speaker a degree of control as an adult-artist that she clearly lacked as a child. But there is a sig-nificant trade-off: non-particularized as the father's acts often are presented (in "Looking at My Father" we are told that "he's a tease, / obsessive, rigid, selfish, sentimental," generic qualities that could be applied to many parents; *GC*), the poetry risks sounding less intensely private, and, consequently, risks minimizing the damage the father caused. In *The Father*, his silences become a recurrent theme. When in "His Stillness" his doctor informs him his cancer is beyond cure, his response is "like a holy man," a dignified "Thank you": "I had not remembered / he had always held still and kept silent to bear things, / the liquor a way to keep still. I had not / known him." The speaker's hostility toward her father evident in earlier poems is significantly toned down in this book; the emphasis here is on the absence of love and the speaker's coming to terms with that fact. The speaker clings to details: his striking a match and drawing on a cigar provided "his only song . . . / it was that song or none." The reader who complains that Olds creates a space around her poems in which plot continuity is suggested but left unfulfilled, the reader who wonders whether the speaker extracts an apology from the father and if the pains of the past are smoothed over in a final emotionally-charged dialogue, misses the point of this book. It is precisely the silence of the father that creates an enormous emptiness that these poems try to fill, silence that provokes multiple conjectures as to who the father is and why his dying and death so confound the speaker. "I had stopped / longing for him to address me from his heart / before he died," Olds writes in "The Want." The irony of "Last Kiss" is that the father's impatience with his daughter, with her suitcases packed as she must leave him, probably for the last time, to return to her world, prompts his exasperated "Last kiss!": "To plead that I leave / my father asked me for a kiss! I would not / leave till he had done so, I will not let thee go except thou beg for it." Although echoing Jacob's demand of the angel with whom he wrestles all night, no blessing is requested by the speaker of her father, and none is offered.

The silencing of the father, as well as the speaker's refusal to damn the father and assert that the speaker herself emerged irreparably scarred from her seemingly traumatic childhood experiences, suggests Olds's intentional willingness to avoid the label "confessional" poet, her resistance to make poetry centered on anger and shame. The conventional view that confessional poetry is practiced primarily by Lowell, Plath, Sexton, and others, has been challenged by Laurence Lerner, who argues that the term is far more amorphous than contemporary critical practice would indicate. An attempt to define the term draws attention to these concerns: "Confession is something that causes us shame . . . confessional poetry deals with experience that it is deeply painful to bring into public, not because it is disgusting, nor because it is sinful, but because it is intensely private" (Lerner 64). The conclusion to "The Chute" swerves away from any expression of shame at having a sadistic father. The historical analogue for understanding the father's action in "The Departure" allows Olds to avoid sounding "intensely private." Lerner argues that some poetry, post 1950s American especially, which gets labelled "confessional" does reveal raw experience, the psyche under intense strain, presumably the author's own and factually accurate, and demonstrates "narrative courage," yet it does not deserve the label poetry. His concluding thought seems particularly appropriate when we think of Olds's work: "lyric poetry was never wholly detachable from confession, just as, if it is to have any claim to be poetry, it can never be wholly identified with it" (Lerner 66).

Olds is careful to avoid painful revelation overwhelming her aesthetic form. Olds's speaker never asserts that her relationship with her father significantly scarred her: the thrust in her accounts of her father is that she survived and with the tool of language will describe what it feels like. In an early poem, "Nurse Whitman," she equates her task as daughter / artist with that of America's greatest poet in his finest non-literary role: "You bathe the forehead, you bathe the lip, the cock, / as I touch my father, as if the language / were a form of life" (*Satan Says*). Her language not only reclaims the past but also serves a therapeutic function for the speaker. In the same book, in two other poems which feature the father when the family was still together dysfunctionally, the speaker concludes that she is a "survivor" ("That Year" and "Time-Travel" in *Satan Says*). "Time-Travel," like many of Olds's poems, replaces the father's speech with his physical presence, which is lovingly described. In a dream-like episode the adult speaker re-visits a lakeside house in the summer of '55. Looking for her father, she finds him and silently observes his appearance. What follows includes the second and part of the third stanzas.

> I can possess him like this, the funnies
> rising and falling on his big stomach,
> his big solid secret body
> where he puts the bourbon.
> He belongs to me forever like this,
> the red plaid shirt, the baggy pants,
> the long perfectly turned legs,
> the soft padded hands folded across his body,
> the hair dark as a burnt match,
> the domed, round eyes closed,
> the firm mouth. Sleeping it off
> in the last summer the family was together.
> I have learned to walk
>
> so quietly into that summer
> no one knows I am there. He rests
> easy as a baby. Upstairs
> mother weeps. . . .

The prompt for the mother's weeping can be presumed only by intratextual readings, and then only indirectly. This is the outline of a frequently brutal man in repose. The speaker's desire to "possess" the father approximates the painter's desire to accurately capture her subject on canvas: for a figure so crucial in the emotional life of the speaker, the father remains mysteriously two-dimensional. What does the speaker think of the father, then (1955) and in the present time of the poem? Olds consistently leaves a gap where one expects to find personal reflection. The adult speaker, the time-traveler, locates her teenage self in this fractured family setting literally by the shore-line, isolated, confused, wary of her family: "She does not know / any of this will ever stop. / She does not know she is the one / survivor" (*SS*). The opening line asserts that the speaker has "learned to go back" to this scene from her past; what she has learned from it remains unstated, though the ending emphasizes the speaker's distance from the brutality of the father.

The dramatic tension is minimized as the antagonist sleeps and the speaker claims a personal victory. "Time-Travel" opens the section titled "Journey" in *Satan Says*. And the journey of the speaker's efforts to describe and understand the behavior of her father and his influence on her continue throughout her work, frequently in poems that capture the physical presence of the father. "The Ideal Father" contrasts two versions of the past as the speaker pries apart idealization and painful memory: the hair, skin, even the penis of the idealized father are "perfect as a textbook example," yet the speaker also must remember the man who "slapped the glasses off a / small girl's face" (*DL*). The honesty with which the speaker avoids blurring idealization and painful memory is evident in other poems that bluntly acknowledge the speaker's inevitable burden of the father's inheritance: "Finally I just gave up and became my father / ... I saw the whole world shining / with the ecstasy of his grief, and I / myself, he, I, shined ..." ("Fate" in *DL*). Again, the reader's frustrations surface as the speaker swerves from telling *what* she sees from this new perspective of merging with the father. The speaker has adopted the "likeness" of a dangerous man, and even praises her husband's willingness to trust her: "As I see you / embracing me, in the mirror, I see I am / my father as a woman, I see you bravely / embrace him, in me, putting your life in his / hands as mine" ("Poem to My Husband from My Father's Daughter," *SS*). The father is both dangerous and pathetic, and the speaker's strength is her ability to turn into art the pain and weirdness. She is a survivor "possessed," as the title of another poem labels this dark passion. "Never having had you, I cannot let you go ..." (*DL*). And this feeling, the speaker urges us to believe, must be reciprocal, though her father might only "realize" this after his death. The speaker fantasizes that with a newly acquired afterlife voice he will account for her effect on him: "She could / speak, you see. As if my own / jaws, throat, and larynx had come / alive in her" ("When the Dead Ask My Father about Me"). This poem, included in *The Father*, and the final poem of this same book, "My Father Speaks to Me from the Dead," demonstrate both the speaker's flagrant ego and her quest for a love that is now—and has been for many years—impossible to achieve. He speaks of her knees, curls, face, and womb. (Olds once asked, "Is there anything that shouldn't or can't be written about in a poem?" (Campbell) and almost in response pushes against poetic bounds here as her father asserts, "when I touched your little / anus I crossed wires with God for a moment.") Though he recalls her baby body quite well, he stops at this surface and will not be bold to imagine her emotional core: "I made you, when I say now that I love you / I mean look down at your hand, move it, / that action is matter's love, for human / love go elsewhere."

As the dying of the father is the subject of this latest work of Olds's, he escapes, quite literally, from any effort the reader imposes to plot the father–daughter relationship. The breathless speaker of "The Race" runs through an airport to catch a plane in order to fly to her dying father's bedside, "to touch him again in this life." The poem concludes in an open-ended manner: "I walked into his room / and watched his chest rise slowly / and sink again, all night / I watched him breathe." Perhaps her walking suggests a last minute reluctance: she is still not mentally and emotionally prepared to discuss the unresolved conflicts that "The Victims" and other poems indicate she feels. No attempt is made here to bring closure on the father–daughter relationship, let alone to assess its impact on the speaker. Expectations that the poet will provide narrative coherence are frustrated.

The speaker's shift from "ran" and "raced" to "walked" also suggests a reluctance to view her dying father's body, or at least a steeling of her emotions to confront the sight of her father's disease-ravaged body. In many other poems, though, the father's body, specifically the signs of its painful decay, become the poem's subject matter. His thick, heavy sputum floats in a glass on a table next to his hospital bed—"I think of it with wonder now"—and the glass acquires symbolic proportions akin to Stevens's jar in Tennessee: it would "shimmer there on the table until / the room seemed to turn around it / in an orderly way" ("The Glass"). What the speaker knows when she sees her father as a victim, dying of cancer, is that they are connected, not by their shared experiences, not even the ones portrayed as traumatic for the speaker in numerous poems, but connected in their bones and blood, their bodies a physical conjunction that transcend all darker memories of abuse. How the father was transformed from a handsome man courting the speaker's mother to an abusive father to a horizontal body with his life slowly excised from him is *not* the subject of Olds's poems. The poems that treat the dying and dead father minimize who the father is. Instead, his dying and death propel the speaker into the mysteries of her assumed inheritance from him. Half of the speaker's pre-embryo state she imagines as she washes the face of her dying father in "Last Acts":

> . . . I want
> to be in him, as I was once inside him,
> riding in his balls the day before he cast me—
> he carries me easily on his long legs up the
> hills of San Francisco in war-time, I am
> there between his legs where I belong,
> I am his flesh, he can love me without
> reserve, I will be his pleasure.

From the testicles descended, Olds derives this physiologically sound, though fantastically imagined, image.

In one of Olds's more audacious poems, "The Swimmer," the speaker throws herself into the sea, emptying herself in the process of memory and emotion as she merges with the matter of her father:

> I am like those elements my father turned into,
> smoke, bone, salt. It is one of
> the only things I like to do
> anymore, get down inside the horizon
> and feel what his new life is like, how
> clean, how blank, how griefless, how without error—
> the trance of matter.

How else, this poem seems implicitly to be asking, can the death of the other be transcended? The emotional distance the father maintained, both when the speaker was a child and as he is dying, prohibits a communion of love between father and daughter in his final days; absent the heart, the father's body still remains as an object the speaker can attend to lovingly with language. She highlights the impersonality of the mechanism of the body: the contents of his catheter bag, the "sucking snap / when his jaws draw back" ("Death and Morality"), his skin, eyes, and open mouth, the weight of his ashes in their urn. But she is not crudely literal. With a motif of birthing (used throughout *The Father*), the speaker internalizes his death:

> . . . my father
> moves, hour by hour, head-first,
> toward death, I sense every inch of him moving

> through me toward it, the way each child
> moved, slowly, down through my body . . . ("The Pulling")

The poems that recall the dead father do not allow the other to remain the other: the speaker absorbs the father into herself. The speaker's breast self-examination prompts recollections of the father's cancer, dying, and death. A live connection between father and daughter prevents her from shaking free of him.

> . . . when I
> lie down and get ready to die,
> prepare to find a sphere hard as a
> wizened pea-seed buried in my breast,
> I can feel myself
> slip into my father
> wholly, deep inside his flesh
> as if into a death-canoe
> fitted tight to the body. ("The Exam")

For the reader to demand a level of insight beyond what Olds offers here would be to expect pat generalities or religious sentiment. Religion is referred to rarely in *The Father*: in "His Terror," only a ritual act—eating the Eucharist, symbolically, the body of the divine Father—is accounted for, an act drained of spiritual significance. The poem shifts from the father's contact with his minister to the speaker's concern that a cry of pain or terror he has long stifled will break loose. Olds's efforts to plot the father–daughter relationship and the father's death-slide always skirt the safe truism. To expect a more specific account of the speaker's revelations is simply unwarranted. Instead, the poet's fearlessness must be acknowledged.

In Olds's previous works, the speaker's sympathy expands to the past, as the father's emotionally shortchanged boyhood is imagined: "When I love you now, / I like to think I am giving my love / directly to that boy in the fiery room, / as if it could reach him in time" ("Late Poem to My Father," *GC*). And her awareness of her father's idiosyncrasies stretches into the future, as the speaker recognizes the passing of his traits on to her children: "Sometimes my daughter looks at me with an / amber black look, like my father / about to pass out from disgust . . ." ("The Sign of Saturn," *DL*). No reader should be tricked into believing, though, that metaphorically pushing out the father's corpse in the canoe means the speaker is released from him. The plot of this relationship might very well continue as long as Olds writes. The past cannot be neatly confronted, interpreted, and resolved. Some plots resist a tidy closure.

NOTES

1. The following abbreviations are used for the titles of Sharon Olds's books: *SS* (*Satan Says*), *DL* (*The Dead and the Living*), and *GC* (*The Gold Cell*).

2. Hunt, Douglas, ed. *The Riverside Anthology of Literature*. 2nd ed. Boston: Houghton Mifflin, 1991.

WORKS CITED

Campbell, Katie. "Sharon Olds." *Contemporary Poets*. Ed. Tracy Chevalier. 5th ed. Chicago: St. James Press, 1991. 719–720.

Lerner, Laurence. "What is confessional poetry?" *Critical Quarterly* 29 (Summer 1987): 46–66.

McEwen, Christian. "Soul Substance." Rev. of *The Gold Cell*, by Sharon Olds. *The Nation* 11 April 1987: 472–475.

Olds, Sharon. *The Dead and the Living*. New York: Knopf, 1984.

———. *The Gold Cell*. New York: Knopf, 1989.

———. *The Father*. New York: Knopf, 1992.

———. "The Prepositions." *The New Yorker* 2 April 1990: 48.

———. *Satan Says*. University of Pittsburgh Press, 1980.

HELEN VENDLER

Rita Dove: Identity Markers

A primary imaginative donnée for the black poet Rita Dove—as for any other black poet in America—has to be the fact of blackness. Since we have not yet become a color-blind country, any black writer must confront, as an adult, the enraging fact that the inescapable social accusation of blackness becomes, too early for the child to resist it, a strong element of inner self-definition. A black writer thus composes both with and against racial identity. The tradition of American black poetry, only partially recoverable, displays a powerful array of responses to blackness, from the heartfelt Christian promise of the spirituals to the dialect-recovery of Dunbar and his imitators; from the social worldliness and urban language of the blues to the steely anthropological elegance of the poetry of Jay Wright. The history of a poet like Langston Hughes, at last fully available in the biography by Arnold Rampersad, can be read as a lifelong search for stances to take toward, against, and within blackness—from early Whitmanian inclusiveness to African *négritude*, from African *négritude* to idealistic Russian communism, from Russian communism (which turned out to be racist, too) to Harlem social commentary. Hughes's most candid social portraits of Harlem were, until recently, censored from mainstream anthologies, black and white alike, in favor of his more idealistic and mournful work; but, as we can now see more clearly, Hughes's poetic practice of social portraiture was one almost

From *Callaloo* 17, no. 2 (Spring 1994): 381–98. Copyright © 1994 by *Callaloo*.

entirely unrestricted, imaginatively speaking. But this wonderfully inclusive inventory was restricted in another way: lexically and syntactically, it limited itself to language that the most uneducated person could hear and understand. For a man of Hughes's far-ranging mind and reading, that linguistic self-restriction was a sign of unquestioned moral commitment to the black reader; within it, moved by the syncopated rhythm of boogie-woogie and by the unembarrassed explicitness of the blues, he recreated in the simplest possible words the street scenes he saw around him—the pimps, the faithless lovers, the pregnant adolescents, the practical cleaning-women, the weary mothers, the bewildered unemployed.

But a young intellectual like Rita Dove, growing with Hughes the most obvious literary role-model among older black poets, would have found her own inner life asking for more than a populist linguistic practice; yet she would have taken, I imagine, the stern commitment of Dunbar and Hughes and Brooks to a poetry understandable by all as a moral warning against a style cavalierly hermetic. I want to take up, as an example of the difficulty of writing lyric in America, Dove's experiments in the representation of her inner life, insofar as that representation reflects on blackness. I will be neglecting the handsome poems Dove has written that do not take blackness as one of their themes—notably, many of her poems on travel, on motherhood, and on aesthetic experience.

Rita Dove, now the Poet Laureate of the United States (a one-to-two-year post that used to be called, more accurately, "Consultant in Poetry to the Library of Congress"), was born in Akron, Ohio, in 1952. Her father was a research chemist for the Goodyear Tire and Rubber Company, and she first began to learn German at school in early adolescence, because she had been frustrated by the presence of her father's reference texts in German—the only books in the house she could not read. She was a National Merit Scholar at Miami University in Ohio, graduated *summa cum laude*, and went on a Fulbright Fellowship to the University of Tübingen; after that, she took an M.F.A. at the Iowa Writers' Workshop. She is now Professor of English at the University of Virginia, is married to a German novelist whom she met at Iowa, and has a daughter. During the 1980s, she published four books of poetry: in 1980, *The Yellow House on the Corner*; in 1983, *Museum*; in 1986, *Thomas and Beulah* (a sequence about grandparents' lives, which was awarded the Pulitzer Prize); and in 1989, *Grace Notes*.

Ideally, I would plunge immediately into Dove's notable successes; but because the problem of blackness is a thematic one, I have to address her initial difficulties in travelling that thematic path before coming to poetically workable solutions. No black has blackness as sole identity; and in lyric poems, poems of self-definition, one risks self-curtailment by adopting only a single identity-marker. A young poet, not yet well-acquainted with the reaches of her own identity, is more likely than someone older to focus on a single aspect of self; and we can see Dove focusing in this way in her first book, where she attempts to school herself in black historical memory. She writes, for instance, a dramatic monologue for a female slave petitioning, in 1782, to be set free:

> I am Belinda, an African,
> since the age of twelve a Slave.
> I will not take too much of your Time,
> but to plead and place my pitiable Life
> unto the Fathers of this Nation.[1]

Belinda has only two identity markers: she is female and she is a slave. Nearby in Dove's first book there is another monologue spoken by a house slave, probably female.[2] In yet another of these slave monologues, Dove widens her canvas by speaking as a man; we follow the abduction back into slavery of "Solomon Northrup / from Saratoga Springs, free papers in my pocket."[3] Dove (a cello and viola da gamba player herself) gives Solomon Northrup a violin under his arm to bring him closer to herself. She learns, through yet other poems, to find black personae who are close to her by reason of their intellectuality, and it does not stop her that they are men; such men are closer to her than a female persona like Belinda who, though of Dove's gender, would not possess those conceptualizing and linguistic drives that make a poet. Dove writes, for instance, about David Walker (1785–1830), a black Boston shop proprietor and pamphleteer. He slips his illegal pamphlets into his customer's pockets; his customers sew them into their coat-linings, but when these men are arrested, the pamphlets are discovered and subsequently read aloud in court. "*Men of colour, who are also of sense,*" one of the pamphlets begins:

> Outrage. Incredulity. Uproar in state legislatures.
>
> *We are the most wretched, degraded and abject set*
> *of beings that ever lived since the world began.*
> The jewelled canaries in the lecture halls tittered,
> pressed his dark hand between their gloves.
> Every half-step was no step at all.[4]

Many of Walker's fellow-blacks in Boston can't see the point of his protest; and finally, Walker's radicalism appalls even the abolitionist press. At forty-five, he is found dead in the doorway of his shop.

These historical personae, taken one by one, female and male, represent Dove's first, characteristically objective, steps toward the representation of her own identity as a black. She is not afraid to transgress, in choosing to use a male surrogate, the usual feminist laws of political correctness. She also transgresses the unspoken law by which a black writer is dissuaded from calling attention to divisions within the black community itself. A historical vignette, "The Transport of Slaves from Maryland to Mississippi," from Dove's first book, recounts how, in 1839, "a wagonload of slaves broke their chains, killed two white men, and would have escaped had not a slave woman helped the Negro driver [of the slavemaster's wagon] mount his horse and ride for help." "*I am no brute,*" says the slave woman. "*I got feelings. / He might have been a son of mine.*"[5] The slaves were re-captured because of the Negro driver's loyalty to his white master, to whom he reported their escape.

Dove is willing to narrate, without prejudice, the Negro driver's conflict between economic loyalty and race-loyalty, and the Negro woman's conflict between group-loyalty to her fellow escapees and race-loyalty to the driver. The many faces of division within the black community are part of her subject, as they were part of Langston Hughes's subject also. In her early years as a writer, Dove entered a literary scene where both assimilation and separatism had powerful voices in their favor, and her first book shows, in the tragic anecdote of the transport of slaves, as well as in the account of the repudiation of David Walker by the Boston abolitionist press, her willingness to make her readers uneasy. Yet even the best of her historical narratives become somewhat stagy in their strained joining of the exigencies of plot to lyric implication. The lyric has not created the plot, as it should have done (and as it does in the best narrative lyrics, like "The Rime of the Ancient Mariner"); history has given the plot, and the lyric has had to dance to its tune.

Even when freed of historical circumstance, Dove's "slave poetry" exhibits a certain awkwardness in its wish to achieve historical linguistic probability. The poem ironically entitled "The Slave's Critique of Practical Reason" transcribes the slave's decision, as he picks cotton, not to attempt an escape; the slave speaks in a "folksy" language that nonetheless unconvincingly drops into—or rises towards—complex vocabulary and metaphor:

Ain't got a reason
to run away—
leastways, not one
would save my life.
So I scoop speculation
into a hopsack.

I scoop fluff till
the ground rears white
and I'm the only dark
spot in the sky.[6]

Against these relatively unsuccessful historical excursions in a lyric time-machine, Dove's first book sets sudden contemporary glimpses that are bravely achieved, like the "odyssey" of six black adolescents out on the town in a car:

We six pile in, the engine churning ink:
We ride into the night.
Past factories, past graveyards
And the broken eyes of windows, we ride
Into the gray-green nigger night. . . .
In the nigger night, thick with the smell of cabbages,
Nothing can catch us.
Laughter spills like gin from glasses,
And "yeah" we whisper, "yeah"
We croon, "yeah."[7]

This may owe something to Gwendolyn Brooks' "We Real Cool," but it avoids the prudishness of Brooks's judgmental monologue, which though it is ostensibly spoken by adolescents, barely conceals its adult reproach of their behavior.

Even as she was sketching historical personae and contemporary adolescents in her attempts to represent blackness, Dove was writing color-neutral poems. In fact, the best poem in *The Yellow House on the Corner* has not a word to say about the fraught subject of blackness. It is a poem of perfect wonder, showing Dove as a young girl in her parents' house doing her lessons, mastering geometry, seeing for the first time the coherence and beauty of the logical principles of spatial form. The poem "Geometry" is really about what geometry and poetic form have in common; and its concluding adjectives, "true" and "unproven," are revealing ones with respect to Dove's poetry:

Geometry

I prove a theorem and the house expands:
the windows jerk free to hover near the ceiling,
the ceiling floats away with a sigh.

> As the walls clear themselves of everything
> but transparency, the scent of carnations
> leaves with them. I am out in the open
>
> and above the windows have hinged into butterflies,
> sunlight glinting where they've intersected.
> They are going to some point true and unproven.[8]

As the windows jerk free the ceiling floats away, sense-experience is suspended; during pure mentality, pure transparency, even the immaterial scent of carnations departs. The magical transformation of the windows into butterflies is perhaps brought about as the geometrical word "intersection"—by way of the word "insect"—suggests the wings of Psyche. The poem illustrates Dove's sure way with images, which are always, in her poems, surrogates for argument. She often avoids proof by propositions in favor of the cunning arrangement of successive images, which themselves enact, by their succession, an implicit argument.

Here, for instance, from a poem called "D.C." (the "District of Columbia" in which the city of Washington is located), is Dove's indictment of the city. She begins with its most visible synecdoche, the obelisk-shaped Washington Monument, a "bloodless finger pointing to heaven," its bloodlessness a figure for heartlessness. She ends with the Monument, too, as its image lies reflected in the long pool at its base; this time, the obelisk is the cue stick of a billiard-game, "outrageous" because of the gambles with lives taken in this increasingly black city. In between are other images—impartially threatening here, seductive there—of Washington:

> A bloodless finger pointing to heaven, you say,
> is surely no more impossible than this city:
> A no man's land, a capital askew,
> a postcard framed by imported blossoms—
> and now this outrageous cue stick
> lying, reflected on a black table.[9]

A passage like this helps to define Dove's imagination, which is rapid, extrapolative, montage-like and relational.

The most interesting implicit commentary by Dove on her own imagination comes from a memory recalled in her fiction. The young woman protagonist of the story called "First Suite" has driven across the country to the school where she will be teaching, and arrives, exhausted, a day early. The school nurse tells her to rest on a cot in the school sickroom. As her eyes adjust to the darkened room, she takes in her surroundings, seeing first some cotton swabs, "ranged in a misty circle around the barely visible rim of a jar." She sees a digital clock, too. On that slender basis—a glass jar with swabs and glowing digital numbers—her imagination begins to work:

> I could imagine the rest of the glass and the wooden sticks as they drew together in a perfect cone, then going on to form the mirror image of that cone, like a severe hourglass. The orange ciphers of a digital clock flared: 9:59, 10:00. I knew I would sleep fitfully until I had seen 11:11—markings in the sand, reckonings. Four marks and a diagonal slashing the four—a numerical group. The Babylonian merchant drew his staff through the sand, eight bunches of fire-wood—see, I have forty bushels of fine Egyptian cotton to trade.[10]

The glass (because of the proximity of the clock) becomes an hourglass as its cone of swabs is geometrically projected into a mirror-cone, like a Yeatsian gyre; the hourglass conjures up sand; sand conjures up Egypt; the wooden sticks of the swabs create the eight bunches of firewood for sale by the Babylonian merchant, as the hospital gauze lying unremarked beside the swabs (but soon to be noticed) creates the bushels of Egyptian cotton. The speaker's observation of the digital clock-numbers leads to a counting obsession, which compels her to stay awake till the numbers regulate themselves into perfect symmetry at eleven minutes after eleven—four marks in the sand, which become marks made by the staff of the Babylonian merchant.

Some such idiosyncratic associative process lies behind most of Dove's poems. "Association," however, is perhaps too languid a word to use of this process, since it has strong elements (visible in the excerpt I have quoted) of obsessive behavior. Until something has been done to reality, some operation performed upon it, this poet is restless. Things seem radically incomplete when they present themselves, in life, for inspection. To make things "perfect," the mind must extrapolate the cone made by the wooden sticks of the cotton swabs until it makes the more "integrable" image of an hourglass, itself dictated by the clock; the hourglass, then must find its pictorial completion in sand; a use must be found for the image of sand, and Egypt is brought in; the clock must be watched until the numbers "come right"; the gauze, in order to enter the Egyptian fantasy, has to be fitted into a non-medical use; the sticks of the swabs must undergo a change in scale and become firewood, and so on. The almost inhuman elation felt by the young girl at the end of the poem "Geometry" can now be better understood: once the theorem is proved, an incessant anxiety is given momentary relief, and the soul is briefly untethered, relieved from the confining pressure of internal cognitive difference. All of the images presented to sight in the fictional excerpt I have quoted are in fact elements of such a "theorem" and must be somehow put into a relational syntax by means of such processes as extrapolation, completion, adjustment, coupling, enlargement or diminution of scale, and so on. When they all achieve a mental "fit," the protagonist can go to sleep, even without waiting for the magical symmetry of 11:11: as she says, "11:11 clicked by unnoticed; I slept until the door opened."[11] It was enough, for the relief of her anxiety, to have conceived in her mind the point at which the clock numbers would be no longer asymmetrical, as they had been at 9:59 or 10:00.

Dove does not always achieve her "fit." Even in an ultimately successful poem she is sometimes misled en route, as she tells us in a very interesting set of remarks on an extraordinary poem called "Parsley," which appears in her second collection, *Museum*. "Parsley" attempts to deal with blackness by moving out of the predicament of African Americans, looking instead at an incident in the lives of migrant Haitian workers in the Dominican Republic where, as Dove's note[12] tells us, Rafael Trujillo in 1937 "ordered 20,000 blacks killed because they could not pronounce the letter 'r' in *perejil*, the Spanish word for parsley."[13] The Haitians, speaking Creole (Kréyol), could not roll their "r"s in the Spanish Fashion; and as each failed the test of saying *perejil* correctly, he or she was killed.

"Parsley" has two parts, the first a song sung by the Haitian cane-cutters, the second a depiction (in free indirect discourse) of the dictator's thoughts as he plans the execution order. Dove has spoken of her false starts in writing "Parsley":

> When I wrote the poem I tried it in many different ways. I tried a sestina, particularly in the second part, "The Palace," simply because the obsessiveness of the sestina, the repeated words, was something I wanted to get—that driven quality—in the poem. I gave up the sestina very early. It was too playful for the poem. A lot of the words stayed—the key words like *parrot* and *spring* and, of course, *parsley*. The first part was a villanelle. I thought I was going to do the entire poem from the Haitians' point of view. And that wasn't enough. I had this villanelle, but it wasn't enough. And there was a lot more that I hadn't said, so I tried the sestina and gave that up.[14]

The "lot more" that Dove had not said after she wrote her song for the cane-cutters turned out to be Part II, her eerily-imagined monologue for Trujillo:

> It fascinated me that this man would think of such an imaginative way to kill someone, to kill lots of people; that, in fact, he must have

gotten some kind of perverse joy out of finding a way to do it so that people would speak their own death sentences.[15]

In these remarks we can see Dove's attraction to obsessive forms like the sestina and the villanelle, but we can also see her principled refusal of their attraction when such "playfulness" threatens to interfere with a more important part of the poem's "fit," its moral seriousness. We can also see Dove's inveterate wish to imagine and understand, if not to forgive, the mind of the victimizer as well as the mind of the victims. Poems of victimage, told from the point of view of the victim, are the stock-in-trade of mediocre protest writing, and they appear regularly in African American literature. The position of victimage, and victimage alone, seems imaginatively insufficient to Dove, since it takes in only one half of the world. That half has of course great pathos, and we hear that pathos in the song she writes for the cane-cutters. Its initial reference to a parsley-green parrot in the dictator's palace remains obscure until the second half of the poem. The cane-cutters sing:

There is a parrot imitating spring
in the palace, its feathers parsley green.
Out of the swamp the cane appears

to haunt us, and we cut it down. El General
searches for a word; he is all the world
there is. Like a parrot imitating spring,

we lie down screaming as rain punches through
and we come up green. We cannot speak an R—
out of the swamp, the cane appears

and then the mountain we call in whispers *Katalina*.
The children gnaw their teeth to arrowheads.
There is a parrot imitating spring.

El General has found his word: *perejil*.
Who says it, lives. He laughs, teeth shining
out of the swamp. The cane appears

in our dreams, lashed by wind and streaming.
And we lie down. For every drop of blood
there is a parrot imitating spring.
Out of the swamp the cane appears.[16]

As she does in this quasi-villanelle, Dove characteristically opens a poem with an oblique and unexplained sentence. The ineluctable reappearance of the fast-growing sugar-cane, no matter how often it is cut down, is enacted, musically, in the exhausting persistence of the phrase "the cane appears"; but its recurrent drone is sharply countered by the menacing appearance of the "General," who, so to speak, will not permit the natural (if enslaving) villanelle-song to continue.

The almost-sestina of the General has seven stanzas of seven or eight lines each, and a single, detached, one-line conclusion. It is too long to quote whole, but in summary it reveals that the parrot had belonged to the General's dead mother, and that in her village, when a woman bore a son, the men of the town wore celebratory sprigs of parsley in their capes. The General, deranged since his mother's death, and hearing the parrot repeatedly call his name in her voice, feels that he, as her son, is dishonored by the presence, in his country, of people who cannot pronounce her language, cannot, with the word "parsley" correctly pronounced, celebrate his male existence. The General, too, lives in the continual anxiety of the obsessive-compulsive; his relief comes by killing. He haunts his mother's room in the palace,

> the one without
> curtains, the one with a parrot
> in a brass ring. As he paces he wonders
> Who can I kill today. And for a moment
> the little knot of screams
> is still.

He orders, for the parrot, his mother's favorite pastries, and as they arrive, "The knot in his throat starts to twitch." He hears the Haitians singing a Spanish song, "Mi madre, mi amor en muerte," and is irritated by their inability to pronounce the "r"s:

> Even
> A parrot can roll an R! In the bare room
> the bright feathers arch in a parody
> of greenery, as the last pale crumbs
> disappear under the blackened tongue. Someone

> calls out his name in a voice
> so like his mother's, a startled tear
> splashes the tip of his right boot.
> *My mother, my love in death.*

The general remembers the tiny green sprigs
men of his village wore in their capes
to honor the birth of a son. He will
order many, this time, to be killed

for a single, beautiful word.

The general sense of certain Spanish words has been permanently eroticized
by their association with his mother, and, as obsessed with language as any
poet, he kills to defend his mother's honor. Rita Dove enters the dictator's
mind, and imagines a sinisterly plausible motive for the mass executions
based on a bizarre word-test. Dove's stanzaic imitation of Trujillo's disin-
tegrating yet obsessively circling monologue is a wonderful piece of imaginative mortise-and-tenon work. The poem represents, in Dove's career, a
dramatic advance, imaginatively speaking, in the treatment of blackness.
It also marks Dove's continued watchful distance from pure lyric; she is
nowhere to be seen in her poem.

   This changes with the supremely confident poem "Agosta the Winged
Man and Rasha the Black Dove," which appeared in the same collection.
Though the American Rita Dove is, once again, nowhere to be seen in the
poem as a lyric "I," her surrogate is present as "Rasha, the Black Dove." When
Dove was a Fulbright student in Germany, she came across a painting of two
Berlin sideshow "freaks" of the 1920s. The portrait, by the artist Christian
Schad (1894–1982), was painted in 1929; the title of the portrait is "Agosta
the Winged Man and Rasha the Black Dove." It is reproduced on the cover of
Museum, and shows Agosta—his naked torso deformed by a bone disease that
causes his ribs and scapulars to point out through his skin like wings—and,
seated below him, his fellow circus-freak—a perfectly normal and handsome
woman whose only freakishness (in the Berlin of 1929) was that she was
black. Rita Dove, herself black, found herself confronting Rasha the Black
Dove of Schad; it is no wonder the portrait generated one of Dove's most
gripping poems.

   The poem is voiced indirectly through Schad the (white) painter. At
first he thinks that his own scrupulous and dispassionate eye is "merciless"
as it sees and reproduces, in unadorned and unconcealed directness, the two
figures—one medically, the other socially, marginal—set aside as freaks by his
society. But then he repents, and thinks, "The canvas, / not his eye, was merciless." It is the exaction of his medium, the stylized accuracy demanded by the
portrait-genre, that guarantees the mercilessness of his work. But at the close,
as Schad comes to a final decision about the composition of the two figures,
he changes his mind yet again:

> Agosta in
> classical drapery, then
> and Rasha at his feet.
> Without passion. Not
> the canvas
>   but their gaze,
>   so calm,
> was merciless.[17]

It is the stigmatized figures, heroically posed, gazing out forever at those who gaze at them, who are "merciless." True, the artist's eye, with its absence of distorting, revulsive "passion" before these "freaks," plays a role; true, the canvas which confers, in its recollection of the history of portraiture, classical drapery on this "ignoble" couple also plays a part; but it is *what* is rendered through eye and generic convention—the socially-marked persons of Agosta and Rasha in 1929 Berlin—that mercilessly indicts German culture. As the young Rita Dove saw her counterpart—a Madagascan woman who could find work only by agreeing to dance entwined with a boa constrictor, and who was given the circus sobriquet of "The Black Dove" in order to recall the old emblem of serpent-and-dove—she knew *something* had to be merciless. In deciding on subject-matter, Dove does not discount either the painterly eye or genre-convention, but she asserts that eye and head have to bend their attention on deep and consequential things, and that those things must "gaze" out at the beholder so as to compel a returning gaze, one coupled with self-examination.

It is evident from such a poem, and from its attention to a painting by a white artist of a stigmatized black woman, that Dove has thought hard about medium, message, and artist as they cooperate to make art. No black artist can avoid the question of skin color, and what it entails, as subject matter; and probably the same is still true, to a lesser extent, of the woman artist and the subject matter of gender. And yet if these important subject matters are not presented by a dispassionate eye and a trained hand, the result will not be art, and will not exert a gaze prompting the beholder to examine his own conscience.

It was Dove's next book *Thomas and Beulah*, that won the Pulitzer Prize in 1986. The book springs from the history of Dove's maternal grandparents, who migrated North (each from a different Southern state) and married in Ohio. The life they made in Akron between marriage and death is the subject matter of the poems, written as two sequences, the first for Thomas, the second for Beulah. Dove solves the "color question" here by having everyone in the central story be black; daily life, then, is just daily life, even though it is in part controlled by a white context appearing only on the edges of the story. The gender question is treated in the poem even-handedly, as Dove, who never appears in person in the book, writes in sympathy with both Thomas and Beulah, often reproducing their own sense of themselves in free indirect discourse. Dove no longer looks to the antebellum slave record, nor to exotic collective massacres, nor to interwar Berlin, to revive history; she records it instead as the account, living vividly in contemporary memory, of the industrial and domestic servitude of two ordinary American people in the earlier twentieth century. Dove integrates here two areas she had earlier tended to keep separate—"low" art as in "Nigger Song: An Odyssey," and "high" art as in "Agosta." In *Thomas and Beulah*, she keeps the individual sequences as elegant in structural form as a *lieder* cycle, while letting colloquial black talk run freely through them. The story of Thomas and Beulah unrolls through brief snapshots (the history of their children, for instance, appears in Thomas' four disappointed words—"Girl girl/girl girl"[18]). It is a common story—both parents working in marginal jobs for low pay, Thomas in the Zeppelin factory, Beulah as a domestic and a milliner; Thomas' eventual lay-off in the Depression; Beulah's disappointment in marriage and exhaustion in maternity; and finally their illnesses and deaths in poverty. But the sequences are punctuated by the ordinary satisfactions, too: making hair pomade, attending a daughter's wedding, buying—at a church rummage sale—an encyclopedia with "One Volume Missing," *V* through *Z*—"for five bucks/no zebras, no Virginia,/ no wars."[19]

From this rich double-sequence of 44 poems (23 for Thomas, 21 for Beulah) I want to take as my example one of the poems that treats the life of a black person without the context of whiteness, as simply one life among others. The poem "Aircraft" depicts Thomas working as riveter in an airplane factory, in what should have been the heady days of a steady paycheck. But Thomas is not happy, as he faces yet another morning of his work:

> Too frail for combat, he stands
> before an interrupted wing,
> playing with an idea, nothing serious.
> Afternoons, the hall gaped with aluminum
> glaring, flying toward the sun; now
> though, first thing in the morning, there is only
> gray sheen and chatter
> from the robust women around him
> and bolt waiting for his riveter's
> five second blast.

The night before in the dark
of the peanut gallery, he listened to blouses shifting
and sniffed magnolias, white
tongues of remorse
sinking into the earth. Then
the newsreel leapt forward
into war.

Why *frail?* Why not simply
family man? Why wings, when
women with fingers no smaller than his
dabble in the gnarled intelligence of an engine?

And if he gave just a four second blast,
or three? Reflection is such

a bloodless light.
After lunch, they would bathe in fire.[20]

The things here that make Thomas unhappy are not blackness and white oppression—not at all. He is unhappy because he has been refused induction into the army, as "too frail for combat"; and he is unhappy because women outclass him at work; they get the interesting work of assembling "the gnarled intelligence of an engine" while he is nothing but a riveter of airplane wings. The only form of vengeance for these insults that Thomas can conceive as within his power would be to disobey his working orders, and give to his rivets, instead of the prescribed five-second tightening-time, "just a four second blast, or three." He merely plays with this dangerous idea, but even his telling himself that it is "nothing serious" means that he has thought of it enough to repudiate it.

Why does it seem so extraordinary to have a black man treated as an ordinary person, with ordinary physical and social resentments? Somewhere in the background, of course, Thomas's blackness tacitly figures, if only his poverty—he has to sit in "the peanut gallery" of the moviehouse. But Dove's picture of a mind that is occupied with induction-disappointment and gender-jealousy is both particular enough not to attempt a false "universality" and humdrum enough to make Thomas like many other men, white as well as black. With her usual cunning, Dove presents Thomas' interior monologue in interlocking thematic snippets, concerning A) War, B) Disobedience, C) Masculine Fire, and D) Women. The sequence of these elements, abstractly rendered, would look like this:

A: Draft-board insult—induction denied
B: Thought [of possible work-disobedience]—dismissed
C: Afternoon brilliance of light, obscuring factory environment
D: Contrasting morning grayness and chatter of women, linked
B: Prescribed order of riveting

D: Flashback to moviehouse, with Thomas longing (remorsefully)
for extramarital sex
A: Newsreel of war

A: Induction insult remembered
D: Defense against infidelity; assertion of marital bond
A/D: Insult repeated—women have better jobs in war-work

B: Thought of vengeance (in reprisal for insults) once again
entertained—this time clearly defined as subversion of orders—
but reflection if dismissed as

D: A bloodless light like the gray light of morning, time of the
chatter of women
C: Longing for fiery brilliance of afternoon.

If we turn this scheme into a string of code, its DNA reads:

ABCD: 10 lines
DA: 7 lines
ADA/D: 4 lines
B: 2 lines
DC: 2 lines

As the space of each successive stanza becomes more constricted, the tension between insult and vengeance—between a longed-for masculine fiery glare and the actual gray female superiority—grows. Dove fleshes out each of her elements—ABCD—by tiny vignettes, so that each takes on characteristic sensual force; and she links the elements of the vignettes by an immediate musicality, as *gaped* matches *glaring* and *gray*, *bolt* is echoed by *blast*, *gallery* presages *magnolias*, *sinking* joins *leapt*, *intelligence* eerily connects to *engine*. The early separate *w*'s of *wing*, *with*, *women*, and *white*, suddenly flare into a flurry of repeated *w*'s: *war*, *why*, *why*, *why*, *wings*, *when*, *women*, *with*—eight words beginning with *w* out of thirteen successive words:

... war.
Why *frail?* Why not simply
family man? Why wings, when
women with. . . .

One can almost hear Thomas' frustrated stutter accompany his three successive indignant questions. It is not cowardice that makes Thomas draw back from vengeance, nor patriotism that prevents his impulse to sabotage the firmness of his rivets. It is rather the fact that abstract and "bloodless" reflection is not natural to him; he lives in a world of work, visuality, and sexual desire, not a second-order world of thought. To comfort himself, he turns his mind to the satisfying masculine exaltation of aluminum glare in the afternoon sun, as the word *fire*, with which the poem ends, satisfyingly combats and "replaces" the insult *frail*, with which the poem had begun. Of course, if the two words did not share three essential letters, the replacement would not seem so poetically satisfying.

Thomas and Beulah represents Dove's rethinking of the lyric poet's relation to the history of blackness. No longer bound to a single lyric moment, she lets the raw data of life (perceived by a man and by his wife at the same epoch and in the same circumstances) become pieces for a reader to assemble. The sure hand of form supports each life-glimpse: cunningly counter-balancing each other into stability, the tart and touching individual poems add up to a sturdy two-part invention, symbolizing that mysterious third thing, a lifelong marriage, lived, it is true, in blackness but not determined by blackness alone.

This important discovery—that blackness need not be one's central subject, but equally need not be omitted—has governed Dove's work since *Thomas and Beulah*. Various poems and sequences in *Grace Notes* (1989) have adopted this attitude, neither focusing exclusively on race nor excluding it from presence when it comes up.[21] The aesthetic level from which this balancing of subject-matter arises has nothing much to do, I think, with blackness. It comes from Dove's discovery (as she puts it in a poem called "Particulars") that life exhibits a "lack of conclusion," and presents an "eternal *dénouement*."[22] For a poet obsessively concerned with "fit," with what "Particulars" dryly calls "agenda"—having one's "second coffee at nine ... / crying every morning, ten sharp—," the recognition of the repetitiveness of that pattern makes the notion of "particular sorrow" moot. The newly-learned "secret" of life—that it lacks conclusion, is always unknotting what it has knotted—is the most devastating secret a poet like Dove, loving conclusiveness, could learn. "Each knot of grief, / each snagged insistence"[23] is now subject to being unwound; and somehow the poems will have to insist on the temporariness of their psychic states rather than on conclusiveness and "fit" alone. This means the abandon of the "dovetailing"—and the pun is justified—which was, aesthetically, so enormously reassuring in a poem like "Aircraft." I think Dove is not yet sure of what can replace dovetailing in the terms of formal construction. But she knows thematically that exploration of un-dovetailed conditions and unknown places is what lies in store for her. I will take up, then, from *Grace Notes*, two examples of Dove's new style, both dealing in some way with blackness.

Blackness begins, but does not end, a poem called "Stitches"; the poet slips and falls, breaking open an old scar so that she has to be taken to the hospital Emergency Room to have the wound stitched. During the poem, she carries on a sardonic dialogue (in italics) with herself, first in self-reproach for carelessness, then in self-reproach for her instant metaphorizing of the doctor's stitching of her wound. In the beginning of the poem, the tear in the flesh is immediately interpreted by the first, inveterate referent for any black, blackness—which always threatens to be the only referent for self, closing down other facts of identity:

> When skin opens
> where a scar
> should be, I think nothing but
> "So I *am* white underneath!"
> Blood swells then
> dribbles into the elbow.

At the end of the poem, we meet first the witty set of metaphors about the doctor stitching the wound (including a last invoking of blackness, skin being seen as "topsoil"), and then the poet's self-reproach for her automatic wish to trope everything, no matter what the occasion. Blackness is forgotten in favor of critical self-interrogation:

> The doctor's teeth are beavery, yellow:
> he whistles as he works, as topsoil
> puckers over its wound. Amazing
> there's no pain—just pressure
> as the skin's tugged up by his thread
>
> like a trout, a black line straight
> from a seamstress' nightmare: foot-tread
> pedalling the need right through.

You just can't stop being witty, can you?

Oh, but I can. I always could.[24]

The self that hates wit, and utters the sardonic baiting line, is the same self that makes wit. The more interesting alternative self, emerging only in the rebuttal closing the poem, is a non-ironic one, always present but sometimes choosing, by allowing wit its play, to refrain from "earnestness."

That "earnest" self is the self of most first-generation black American poets. It was first countered in a sustained way by Langston Hughes, who took on the wit and gallantry of the blues as an antidote to plangency or indignation. The "earnest" self behind "Stitches" cannot any longer use the sophisticated and oblique "arrangements" of the artificer-self; and so "Stitches" is told chronologically, in the order of its happening, rather than by the process of reflective faceting which organized a poem like "Aircraft." "Stitches," as it progresses, literally shows blackness being forgotten in favor of the more urgent inner aesthetic conflict between earnestness and wit. And yet by admitting that her first, instinctive response to a wound was her assertion of inner whiteness, Dove shows blackness as an ever-present, unsheddable first skin of consciousness, a constant spur to "earnestness" against the aesthetic playfulness of poetic wit.

The last poem I will mention is one I perhaps do not entirely understand. It is called "Medusa,"[25] and plays (I think) with the idea of blackness as conferring gorgon-status on a black female. Sexual feeling is identified with an underground cave-like liquid darkness which the eye, that "hairy star," cannot reach and is in danger of forgetting:

> I've got to go
> down where my eye
> can't reach
> hairy star
> who forgets to shiver
> forgets the cool suck
> inside

In a famous poem, "I, Too," published in 1932, Langston Hughes prophesied eventual justice for the American black—that he would be invited to leave his ignominious place in the kitchen and join in the general feast at the table. And yet, for Hughes, justice alone does not suffice. Hughes ends his poem with a vision that was astonishing at its moment in the 1930s—that the aesthetic of America will change, and that the black body, which seemed a thing of revulsion, and the black soul, which seemed a thing apart, will be seen, amazingly, as *beautiful*:

> Tomorrow,
> I'll be at the table
> When company comes.
> Nobody'll dare
> Say to me,
> "Eat in the kitchen,"
> Then.
>
> Besides,
> They'll see how beautiful I am
> and be ashamed—
>
> I, too, am America.[26]

Dove's "Medusa" is a descendant of "I, Too," and embodies a comparable prophecy: that the despised Medusa, once she is truly seen and loved, will become a star (even a constellation) in that process that "stellified" Bernice's and Belinda's hair:

> Someday long
> off someone will
> see me
> fling me up
> until I hook
> into sky

What is the price that must be paid by the person who learns to see and love the gorgon? He must "drop his memory" of his former aesthetic, as America will learn, in Hughes's prophecy, to think beautiful what it formerly thought, under a more restricted aesthetic, repellent. And what will happen to Medusa once she is stellified? Her hair, once represented as serpentine, but in reality a liquid darkness with its "cool suck" and "shiver," will become, in the astral cold, something like a halo of icicles: "My hair/ dry water." Let me reproduce this mythological tale of the redemption of blackness once more:

> I've got to go
> down where my eye

can't reach
hairy star
who forgets to shiver
forgets the cool suck
inside

Someday long
off someone will
see me
fling me up
until I hook
into sky

drop his memory

My hair
dry water[27]

This manner of dealing with blackness—non-autobiographical, mythological, cryptic—is at the opposite pole from the journalistic demeanor of
"Stitches," or, looking back, from the historical focus of the slave narratives,
the geographic exoticism of "Parsley" and "Agosta," and the realistic story of
Thomas and Beulah. The severe geometry of form in "Medusa" suggests the
power of Dove's writing to embody a black identity without being constricted
by it to a single manner. More than any other contemporary black poet, Dove
has taken on the daunting aesthetic question of how to be faithful to, and yet
unconstrained by, the presence—always already given a black American—
of blackness. She earns, by a poem like "Medusa," her epigraphs prefacing
sections of *Grace Notes*—Cavafy's clear-eyed advice, "Don't hope for things
elsewhere,"[28] and Claude McKay's celebratory remark on "the dark delight
of being strange."[29] When Whitman remarked, in the *Song of the Exposition*,
that the Muse had left Greece and had come to inhabit America—"She's
here, installed amid the kitchen ware!"—he, along alone our nineteenth-cen-
tury poets, might have foreseen that in one of her incarnations this American Muse would be one with the terrifying Medusa-face of slavery—but a
Medusa who would become, by taking her liberty into her own hands and
opening herself to a recognizing love, an American icon of the beautiful.

Notes

1. Rita Dove, *Selected Poems* (New York: Pantheon, 1993), p. 28. All quotes
from the first three collections of Dove's poetry are taken from this volume.

2. *Ibid.*, p. 29.

3. *Ibid.*, p. 31.

4. *Ibid.*, p. 30.

5. *Ibid.*, p. 32.

6. *Ibid.*, p. 38.

7. *Ibid.*, p. 14.

8. *Ibid.*, p. 17.

9. *Ibid.*, p. 22.

10. Rita Dove, "The First Suite," (from a novel-in-progress), in *Black American Literature Forum* 20 (Fall 1986), p. 244. The passage, somewhat cut, appears in Dove's novel, *Through the Ivory Gate* (New York: Pantheon, 1992), p. 19. What is cut out is the imagination: the extrapolated cone, the obsessive relation to the digital numbers, and the fantasy of the Babylonian merchant. These would all be entirely at home in a poem by Dove; her cutting them out of her novel suggests that she has not yet come to a desirable integration of her imaginative with her tale-telling impulses.

11. *Ibid.*, p. 245.

12. *Selected Poems*, p. 136.

13. Here and elsewhere the correct date of the Haitian massacres, 1937, is mistranscribed as 1957. The event is described by Robert D. Crassweller, in his biography *Trujillo* (New York: Macmillan, 1966), pp. 154–56, as follows:

> The terrible events of the thirty six hours that began on the night of October 2 . . . had surely been planned well in advance, as a kind of military operation . . .
>
> In Santiago alone the [Dominican] Army rounded up between one and two thousand Haitians, herded them into a courtyard formed by government buildings, and systematically decapitated them with machetes, this weapon being used whenever possible in preference to firearms in order to simulate a spontaneous attack by an enraged Dominican peasantry. In Monte Cristi another large group of Haitians was marched at gunpoint to the end of the harbor pier, with arms bound, and simply pushed into deep water to drown. . . .
>
> A crude test was adopted to probe the claim of Dominican nationality which the terrified Haitians often cried out. Everyone was asked to say the Spanish word *perejil*, and those who pronounced it "pelegil" were damned as Haitians and cut down without further ado. . . .
>
> The number of those who perished in these October hours will never be known with accuracy. . . . Estimates range from a low of 5,000 to a high of 25,000. The Haitian Government at one time put forth a figure of 12,000 fatalities, and Trujillo in later days spoke of 18,000. A figure between 15,000 and 20,000 would be a reasonable estimate, but this is guesswork. . . .
>
> An almost incredible time elapsed between the killings and the world's knowledge of them. The first public mention appeared in *The New York Times* on October 21, seventeen days after the events. . . . It reported rumors of a border clash in which "several Haitians" had been shot.

Crassweller does not give a specific source for the story about the test-by-pronunciation. Jesús de Galindez, in *The Era of Trujillo*—published only in 1973 by the University of Arizona Press, Tucson, but submitted as a doctoral dissertation at Columbia University in 1956, shortly before Galindez disappeared, probably kidnapped and murdered by Trujillo forces—does not mention the test; he does say that "private sources mention 20,000 and even 25,000" killed (p. 209).

14. "Conversation with Rita Dove," ed. Stan Sanvel Rubin and Earl G. Ingersoll, *Black American Literature Forum* 20 (Fall, 1986), pp. 230–31.

15. *Ibid.*, p. 230.

16. *Selected Poems*, p. 133.

17. *Ibid.*, p. 100.

18. *Ibid.*, p. 158.

19. *Ibid.*, p. 163.

20. *Ibid.*, p. 160.

21. However, Dove can still write a poem where race is the central concern, like the relatively unsuccessful "Arrow," which fails because it has no imaginative interest in the lecturer whom it accuses of racism.

22. Rita Dove, *Grace Notes* (New York: W.W. Norton, 1989), p. 31.

23. *Ibid.*, p. 43.

24. *Ibid.*, p. 51.

25. *Ibid.*, p. 55.

26. Langston Hughes, *Selected Poems* (New York: Vintage, 1990), p. 275.

27. *Grace Notes*, p. 55.

28. *Ibid.*, p. 57.

29. *Ibid.*, p. 45.

JEANNE PERREAULT

New Dreaming: Joy Harjo, Wendy Rose, Leslie Marmon Silko

We come to dream this reality
sus
    pended
            between the arcs of
space & time.

                  (Sanchez "Open Dream Sequence" 228)

I. Introduction: Beautiful Dream

In the work of the Native American writers I am discussing here, dreaming constitutes a semiotic field in which realities are made in the naming. Within the parameters of such a dream-field the past can be reclaimed; the present revised, and a future made possible. In this literary dreaming, the past leaks into the present just as the spirit vision spills over into the material world. All categories demarcating degrees of realness come apart at the seams. Any artist may be said to work in the interstice "between the arcs of / space & time," but in the poems of many contemporary Native American writers the reality that is dreamed there draws the arcs of place and movement and time into a great circle.[1]

The poetry asserts that even the worst moments of the past must be faced, the most painful of historical fragmentations accepted if the circle is to

From *Deferring a Dream: Literary Sub-Versions of the American Columbiad*, pp. 120–36. Copyright © 1994 by Birkhäuser Verlag Basel.

61

be realized. Black Elk articulates such a moment, naming and mourning it, as he gives testimony of the slaughter at Little Big Horn:

> When I look back now from this high hill of my old age, I can still see the butchered women and children lying heaped and scattered all along the crooked gulch as plain as when I saw them with eyes still young. And I can see that something else died there in the bloody mud and was buried in the blizzard. A people's dream died there. It was a beautiful dream. . . . the nation's hoop is broken and scattered. There is no center any longer, and the sacred tree is dead. (419)

The past refuses its boundaries. As witness, Black Elk testifies not only to his original experience but also to the immutability of that sight. "I can still see," he tells us, and such perpetuated seeing refuses dissolution, and requires his audience to see with him from the doubled place of metaphor. The "high hill" of his old age and the height from which he looked down on his slaughtered people overlap in figural space. But the "bloody mud," the bodies "heaped and scattered" that existed in the past and shape the present do not confine his vision. He sees "something else," something beyond the fact or the memory of murder. Black Elk sees the not-visible, the death of his people's dream. The "dream" and the "people" coalesce in Black Elk's vision, and the people's dream is not of something, but is them.

The "beautiful dream" that Black Elk mourns is, however, not dead, and the people are not vanishing.[2] Though the grief and loss that he expresses continue to pervade the lives and the writings of Native Americans, that ongoing anguish is not the only truth. Another generation of Native speakers is making another dream emerge. Abenaki poet Joseph Bruchac describes that hope, quoting Ray Young Bear, 'from spiritual strength there came survival,' then going on:

> When we combine that spiritual power with the kind of intellectual awareness which characterized the best of our elders for untold thousands of years as they struggled to survive, knowing that life was not meant to be easy, we find ourselves with a body of art which dreams the tribal past into tradition . . . which points out the paths to survival.[3]

Bruchac, and others, claim a new dream, nourished by the old ways and the old strengths of intellect and spirit, informed by ongoing struggles. The "body of art" in Bruchac's image takes up the agency of dreamer, and enacts the dreaming that is the result of these connections. The artists link past to present, and the "tribal past" is recreated, not as fossil or museum piece but as active participant in survival. Black Elk's despair is not forgotten, but it is only one part of the story.

Various dreamings complicate the writing of Native American poets Joy Harjo, Wendy Rose and Leslie Marmon Silko. Harjo, Rose and Silko participate in those transformations that "dream the tribal past into tradition" and through their acts of resistance make the "space[s] in the margin . . . a site of creativity and power" (hooks 23). Each writer addresses herself to history, finding in the past and the "living present" the not-lost traditions with the old stories "rattling under [the] hand / like greasy sun dried gambling bones" (Rose "Story Keeper" 25–27). In my discussion of contemporary poets, I undertake two distinct, but crucially linked, tasks. First I look to a handful of poems in which these three writers enact the complex intersections of past and future. This main body of the paper reads the procedures by which historical-mythical-poetic transformations occur: Joy Harjo takes up the dream spaces necessary to claim the waking present; Wendy Rose, bringing old, untold stories into play, gives tongue to those whose words were stolen; and Leslie Marmon Silko mocks eurocentered history with a dreamlike revisionist "origin" myth in which the Columbiad is set into motion. The paper concludes with a brief but necessary examination of the critical act when texts are cultural productions of a marginalized people and the reader is (uncomfortably) centralized by her membership in the dominant (here, white) group.

II. Joy Harjo: "through the dream"
Looking for "paths to survival" in the face of history produces the complex present Joy Harjo describes in the poem "Anchorage":

> on a park bench we see someone's Athabascan grandmother, folded
> up, smelling like 200 years of blood and piss, her eyes closed against
> some unimagined darkness. (14)

The old woman is not anonymous, but a relative in the honoured place of elder and "grandmother," and tribally named. Her eyes are closed, not in dreaming, but in a darkness that is "unimagined"—an ambiguity of agency suggesting both that the women passing her cannot know what the Grandmother has faced and that the darkness is unrelieved by dreams. The women struggle to take on her reality, asking, "What can we say that would make us understand / better than we do already?" The answer they give themselves helps us understand Bruchac's "dream." In response to the question, "what can we say?", Harjo answers:

> Except to speak of her home and claim her as our own history, and
> know that our dreams don't end here. (14)

Claiming the history, and remembering "home" embodied in the old woman
lost in her "unimagined darkness" may be an aspect of the "historical
memory" Rayna Green evokes when she asserts "history is for us the living present. Sometimes it chokes us, sometimes it breaks our hearts again"
(63). Harjo's embrace of the past does not contain or delimit the present,
nor does it foreclose the future. The poem may even suggest that Harjo
sees drunkenness, though tragic, as a mode of resistance to the demand for
assimilation, "a method of survival under cultural duress and the stress of
acculturation in the white world" (Vizenor 308). That their dreams "don't
end here," however, in this place of destruction is crucial to survival. And
survival is explicitly the issue as Harjo ends the poem with allusion to "the
fantastic and terrible story of all our survival, / those who were never meant
/ to survive . . ." (14).

Among Joy Harjo's survivors is the figure of Noni Daylight, another
presence to be claimed. Rayna Green observes that Harjo is "always on the
road" (*That's What She Said* Green 7) often out there with Noni Daylight
grappling with a "living present" that takes her through the hard places that
a not-quite-young urban Indian woman might encounter. Noni Daylight
appears in several of Harjo's poems, tough, funny, sexy, thoughtful, resisting
stereotypes and trying to find her way home. In the poem "She Remembers
the Future," Noni Daylight

> feels the sky
> tethered to the changing
> earth, and her skin
> responds, like a woman
> to her lover. (46)

She talks with "The otherself," asking

> Should I dream you afraid
> so that you are forced to save
> yourself?
>
> Or should you ride colored horses
> into the cutting edge of the sky
> to know

that we're alive
we are alive. (46)

The poem "Heartbeat" seems to be the evolution of that dream, for Harjo begins it with the bald assertion, "Noni Daylight is afraid" (37). She is afraid because

The pervasive rhythm
of her mother's heartbeat is a ghostly track
that follows her

and threatens to "lull her back." The past, here, is terrifying, and the possibility of facing her history and her dreams is so threatening that she takes LSD to keep her awake. The sounds of the mother's heartbeat prevent Noni Daylight from hearing her own: "She wanted . . . a way to hear / her heart, her own heart." The past and the living present in conflict drive her out into the night:

These nights she wants out.
And when Noni is at the edge of skin she slips
out the back door. She goes for the hunt, tracks the
heart sound on the streets
of Albuquerque. (37)

Toying with suicide, her fear and "the heartbeat" are constant noises as she drives through the city night with the four doors of her car unlocked. The poem's authoritative voice tells us

she waits
for the moment she has hungered for,
for the hand that will open the door.
It is not the moon, or the pistol in her lap
but a fierce anger
that will free her. (37)

In this poem, Noni Daylight becomes a figure for the desperate anxiety of those for whom the past eclipses the present. The past, figured as mother's heartbeat, incorporates, quite literally embodies, the personal territory of birth and family, as well as the ancient reverberations of the beating heart of the earth and the ancient traditions that track her. Frantic to escape,

Noni Daylight takes her fear with her, inverting her position as prey as she
"goes for the hunt." She will "track the / heart sound" in a most unlikely
context: the streets of Albuquerque. Harjo's inversion of hunter and hunted,
of mother's heartbeat and Noni Daylight's own, elaborates a sense of possibility: the contemporary urban world cannot be escaped, it must be faced;
and what facing it means is facing the self. Here, however, "self," her own
heartbeat, carries the "ghostly track" of the past. Facing the dangers of the
present (a woman alone in an unlocked car in a big American city at night
is necessarily afraid), she is eager to provoke a crisis that will shatter her
fear, that will "free her." The gun, the means by which the despair of many
Native Americans is expressed, will here be turned away from herself, will
defend her against the attacker she is waiting for. But Harjo's voice cuts
through Noni Daylight's fear of the past and of the present:

> It is not the moon, or the pistol in her lap
> but a fierce anger
>   that will free her. (37)

Resistance here is explicit. Its source is neither the mystical power of the
moon, nor the mechanical violence of the pistol, but the transformation of
fear into "fierce anger." Both terror and rage have the same sources, and neither can be evaded or escaped. When Noni Daylight is "at the edge of skin"
she is at the mediating moment between inner and outer, past and present,
white and Indian. This is the site of engagement that makes up the moment
in which her anger can be felt, and that "will free her." Going out to meet
what she fears, she wills survival.

III. Wendy Rose: Dreaming Ghosts

Like Noni Daylight, living at the "edge of skin" between past and present,
on the hunt for her own heartbeat, Wendy Rose also grapples with survival,
which is, after all, the first line of resistance. For her this means taking on
the ghosts that come to her (in part) as stories, making demands, forcing
connection, requiring commitment. Rose's ghosts are not fixed in legend or
tale. She notes with some surprise how active a force the ghosts are, inhabiting, ambiguously, the traditional ways: "Oh they make us dance / the old
animal dances" ("Story Keeper" 25–27). But Rose's ghosts also come from
the mixed channels of her mixed blood, "haunting" the poet with sinister
hybrid images in "The Poet Haunted"

> The ghosts are attacking me
> crowding up from the years

like coyotes or priests
rosaries rattling between claws and teeth. (41–42)

Here the bestial and the clerical collapse into each other, each bringing
to the attack its own characteristic weapons, presented in uncharacteristic
ways. We must note that since Coyote is, of course, the primary trickster
figure in South West Indian stories, the tricky elements of the priest are
also in play. The ghost figures that haunt her crowd into her consciousness
and must be recognized. Rose chants the ghosts into their names, bringing
the losses that we might have expected into reality alongside the odd and
discordant ghostliness of an insubstantial present:

Ghosts these fathers
Ghosts these children
Ghosts these clans
Ghosts these pictures
Ghosts these dancers
Ghosts these gods
Ghosts these afternoons
Ghosts these pills
Ghosts these kittens. (41)

Inhabited, chaotic, suffering, haunted, the poet's chanting makes order as she
instructs the reader to "understand now / how ghosts are made." Individual
and collective history, "ghosts left alive / ghosts dying," walking through her,
mark the poet as the site of her own "massacre." Her own being evokes the
massacre at Wounded Knee in which 350 Sioux men, women, and children
were murdered by the US Seventh Cavalry while dancing the Ghost Dance
in an attempt to bring back the old ways. The poet, confronting her tribal,
historical, and personal past through the ghosts, chanting their existence,
declares the memories, the feelings, and the objects as having an autonomy
that she must recognize. The everydayness of "kittens" and "pills" leans into
the ghostly as ordinary reality seems emptied out of its own substantiality,
while the figures from the past, "these clans," "these gods," "these dancers"
are brought into immediacy. The repetition of "Ghosts these . . ." brings the
figures before our eyes while it declares their other-worldliness. The chanting itself, with its reverberations of ancient song, is one of the ways Rose
subverts the unwieldy alienation of the present from the past and brings
both into a common dimension of existence. By speaking her own ghosts,
Rose makes herself into a ghostly presence that haunts the reader, and we
understand "how ghosts are made" in at least one way.

Taking on the task of speaking the ghosts may have been authorized by the instructions her father gave her in "What My Father Said":

Begin, he said, by giving back;
. . .
Remember them
think of those ones
that were here before,
remember
how they were hungry. (19)

The poem concludes

remember to speak,
to smile, to beckon,
        come and eat
        come and eat
        live in my tongue
        and forget
        your hunger. (19–20)

The "ones that were here before" can ease their hunger with words, can eat the language of the poet. To give voice is to give back to those who could be forgotten, and the father's injunction "Remember . . . remember" can be fulfilled only in speaking.

The poem sequence entitled *The Halfbreed Chronicles* suggests how widely Rose understood her father's words. The series consists of the voices of those who live only in the poet's tongue because the betrayals and ironies of history have silenced their own. The "Halfbreeds" for whom Rose speaks, speak for her, of course. The invitation to "live in my tongue" beckons most strongly in poems devoted to Julia Pastrana and Truganinny. Like all the poems in *The Halfbreed Chronicles*, both "Julia" and "Truganinny" open with documentary epigraphs that provide basic information about the central figure of the poem. Rose engages with genocide as an aim of history and as trope informing us that Truganinny, said to be the last of the Tasmanians, had seen the stuffed and mounted body of her husband

and it was her dying wish that she be buried in the outback or at sea [for she did not wish her body to be subjected to the same indignities.] Upon her death she was nevertheless stuffed and mounted and put on display for over eighty years. (56)

Truganinny speaks her last wish, whispering

> You will need
> to come closer
> for little is left
> of this tongue
> and what I am saying
> is important.
>
> I am
> the last one. (56–57)

Intimate with this dying and dying out, the poem invites engagement and offers it: "Take my hand" . . . "Do not leave." The context provided by the epigraph and the urgency of Truganinny's plea make the cruelty of her body's fate echo past the tragedy of her individual death. Her real horror is being left in the hands of the destroyers, having to depend on them for the proper treatment of her body. The last stanza reads:

> Please
> take my body
> to the source of night,
> to the great black desert
> where Dreaming was born.
> Put me under
> the bulk of a mountain
> or in the distant sea,
> put me where
> they will not
> find me. (57)

Rose speaks out of an understanding of the power of "Dreaming" in Aboriginal culture.[4] "Where Dreaming was born" is the source of significant life, and the place both in and beyond location where spirit and body will be safe.

Similarly, Julia Pastrana, a Mexican Indian afflicted with facial deformities and long body hair, billed as "the Ugliest Woman in the World" in her 19th Century circus act died in childbirth. Her husband-manager had woman and infant stuffed and travelled the circus route with them. Their bodies were on display in Europe and North America as recently as 1975 (69).

In "Julia," Rose also gives her figure a voice with which to speak. In a formal address, Julia also begs for reassurance, saying, "Tell me it was just a dream / my husband" while she describes her strange, prophetic nightmare: "I had become hard / as the temple stones." The poem concludes with her pleading

> Oh my husband
> tell me again
> this is only a dream
> . . .
> tell me, husband, how you love me
> for my self one more time. (71)

Because of the information contained in the epigraphs, these living voices of wish and dream seem to speak through the horrific image of the embalmed women. The reader is figured, in part, as viewer, the white reader as intended audience for the original degradation and exploitation of the trophy. But the reader is also addressed by both "Truganinny" and "Julia" as the trusted survivor. In "Julia" the reader is "husband" waiting to make use of the corpse of this tenderly speaking woman. In "Truganinny" the reader is a "you" who may help protect her body as "they" wait. The "you" that Rose imagines was either powerless or a betrayer, as Truganinny's stuffed body was indeed displayed for over eighty years. The trust that informs the speakers in both poems provokes recognition of the shameful role we play as museum audience, entertained as the living are turned into the dead for commodification and trophies of power.

Placing these poems under the heading "Halfbreed Chronicles," Rose is doing more than inverting the racist epithet and claiming a name. The collection, which includes poems about Robert Oppenheimer, "father" of the atomic bomb, and Isamu, Japanese American sculptor, suggests that the being lost or stolen away from her/himself becomes a kind of "halfbreed." Rose discusses this in an interview speaking of her own history as Hopi, Scots, Irish, and Miwok. She says "in *The Halfbreed Chronicles* I come to terms with that half-breededness [sic] . . . it's a condition of history, a condition of context, a condition of circumstance . . . We are in fact all half-breed in this world today" (Coltelli 123). The ghost of that story speaks for Wendy Rose, self divided away from its body, its roots.

That division, and the display and performance of the body used against the deepest self, for another's purpose, make the figures of Julia and Truganinny available for Rose's appropriation. To give speech to the body is not only to correct an historical silence, but to resist the silences of the present. When the living voice is heard through the initial, epigraphic image of the stuffed corpse, we must wonder if Rose is not only asserting an historical tragedy but demanding that we see the image of the aboriginal fixed in European culture as a parallel colonized object of display, one that her poems put before us while in the same moment refusing the indignity of that silenced body.[5] These poems thus work as emblems of the relation of whites to contemporary Aboriginal peoples who are "stuffed, mounted, and put on display" as living fossils. As Truganinny or Julia Pastrana speak their dreams, Rose is working to make us hear the speaking voice beyond the fixed image.

IV. Leslie Marmon Silko: Bewitching the Columbiad

Building on the ancient pattern of oral tradition, Leslie Marmon Silko's revision of origin myth enacts another mode of resistance, this time with a strange, menacing embrace. In her first novel, *Ceremony*, Silko uses vernacular alongside traditional storytelling as Betonie, a contemporary healer/storyteller, takes upon himself the right of history and myth making to explain how white people came to be. This tale begins in proper storytelling mode, mixing legend and fairy tale and biblical no-time frames:

> Long time ago
> in the beginning
> there were no white people in this world
> there was nothing European.
> And this world might have gone on like that
> except for one thing:
> witchery. (132–133)

The storyteller explains that

> This world was already complete
> even without white people.
> There was everything
> including witchery. (30)

Perhaps I should explain here that Silko's conception of witches and witchery has no relation to the recuperated figures of European "wise women" traditions. For Silko, witchery, not specific to any racial source, is the root of evil, that which is excited by another's pain, "blood, torture, enslavement" (Tax 17–18). That witchery has an existence apart from whites, that aboriginal peoples were no more free of evil than Europeans, is an ongoing theme in Silko's writing. Betonie corrects the view that whites are the source of evil. He says

That is the trickery of the witchcraft . . . They want us to believe all evil resides with white people. Then we will look no further to see what is really happening. They want us to separate ourselves from white people, to be ignorant and helpless as we watch our own destruction. But white people are only tools that the witchery manipulates. (132)

In Betonie's tale the witch people from all parts of the earth have gathered for a "contest . . . in dark things":

> They were having a witches conference,
> that's what it was
> [. . .]
> they got together
> to fool around in caves
> with their animal skins.

"but this time" the storyteller says "it wasn't enough." The competition in evil power medicines and "disgusting objects" escalates until an indeterminate, unknown figure is the "only one / left who hasn't shown off charms or powers." The others laugh when the last witch has only a story to offer, but this story has more power than any of their spells: it will begin to happen as it is told. The storyteller's friendly, familiar voice is displaced by the witch's "story" as spell and narrative coalesce:

> Okay
> go ahead
> laugh if you want to
> but as I tell the story
> it will begin to happen.
>
> Set in motion now
> set in motion by our witchery
> to work for us. (135)

The story, then, is a magic force, and the story the witch tells is the history of contact and a prediction of the destruction of aboriginal peoples, an explanation of European compulsion and greed, and a sinister celebration of the death put into motion. The narrative/spell describes

> white skin people
> like the belly of a fish

> covered with hair
> who
> grow away from the earth
> [...]
> see no life
> when they look
> [...]
> The world is a dead thing for them
> [...]
> They fear the world
> They destroy what they fear. (135)

The witch details the pattern of destruction familiar to us all, gloating,

> corpses for us
> blood for us
> Killing killing killing killing
> [...]
> Corpses for our work.

The witch ends this chant with the declaration "set into motion now / set into motion" (138). The original storyteller picks up the tale again, bringing the high rhetoric of witchery down to everydayness:

> So the other witches said
> 'Okay you win; you take the prize,
> but what you said just now—
> it isn't so funny
> It doesn't sound so good
> [...]
> Take it back.
> Call that story back.'
> But the witch just shook its head
> at the others in their stinking animal skins, fur and feathers.
> It's already turned loose.
> It's already coming.
> It can't be called back. (138)

The witch's voice ends the story with these words and we are left with the ghastly sensation of an inexorable force now, and still, set into motion, fulfilling that prediction. I have chosen to present much more of the text than is usual in a critical discussion in order to provide a sense of the power in that story.

As in all origin tales, the present, existing outside the boundaries or frame of the story, is illuminated by the witch story. It takes what we know of history, and by making those hairy white-skinned beings (terrified, sterile, violent and senseless) instruments of some force outside themselves, it subverts, even shatters, the European sense of events. Europeans, here, are not the "measure of [a] man," but are constructed as beings, who "see no life," desperately vulnerable to the will of the speaking witch. A different Manifest Destiny is "set in motion," as Silko appropriates and inverts the white fantasy of the Indian as the "uncontrolled, impassioned spirit of evil" (Goldie 71). The magnitude of horror in the story-making witch's words, the shift to a new plane of destruction, makes the other witches seem adolescent, with their "dead babies simmering in blood" in the "big cooking pots" of the Navajo, the Sioux or the "black skinned" or the "slanty eyed" witches. The speaking witch is the antithesis of "uncontrolled" or "impassioned" evil. This voice is deliberate, cold, precise. Neither shifting away from the true devastation of contact, nor attributing real agency to the whites, Silko reasserts a mode of story-telling power. Her storyteller (not the witch, but the narrator), using a contemporary language, is "naming the age" and that, as we know, is the winner's prerogative.

With their dreamings and their hard-edged poetry, Harjo, Rose and Silko are reclaiming the right to name themselves in the context of their history, to articulate loss and rage, and to define survival. Along with resistance comes transformation not only of Native peoples but of all those who have come to aboriginal lands (or texts) with European values in place. For the white reader, this complex process of transformations must include a self-conscious examination of some of the implications of change.

V. Dreaming the Provisional Critic
While contemporary Native American writers are mapping out "paths to survival," white readers/critics must attend to the paths we are mapping. Abdul JanMohamed and David Lloyd observe the tendency of the dominant culture to regard minority cultural productions as "aestheticized form of recreations" (5); and bell hooks warns against the critic whose text declares, "I am still author, authority, I am still the colonizer, the speaking subject" (22). This critic as colonizer, hooks explains, like all colonizers, refuses to hear a discourse of resistance. Only pain can be spoken, and only the language of defeat and deprivation is tolerated (23). Unmasking this power imbalance between critic and text may have a destablizing effect

on the complacency of the dominant-culture critic, but significant trans-formation will require an exploration and embrace of a highly complex conception of "resistance" (Hartsock 33). The conventional perception of resistance as locked into reaction (a stimulus-response dynamic) leads inevitably to Nancy Hartsock's observation that "if resistance succeeded" without modifying the ground of power "we would simply be creat[ing] new oppressions" (33). The resistant critic and artist are both working against a cultural matrix that attempts to channel them away from trans-formations of social realities and towards a recreation of the same old power struggle.

hooks makes a distinction between kinds of criticism: and following her lead, the critic need not take on the position of "colonizer" to the new found land of the text. She suggests that we recognize and reject the val-ues or ideological freight of those readers who have predetermined what a "minority" discourse must be. hooks observes that some white critics demand that marginalized writers "Only speak your pain" (23). I suggest that some white critics enact an alternate, equally oversimplifying, hegemony. They seem to instruct minority writers to "speak *only* in the voice of resistance." Either, indeed, any, injunction is inappropriate. For white critics, accepting the authority of epistemic privilege—to believe, for example, that those who have suffered directly from racism know more about it than those who have not—will give a different shape to critical discourse.

Recognizing that both artist and critic may be vulnerable to the "com-modification of ethnicity," Coco Fusco, Black American film critic, suggests breaking out of the reductive, dialectic cage of resistance as reaction, by mak-ing "the address as complex as possible ... not allow[ing] it to be that easily commodified ... by accepting ambiguity." (25). This movement, whose *effect* is resistant, though it is not *shaped* by defensiveness, echoes Bruchac's asser-tion of a history of "intellectual awareness" and "spiritual power" as essential to Native survival. At this point, we are far beyond questions of "strategy." To see transformation as merely a "strategy of resistance" is to ignore the redraw-ing of cultural reality that Rayna Green undertakes when she says of Native peoples in America: "we are squarely in the middle of that culture. We are not apart from it. . . . we are . . . essential to it. (72) bell hooks' metaphors of marginality and Rayna Green's conception of centeredness direct us towards creativity, speech, and survival, and both writers remind us of the material basis of spatial imagery. The original conflict was for territory. That ongoing struggle now includes a battle for place.

One of the facts of oppression is that there are relatively very few Native individuals involved in academic literary studies. At my university, for example, set in the Canadian west, with six distinct Aboriginal nations living within a hundred miles, if a non-Native person does not teach Native literatures, they do not get taught. In most academic settings, to take up this space, that is, the activity of the critic talking about Native writing, is to *create* that space, to elbow, jostle, argue, for the necessity of its existence. This is not the same as insisting or claiming that it is one's *own* space, but rather to engage one's self as critic in the parallel activities to those whose "space in the margin is a site of creativity and power" (hooks 23). And to have done so, is to recognize that one's relation to the literature is problematically ambiguous.

Meeting this complex address, this critic, then, speaking from the dubiously authoritative subject position granted by the dominant culture (white, but not male), tries to learn to read or speak differently, surrendering the assumptions of authority as they become conscious, yet maintaining the most simple, difficult privilege: that of breaking silence.

NOTES

1. Arnold Krupat makes the useful observation that "the circle" is too easy and totalized an image for critics to rely upon as it is inadequate in the face of "the complex facts of Native American and Western cultural diversity" (42). My aim here is to use that figure in specifically referenced rather than generalized ways.

2. Readers should be aware of the collection of poems by that name: Chrystos, *Not Vanishing*, Vancouver, B.C.: Press Gang Publisher, 1988.

3. Page 17. Bruchac attributes the phrase "dream the tribal past into tradition" to Gerald Vizenor ("Four Skins" 95).

4. See Diane Bell's *Daughters of the Dreaming* for more material on this subject.

5. See Margery Fee's "Romantic Nationalism" in reference to *Tay John* in which Indians are "stuffed and framed" as aesthetic objects (15).

WORKS CITED

Bell, Diane. *Daughters of the Dreaming*. Sydney: Allen & Unwin, 1983.

Black Elk, quoted in *Bury My Heart at Wounded Knee*. Dee Brown. New York: Washington Square, 1970. 419.

Bruchac, Joseph. Introduction. "Dreaming the Tribal Past into Tradition." *Tamaqua* 2.2 (1991): 11–17.

Coltelli, Laura. "Wendy Rose." *Winged Words: American Indian Writers Speak*. Lincoln: U of Nebraska P, 1990: 121–134.

Fee, Margery. "Romantic Nationalism and the Image of Native People in Contemporary English-Canadian Literature." *The Native in Literature: Canadian and Comparative Perspectives*. Ed. Thomas King, Cheryl Carver, and Helen Hoy. Toronto: ECW, 1987. 15–33.

Fusco, Coco. "The Morning Discussion: Theory and the Politics of Location." *Framework* 36: 24–29.

Goldie, Terry. "Fear and Temptation: Images of Indigenous Peoples in Australian, Canadian, and New Zealand Literature." *The Native in Literature*. Ed. Thomas King, Cheryl Carver, and Helen Hoy. Toronto: ECW, 1987. 67–79.

Green, Rayna. "American Indian Women: Diverse Leadership for Social Change." *Bridges of Power: Women's Multicultural Alliances.* Ed. Lisa Albrecht and Rose M. Brewer. Philadelphia: New Society, 1991. 61–73.

———, ed. "Introduction." *That's What She Said: Contemporary Poetry and Fiction by Native American Women.* Bloomington: Indiana UP, 1984. 1–12.

Harjo, Joy. *She Had Some Horses.* New York: Thunder Mouth, 1982.

Hartsock, Nancy. "Rethinking Modernism: Minority vs. Majority Theories." *The Nature and Context of Minority Discourse.* Ed. Abdul R. JanMohamed and David Lloyd. Oxford: Oxford UP, 1990: 17–36.

hooks, bell. "Choosing the margin as a space of radical openness." *Framework* 36. 15–23.

JanMohamed, Abdul R. and Lloyd, David. "Introduction: Toward a Theory of Minority Discourse: What is to be done?" *The Nature and Context of Minority Discourse.* Ed. JanMohamed and Lloyd. Oxford: Oxford UP, 1990: 1–16.

Krupat, Arnold. *Ethnocriticism: Ethnography, History, Literature.* Berkeley: U of California P, 1992.

Rose, Wendy. *The Halfbreed Chronicles.* Boston: South End, 1984

Sanchez, Carol Lee. "Open Dream Sequence" in Green *That's What She Said.* 226–227.

Silko, Leslie Marmon. *Storyteller.* New York: Seaver, 1981. 130–137.

Tax, Meredith. "Return of the Native Americans: Leslie Marmon Silko's Vision Quest" Rev. of *Almanac of the Dead*, by Leslie Marmon Silko. *Voice Literary Supplement* Nov. 1991: 17–18.

Vizenor, Gerald. "Firewater and Phrenology." *Crossbloods: Bone Courts, Bingo, and Other Reports.* 1976. Minneapolis: U of Minnesota P, 1990: 300–319.

———. "Four Skins" *Tamaqua.* 2.2 (1991): 89–104.

JAMES LONGENBACH

Louise Glück's Nine Lives

Vita Nova, Louise Glück's eighth book of poems, begins with this enigmatic exchange between master and apprentice.

> The master said *You must write what you see.*
> But what I see does not move me.
> The master answered *Change what you see.*

Change is Louise Glück's highest value. Each of her books has begun, she admits, in a "conscious diagnostic act, a swearing off" of the work preceding it. But because of what Glück calls in *Vita Nova* her "inflexible Platonism," she is both entranced and threatened by "something beyond the archetype." If change is what she most craves, it is also what she most resists, what is most difficult for her, most hard-won. And if her career has often moved forward at the expense of its own past, *Vita Nova* feels like the inauguration of a different kind of movement. Rather than retreating to an extreme of diction or sensibility, the poems of *Vita Nova* ultimately feel at home in a fluctuating middle ground that is not a compromise between extremes. Near the end of the book, the apprentice recognizes that she has internalized the lesson of the master.

From *Southwest Review* 84, no. 2 (Spring 1999): 184–98. Copyright © 1999 by James Longenbach.

> I have acquired in some measure
> the genius of the master, in whose supple mind
> time moves in two directions: backward
> from the act to the motive
> and forward to just resolution.

These lines characterize two narratives: one involves the place of *Vita Nova* in Glück's ongoing career and the other is the story *Vita Nova* itself tells. To *write what you see* you must first *change what you see*. And if the past is the poet's subject, then the past must change: the inflexible Platonist must realize that the givens of experience are potentially as fluid, as mutable, as its possibilities. "I couldn't even / imagine the past," Glück admits at one point in *Vita Nova*. At another, when she asks herself if she feels free, all she can respond is that she recognizes the patterns of her experience. Throughout her career, Glück has often shown how the future runs on rails that are laid down not only in childhood but in lives preceding our own. But in *Vita Nova* the act of imagining the future is contingent upon the act of reimagining—rather than rejecting—the past. To change what she sees, the poet must write what she sees, changing what she sees in the process.

"The *Vita Nuova*," said T. S. Eliot, "is to my thinking a record of actual experience reshaped into a particular form." Glück's title is brazen: like Dante's, her book is about the struggle to find what Glück calls "discernible form" for harrowing experience: the death of love and the rebirth of vocation. Glück has railed in her essays against narcissism in poetry; she has rejected the automatic prestige of forbidden subject matter. And by exploring the aftermath of a broken marriage in *Vita Nova*, Glück runs the risk—knowingly—of seeming merely sincere. But the real drama of *Vita Nova*, both thematic and structural, is the unfolding dialogue between "material" and "form," the way in which past experience is refigured in the language of poetry. "It must be done by speech," says Dante in Rossetti's translation, "or not at all."

Glück's last book, *Meadowlands*, was distinguished by its surprisingly wide discursive range—brash, vulgar, often funny. And while *Vita Nova* feels less austerely hieratic than much of Glück's earlier work, its poems by and large return to her more typically hushed idiom. But *Vita Nova* in no way signals a retreat. Glück's compulsion to change seems more substantive than ever before because *Vita Nova* does not represent a "swearing off" of the past: it accepts the notion that truly meaningful change must inevitably be partial change—complicit, incomplete. Speaking of her lifelong willingness to discard anything, Glück sees in herself the child she once was, a child "unwilling to speak if to speak meant to repeat myself." In *Vita Nova*, Glück learns to live within repetition, and the result is, paradoxically, something really new: a reconsideration of the structure and function of lyric poetry.

* * *

Since the beginning of her career, the presiding technical problem of Glück's poems has been the placement of the speaker relative to the material. In *Firstborn*, her first book, the speakers seem involved in the emotional dilemma of the poems. But in the books that followed, Glück wrote a poetry distinguished more by its tone than by anything we could think of as a voice. Even the speakers of her dramatic monologues (often mythological figures) did not seem involved in the drama of their own lives. The novelist Michel Tournier has defined myth as "a story that everybody already knows," and it is in this sense that so many of Glück's poems seem mythic, whether their subjects are mythological or not. Her speakers know everything, and since everything has already happened, the poems feel spectral and eerily calm.

The poems also tend to culminate forcefully in their final lines. In 1975, Glück published a group of five poems, four of which would appear later that year in her second book, *The House on Marshland*. "Here Are My Black Clothes" sounds like a *Firstborn* poem; from the start, its speaker is agitated, its gestures dramatic: "I think now it is better to love no one / than to love you. Here are my black clothes." In contrast, "Messengers" is exquisitely placid but ultimately far more moving. Glück describes anyone's encounter with commonplace wild animals—geese, deer—but defers the significance of such encounters until the final lines:

> You have only to let it happen:
> that cry—*release, release*—like the moon
> wrenched out of earth and rising
> full in its circle of arrows
>
> until they come before you
> like dead things, saddled with flesh,
> and you above them, wounded and dominant.

In poems like these, Glück withholds the poem's attitude toward its material (rather than advertising it, as she does in the poems of *Firstborn*), and the result is an ending that directs our experience of the entire poem. "The love of form," Glück would say in *Ararat*, "is a love of endings."

The uncanny power of poems like "Messengers" grows out of acts of willed renunciation: vigorous syntax, energetic rhythms, and colloquial diction had to be banished from this poetry. It is not surprising that from among the five poems published together in 1975, only "Jukebox" remains uncollected: "You hot, honey do she bitch and crab, / her measly and depriving body holding back / your rights?" As these lines suggest, Glück has always remained interested in the poetic possibilities she renounced. But she was unable to find a place for this rough, colloquial diction in *The House on Marshland*, just as Yeats could not have worked the phrase "greasy till" into the symbolic world of *The Wind among the Reeds* even if he'd wanted to.

The diction of *Ararat*, Glück's fifth book, is nowhere as energetic as in "Jukebox," but the poems do register Glück's will to change: throughout this sequence written in the aftermath of her father's death, Glück forged a more intimate, less ghostly tone. But as Glück has recognized of herself, she has "always been too at ease with extremes," and it is telling that after the more colloquial *Ararat* she produced *The Wild Iris*, her most flagrantly symbolic book. It is her *Wind among the Reeds*—a collection of disembodied lamentations and prayers: flowers address their gardener, the poet addresses God, and more profoundly, the poems address each other, creating a self-enclosed world of great poetic extravagance and—astonishingly enough—deep human feeling. But even when the poems adopt a point of view opposed to the poet's, the tone remains consistent:

> But John
> objects, he thinks
> if this were not a poem but
> an actual garden, then
> the red rose would be
> required to resemble
> nothing else, neither
> another flower nor
> the shadowy heart, at
> earth level pulsing
> half maroon, half crimson.

These lines contain the seed of the dissatisfaction that would in turn produce *Meadowlands*, a book of different voices—some of them as rough as "Jukebox." Describing Yeats's development, Paul de Man once argued that *The Wind among the Reeds* was a dead-end because its words seemed only to invoke other words, other associations, having relinquished their referential power. Like the Yeats of *In the Seven Woods*, Glück struggles in *Meadowlands* to let the red rose "resemble / nothing else." More profoundly, she also recognizes that the refusal of resemblance inevitably depends on its perpetuation:

only through metaphor ("the shadowy heart, at / earth level pulsing") may the rose be said to resemble nothing.

Throughout *Meadowlands*, the poet is challenged by the acerbic voice of her husband (who is also Odysseus): "You don't love the world," begins "Rainy Morning"; your "tame spiritual themes, / autumn, loss, darkness, etc" are completely consistent with "the cat's pathetic / preference for hunting dead birds." In response, the poet (who is also Penelope) wants to entertain the possibility of including more of the world in her poems. But given the very nature of poetic language, the task is difficult. In "Parable of the Gift" Glück explains how she inadvertently killed a fuchsia plant by leaving it outside—by "mistaking it / for part of nature." The poem ends with a memory of a friend (who gave her the plant) bringing her "a towel of lettuce leaves":

> so much, so much to celebrate
> tonight, as though she were saying
> here is the world, that should be
> enough to make you happy.

These lines epitomize the dilemma of *Meadowlands*. Glück is tired of reading the world as if it were an emblematic tapestry, yet she finds it difficult to be sustained by natural things alone. What's more, she has trouble distinguishing the natural from the emblematic. "As part of nature he is part of us," said Stevens of the poet, but it's not easy for a poet who mistakes a plant for "part of nature" to take this wisdom for granted.

In "Nostos" (perhaps the most beautiful poem in the book) Glück remembers an apple tree that seemed, year after year, to flower on her birthday: seen once, it immediately became an emblem for consciousness, as did every subsequent apple tree she encountered.

> Substitution
> of the immutable
> for the shifting, the evolving.
> Substitution of the image
> for relentless earth. What
> do I know of this place,
> the role of the tree for decades
> taken by a bonsai, voices
> rising from the tennis courts—
> Fields. Smell of the tall grass, new cut.
> As one expects of a lyric poet.

We look at the world once, in childhood.
The rest is memory.

Like "Messengers," "Nostos" culminates scrupulously in its final lines; it is the
kind of poem Glück has mastered. But as Bonnie Costello suggests, the poem's
delineation of a timeless lyric space is balanced throughout *Meadowlands* by
a desire for disruptive forward motion—"that pulse which is the narrative /
sea." However representative of Glück's achievement, "Nostos" must be read in
dialogue with the rougher poems of *Meadowlands*. The voice exhorting Glück
to abandon "tame spiritual themes" in "Rainy Morning" is really her own: she
wants sincerely to push at the boundaries of what "one expects of a lyric poet."

Even if any word she uses is fraught with emblematic significance and
can never be "natural," the multiple voices of *Meadowlands* allow Glück to
harness words and rhythms that could never have sat comfortably even in
Ararat. She is also free to be funny: the brash or deadpan poems, especially
those spoken by the weirdly prescient son (who doubles as Telemachus),
sound especially humorous when juxtaposed with poems like "Nostos." Still,
this very strength—the achievement of a wholeness of feeling greater than its
parts—may have relieved Glück from the pressure to transform herself more
substantively. No matter how many times Glück writes a poem like "Rainy
Morning," poems like "Nostos" or "Parable of the Gift" nonetheless stand
comfortably beside poems like "Messengers."

If *Meadowlands* first seemed like a sign that Glück were expanding her
range, the appearance of *Vita Nova* now makes *Meadowlands* feel ominously
like a dead end. It offered Glück two mutually exclusive choices: she could
continue to write hushed, luminous poems like "Nostos" or she could write
brash, acerbic poems like "Rainy Morning." But how much more skeptical,
more disillusioned—more pick-your-adjective—could the author of lines like
"your cold feet all over my dick" become? Glück's scrupulous talent for self-
interrogation is capable of generating its own illusions. "Romance is what I
most struggle to be free of," she has said, but there is a romance bound up in
the need never to be deceived, the need always to see through ourselves before
somebody else gets a chance. It is a romance of purity, a romance that leads us
to be more comfortable in extremes than in the middle. More difficult than
heaven or hell, says Glück apropos of Eurydice, is the act of "moving between
two worlds." *Vita Nova* is her book of the difficult middle.

*   *   *

Like *Meadowlands*, *Vita Nova* demands to be absorbed in one long reading. But *Vita Nova* is built around not one but two mythic backbones—the

stories of both Dido and Aeneas and of Orpheus and Eurydice: the book's structure consequently feels like an intersection of various narratives rather than the unfolding of a single one. In addition, Glück's position relative to these narratives is fluid. At one moment the poet will align herself with Dido or Eurydice, but at the next, her condemnation of Orpheus' narcissism will seem directed as much at herself as the lover who has abandoned her: "Tell them there is no music like this / without real grief." Because Glück recognizes her complicity, the poems don't feel neatly opposed to each other even when they take on opposing personae. If *Meadowlands* exteriorized as dialogue the conflicts lyric poems more often interiorize as ambiguity, *Vita Nova* is uttered by a single speaker who contains within herself a variety of overlapping, eccentric positions.

This strategy is appropriate to the book's subject since, as I began by suggesting, the poems of *Vita Nova* concern not so much the breakup of a marriage as the poet's subsequent attempt to reorder her experience—to provide "discernible form" for "available material." On the other hand, the poet is cut off from the future; the marriage she thought was eternal has succumbed to time. On the other hand, she is cut off from the past; she remembers how her mother turned away "in great anger" because she had "failed to show gratitude" for her mother's love: "And I made no sign of understanding. / For which I was never forgiven." This "never" is the dead center of *Vita Nova*: it signifies a past that is beyond our control but which continues to control us, delimiting our experience in the present.

Throughout most of the first half of *Vita Nova*, Glück despairs of the possibility of meaningful change. As in "Nostos," she feels that we enter the world "guilty of many crimes," that the soul is as a result "inflexible." Paradoxically, it is the end of the marriage—the source of despair—that offers an antidote to despair. In "Unwritten Law" the poet seems weirdly grateful to the husband who abandons her: if she gave herself to him "absolutely," he, in his "wisdom and cruelty," taught her "the meaninglessness of that term." He taught her, so to speak, that the word *never* is only as shifting and deceptive as the word *forever*, that the material of our experience is never beyond change.

Our job is not to "recognize [the past] 'the way it really was,'" said Walter Benjamin, but to "seize hold of a memory as it flashes up at a moment of danger." Glück's passionate commitment to change is born of a fear of irrefutable memory—of the possibility that, as in "Nostos," we are permitted to look at the world only once. Throughout the second half of *Vita Nova* she consequently begins to fight back, seizing hold of the past when it threatens to determine her future. In "Nest" she describes a dream in which she watched a bird construct its nest from the "available material" left in the yard after other birds have finished their weaving:

> Early spring, late desolation.
> The bird circled the bare yard making
>
> efforts to survive
> on what remained to it.
>
> It had its task:
> to imagine the future.

The bird's task is of course Glück's. In dreams as in poems she moves—like the master who instructs her—in two directions at once: by moving forward into the future she also moves backward into the past, altering it, command-ing it. In "Condo" her dream even confuses past and future, "mistaking / one for the other."

There is nothing merely innocent or inevitable about the confusion: "*Bedtime,*" whisper the leaves in "Evening Prayers," "*Time to begin lying.*" But however desperate Glück feels in the face of intractable material, her "strug-gle for form" does move toward moments of repose. "Formaggio" begins with lines that sound like the end of a typical Glück poem.

> The world
> was whole because
> it shattered. When it shattered,
> then we knew what it was.

The triumph of "Formaggio" is that it moves beyond what feels like an ending, reconstructing a world. After the world shattered, says Glück, human beings built smaller worlds in the fissures: "blocks of stores" (Fishmonger, Formaggio, Hallie's flowers) are like "visions of safety"; "salespeople" are "like parents" only "kinder than parents." In this "provisional" world the recognition that Glück has "had many lives" is for once liberating. She is even willing to repeat the phrase:

> I had lives before this, stems
> of a spray of flowers: they become
> one thing, held by a ribbon at the center, a ribbon
> visible under the hand. Above the hand,
> the branching future, stems
> ending in flowers. And the gripped fist—
> that would be the self in the present.

These final lines of "Formaggio" are liberating both because of what they say (emphasizing the way in which a self is constructed over time rather than predetermined) and because of the way they follow on the previous lines of the poem. The poem sets a scene—a block of stores on Huron Avenue—and weaves a meditation in and out of the scene, implicitly paralleling the poet's casual movement from store to store: the poem's final image of the self gripping its previous lives feels like the wonderfully unpredictable result of having ended a day's journey in Hallie's flower shop. "The place you begin doesn't determine / the place you end," says Glück in "Nest": coming from the author of "Nostos," this realization is the source of all freedom in *Vita Nova*.

For the simple reason that they repeat language that has already occurred earlier in the poem, the final lines of "Formaggio" feel spontaneous rather than weighty, part of an ongoing process rather than grandly conclusive. Repetition: while Glück laments in "Unwritten Law" that "the mistakes of my youth / made me hopeless, because they repeated themselves," she eventually recognizes in "The Garment" that "when hope was returned to me / it was another hope entirely." To exist in time is necessarily to exist in repetition; to exist successfully in time is to recognize that what is returned to us—hope or despair—repeats the past with a difference. Once we recognize that difference, then the past is changed; it becomes a source of possibility. But however powerful in itself, this realization wouldn't matter much if Glück presented it in poems that, like "Messengers" or "Nostos," carry their weight in their final lines. The real achievement of *Vita Nova* is a new kind of lyric structure, one that embodies a love of the middle rather than a "love of endings."

In the first poem called "Vita Nova" Glück revisits the scene of "Nostos"—the apple tree that determines her experience of all subsequent trees. This time, Glück looks at the scene again and again. Her meditation stutters, returning to the scene of the apple tree with fresh observations. She compares the memory to a scene in the present; she wonders if she's remembered correctly. "Crucial / sounds or gestures" from childhood may be "laid down" like a track, but rather than feeling doomed to repeat them, Glück feels enabled by repetition—"hungry for life." In the poem's final lines, spring repeats itself but with a difference.

> Surely spring has been returned to me, this time
> not as a lover but a messenger of death, yet
> it is still spring, it is still meant tenderly.

The difference is the recognition of mortality—the recognition that we live in time. If "Nostos" offers what "one expects of a lyric poet"—a timeless lyric space—"Vita Nova" offers a new sensibility in a new structure. Like "Formaggio," "Vita Nova" exists more firmly in the repetitive turnings and hesitations of its middle than in its conclusion; it embodies the movement of a story without telling one.

None of these more dialogically structured poems employs the rougher diction that characterized many of the poems of *Meadowlands*. Only the second poem called "Vita Nova" recalls the idiom of *Meadowlands*, and it is telling that this poem concludes with highly charged final lines. It seems to me that after testing her signature idiom in *Ararat*, honing it in *The Wild Iris*, and exploding it in *Meadowlands*, Glück realized that the changes were in danger of seeming cosmetic: her poetic structures—and the determinism they embodied—remained unchallenged. Ellen Bryant Voigt has recently written about how, at least since the New Criticism, we have tended to focus on form, diction, and tone, leaving poetic structure (which is not necessarily coequal with form) to take care of itself. Poems like "Formaggio," the first "Vita Nova," "Aubade," "Castile," "Ellsworth Avenue," or "Lament" do not flagrantly expand Glück's idiom but offer instead a more meaningful change, a change that reaches through a poem's skin to its bones.

These poems seem more intricately dialogical than the poems in *Meadowlands* or *Vita Nova* that are structured as actual dialogues. Since they don't split into different voices, their movement feels endless and manifold rather than end-stopped and oppositional. Because the poems repeat and revise themselves, the dialogues take place within their very linguistic texture. Even if the same thing could be said of the texture of an earlier poem such as "Mock Orange"—

> It is not the moon, I tell you.
> It is these flowers
> . . . .
> I hate them.
> I hate them as I hate sex.

—these repetitions feel static, intentionally wooden, and the poem feels liberated from repetition when its syntax finally arcs across the line:

> In my mind tonight
> I hear the question and pursuing answer
> fused in one sound
> that mounts and mounts and then
> is split into the old selves,
> the tired antagonisms.

In contrast, the dialogical poems in *Vita Nova* seek no liberation from repetition—neither formally nor thematically. (And it is telling that they feature longer lines and less enjambment than most of Glück's earlier poems.) Since Glück has abandoned her staunch determinism, freedom may now be found within the unfolding of the poem rather than at its conclusion. Speaking of Robert Pinsky's "At Pleasure Bay" (a poem structured through the repetition of the phrase "never the same"), Glück has noted that the implication of the phrase changes subtly with each repetition and consequently "stands for recurrence even as it asserts the absence of perfect duplication." She could be speaking here of "Formaggio" or the first "Vita Nova." The poem "finds in shift and movement what lyric [traditionally] uses stopped time to manifest," Glück continues; through its "relentless mobility," it offers "an unfolding, a pattern, as opposed to . . . iconic stasis."

In her own "Castile" Glück does not repeat a single phrase but a group of phrases that recombine throughout the poem in different ways: "orange blossoms," "children begging for coins," "I met my love," "the sound of a train," "I dreamed this." The poem begins by setting a scene:

> Orange blossoms blowing over Castile
> children begging for coins
> I met my love under an orange tree

But Glück immediately questions this memory, wondering if the orange tree might have been an acacia tree, speculating that the memory might have been a dream. The poem seems to start over several times, moving in and out of the scene, simultaneously presenting it and questioning it.

> Castile: nuns walking in pairs through the dark garden.
> Outside the walls of the Holy Angels
> children begging for coins
>
> When I woke I was crying,
> has that no reality?
>
> I met my love under an orange tree:
> I have forgotten
> only the facts, not the inference—
> there were children somewhere, crying, begging for coins

Because each repetition of a phrase occurs in a slightly altered context, the phrases feel both different and the same. And their movement consequently embodies the fluid, errant sense of memory that the poem describes. Near the end of "Castile" she remembers that she gave herself to her lover "completely and for all time"—or so she thought: the poem's final image of movement confirms the vicissitudes both of love and of poetry.

> And the train returned us
> first to Madrid
> then to the Basque country

If the poems Glück has written since *Firstborn* feel like records of events that have already happened—myths—the dialogical poems like "Castile" feel like events that are happening. They are quite simply the most intricate and beautiful poems Glück has ever made.

*   *   *

Glück's embracing of repetition seems to me the crucial development in *Vita Nova*: the structure of the poems, their attitude toward change, and their relationship to Glück's earlier work all depend on it. Having seen repetition as Platonic recollection, in which everything new looks backward to its original source, Glück now understands repetition as Walter Benjamin described it in his magisterial essay on Proust: "Is not the involuntary recollection, Proust's *mémoire involuntaire*, much closer to forgetting than what is usually called memory?" While our "purposive remembering" dissipates "the ornaments of forgetting," Proustian memory looks forward rather than holding us hostage to an unchanging past: it discovers future possibilities by recognizing that what repeats is always subtly different from itself.

"A terrible thing is happening—my love / is dying again," begins "Lament," the penultimate poem in *Vita Nova*. "How cruel the earth," says Glück, "the willows shimmering." Then again: "My love is dying." But surely: "Once is enough." Yet again: "The willows shimmer by the stone fountain." And again: "Once is enough." And again:

> My love is dying; parting has started again.
> And through the veils of the willows
> sunlight rising and glowing,
> not the light we knew.
> And the birds singing again, even the mourning dove.
>
> Ah, I have sung this song. But the stone fountain
> the willows are singing again.

"Ah, I have sung this song": this sigh of recognition is the crowning moment of *Vita Nova*. Throughout "Lament," Glück mourns not the loss of her lover but the loss of her mourning: what will Orpheus have to sing about? The acceptance of repetition (which is the acceptance of mortality) allows memory to become a kind of forgetting; it allows her to imagine a future beyond the death of the death of love. It also enables her to live in the present, in the middle of life, rather than seeking shelter in extremes of language or sensibility. In "Earthly Love" (which stands beside "Immortal Love") Glück describes a couple who were held together by the "conventions of the time," conventions requiring them "to forfeit liberty" without their knowing it. The end of the marriage was in this sense fortunate, since it dissipated the romance of convention. "And yet," says Glück—

And yet, within this deception,
true happiness occurred.
So that I believe I would
repeat these errors exactly.

These are mighty lines for a poet who has said that she disdains the illusions of romance above all else, a poet who has said that she would rather keep silent than repeat herself. The lines themselves repeat the work of another reformed Platonist, the Yeats of "A Dialogue of Self and Soul"—

I am content to live it all again
And yet again

—the Yeats who was astonished at the "bitterness" of *The Tower* and subsequently embraced the fury and mire of experience in *The Winding Stair*. Yeats is, famously, a poet whose every new volume offers a new Yeats; "It is myself that I remake," he counseled readers early on. But Yeats is also a poet whose every line is identifiable as his alone. *Vita Nova* sounds more like the Louise Glück we know than *Meadowlands*, but given the real innovation in poems like "Castile" and "Lament," that familiarity is the book's power. Having recognized that real freedom exists within repetition rather than in the postulation of some timeless place beyond it, Glück now seems content to work within the terms of her art—resisting them from within rather than turning against them. The result is a book suggesting that Glück's poetry has many more lives to live.

VIRGINIA C. FOWLER

And This Poem Recognizes That: Embracing Contrarieties in the Poetry of Nikki Giovanni

One

The most appropriate metaphor to describe Nikki Giovanni's work is perhaps the quilt; she herself invokes this metaphor frequently to describe "Michelle-Angelo's contribution to beauty (*Selected*, 246).[1] Although the quilt as a metaphor for women's writing has become "commonplace" today,[2] it has most frequently been applied to women's fiction, where its connections to various aspects of postmodernism are evident. Elaine Showalter has argued that "the patchwork quilt came to replace the melting-pot as the central metaphor of American cultural identity."[3] Even more recently, artists and scholars like Deborah Gray White, Faith Ringgold, and Patrice Kelly have demonstrated the centrality of quilt making by African American women during slavery, and the connections between this activity and African weaving and textiles; as Angela Dodson has pointed out, "When we dig deep in our history we find people whose livelihoods have been linked to textiles, making and shaping them into long ribbons of colorful cloths we now know as kente, or the neutral tones of mudcloth. The thin strips produced on treadle looms necessitated piecing together smaller fragments."[4] A quilting aesthetic informs the work of many African American women writers, including Nikki Giovanni. In many unique ways the quilt is an apt metaphor for Nikki Giovanni's conception of art; further, the quilt

From *Her Words: Diverse Voices in Contemporary Appalachian Women's Poetry*, edited by Felicia Mitchell, pp. 112–35. Copyright © 2002 by The University of Tennessee Press/Knoxville.

best symbolizes those values and meanings that she associates with black female identity.

When Giovanni makes explicit reference to quilts in her poetry, the attribute she most frequently highlights is their structural composition; in a gesture, perhaps, toward her own southern/Appalachian roots, she nearly always invokes quilts of a log cabin pattern. Even in an early poem like "My House," Giovanni identifies women as the makers of quilts and love as the spirit that urges them on:

> i spent all winter in
> carpet stores gathering
> patches so i could make
> a quilt
> does this really sound
> like a silly poem
> i mean i want to keep you
> warm
>   (*Selected*, 149)

Central here and elsewhere is the fact that the quilt is a whole made of patches or fragments. Equally important is the quilt's ability to provide spiritual and emotional as well as physical warmth, a quality she also wants her poetry to possess. "A Very Simple Wish," for example, opens with her expression of this desire: "i want to write an image / like a log-cabin quilt pattern / and stretch it across all the lonely / people who just don't fit in / we might make a world / if i do that" (*Selected*, 172).

In a somewhat later poem, "Hands: For Mother's Day," Giovanni's celebration of women is actually a celebration of those qualities she associates with black women. The poem initially suggests that gender can bridge the gulf often created by race: "The wives and mothers are not so radically different" (*Selected*, 245). But eventually the speaker acknowledges that "I yield for women whose hands are Black and rough" (*Selected*, 245). At the heart of the poem is one of Giovanni's few extended uses of the quilt metaphor; in the following passage we see that for her the quilt is a metaphor for the struggles, the creations, and the beauty of black women:

> Some people think a quilt is a blanket stretched across a Lincoln bed ... or from frames on a wall ... a quaint museum piece to be purchased on Bloomingdale's 30-day same-as-cash plan ... Quilts are our mosaics ... Michelle-Angelo's contribution to beauty ... We weave a quilt with dry, rough hands ... Quilts are the way our

lives are lived . . . We survive on patches . . . scraps . . . the leftovers
from a materially richer culture . . . the throwaways from those with
emotional options . . . We do the far more difficult job of taking
that which nobody wants and not only loving it . . . not only seeing
its worth . . . but making it lovable . . . and intrinsically worthwhile
. . . (*Selected*, 246)

What Giovanni finds remarkable about black women is their ability "to
make a way out of no way," that is, to create something of beauty and comfort out of the "scraps" thrown away by those who are "materially richer."
These are the kinds of qualities Giovanni repeatedly attributes to and
admires in black women; significantly, she most frequently envisions these
black women as southern and old—as, we will see, her grandmother.

Finally, the quilts made by these women bring spiritual warmth because
they incorporate the past, family history; one of Giovanni's recent poems,
"Stardate Number 18628.190," written in celebration of "the Black woman
. . . in all our trouble and glory," elaborates on the historical function of quilts:

This is a summer quilt . . . log cabin pattern . . . see the corner piece
. . . that was grandmother's wedding dress . . . that was grandpappa's
favorite Sunday tie . . . that white strip there . . . is the baby who
died . . . Mommy had pneumonia so that red flannel shows the
healing . . . This does not hang from museum walls . . . nor will it
sell for thousands . . . This is here to keep me warm. (*Selected*, 19)

The quilt incorporates the vicissitudes of a family's history; it brings
together joy as well as grief, fear as well as hope. It is art designed to comfort
and protect, not to be showcased or made unavailable to average people by
its exorbitant price (Alice Walker's short story "Everyday Use" develops this
same theme).[5] The "This" of the opening line refers to the poem Giovanni is
writing, and we can see once again that she views the quilt as an appropriate
metaphor for her own art. The particular language here is notably personal,
"grandpappa" and "Mommy" being the nomenclature Giovanni actually
uses for her grandfather and her mother, and it can hardly be surprising
that Giovanni's own quilt collection was recently featured in a photograph
of her and her mother as a part of Roland Freeman's *A Communion of the
Spirits: African-American Quilters, Preservers, and Their Stories*.[6] As I hope to
make clear in the following pages, the quilt is a gendered, racialized, and
even region-specific trope for Nikki Giovanni. Until very recently, the love
and strength of black (southern) women it represents in Giovanni's poetry
are adequate bulwarks against a world (usually white and male) that is often

treacherous. Some of the poems she has written since her encounter with lung cancer, however, seem to question the effectiveness of these bulwarks. Simultaneously, as we will see, some of her most recent poems have begun to celebrate black men.

Two

Certain aspects of Giovanni's biography are not unique to her but common to several generations of African Americans. Born in Knoxville, Tennessee, she moved with her family to Cincinnati, Ohio ("Gateway to the South"), in 1943, when she was only two months old. She and her family were a part of what we now call the Great Migration of blacks from the rural South to the urban North. Like many others, Giovanni's parents migrated north to pursue better job opportunities and to escape the racial conditions of the South. In Knoxville, Giovanni's father could find only low-paying, menial jobs, despite the fact that he had a college education. In Knoxville, his children's lives would be constricted by segregation's many rules and regulations. In Cincinnati, where he had moved with his mother when he was himself only a child (a part of an earlier wave of black migration from the South), Gus Giovanni was offered a job at a home for black boys as well as opportunities for future, better-paying professional employment.

Like many other children whose parents migrated to the North but left family in the South, Giovanni and her sister and cousins all returned to Knoxville for summer vacations; moreover, Giovanni lived with her grandparents in Knoxville from the time she was fourteen until she was seventeen, when she left Austin High School and went to Fisk University as an early entrant. Her grandparents' home at 400 Mulvaney Street becomes in Giovanni's work the enduring symbol of safety, happiness, warmth, and security. Even after its literal destruction, it remains, at least imaginatively, her refuge from a hostile world. Importantly, most of the values inscribed throughout Giovanni's poetry are associated with her maternal grandparents. More powerfully than their home at 400 Mulvaney, which was ultimately destroyed in the wake of "urban renewal," her grandparents live on in her poetry as ancestral figures offering wisdom, comfort, and love.

As this brief summary of some of the biographical details of Giovanni's life suggests, both because of her parents' roots in the South and because of her ties to her grandparents, Giovanni may have grown up in the North (although Cincinnati is in reality and not just in name the "Gateway to the South"), but many of the values instilled in her as a child were southern and Appalachian. Like many other African American writers of her generation, however (for example, Toni Morrison), Giovanni tends to identify these values sometimes as "Southern," but more often simply as "Black." When she wants to celebrate black women, for example, her images are most often of southern black women. Although white Americans rarely acknowledge it, many elements of southern culture have some of their deepest roots in Africa. The abiding presence and importance of the past, the significance, even sacredness, of place, the centrality of food and food rituals, the importance of oral tradition—these were central to West African cultures. Similarly, quilts and quilting, which I have suggested are central tropes in Giovanni's poetry, also have African roots. While African American and feminist historians have made significant corrections to the traditional white, male version of southern history, few would venture to assert—as Nikki Giovanni repeatedly does in her lectures—that southern culture, at least in terms of these values, is black.

The process by which black American culture becomes white was definitively described by Langston Hughes in a poem entitled "Note on Commercial Theatre": "You've taken my blues and gone—."[7] White failure to recognize or even to see the ultimate source of some of America's most treasured cultural artifacts stems directly from an overwhelming need to deny both the theft and the original owner; as Hughes's poem indicates, white people have taken black creations and incorporated them into art which is for and about white people and their stories. Black contributions to American culture have been systematically appropriated and then denied. Thus, southern cooking, which incorporates many African features and which also reflects the work conditions of the slaves, is generally viewed (in cookbooks and cooking magazines) as white, while southern black cooking is known as "soul food."[8] The point made in Hughes's poem has frequently been reiterated by Giovanni. In an early essay, for example, she writes about this kind of cultural theft in regard to music: "The blues didn't start with Dixieland or work songs or Gospel or anything but us.... Dvořák's Fifth, commonly called 'The New World Symphony,' is nothing but our music" (*Gemini*, 117). Similarly, in her recent poem "When Gamble and Huff Ruled," she states, "I dislike other people for taking our music our muse and our rap to sell their cars and bread and toothpaste and deodorant and sneakers but never seeming to have enough to give back to the people who created it" (*Love*, 51). Not only is it the case that "Black people don't get paid for anything that we do," Giovanni argues in a very recent poem, but "we watched the white folks record our music ... take our dance to the Great White Way ... and then turn around and ask why we couldn't come up to their standards" (*Blues*, 39). Among the more frustrating and infuriating aspects of American racism is not simply the denial of the horrors of slavery and, in modern times, of racism, but also the erasure of its products; the reality consistently erased is that America, and especially the South, was built from the sweat, the toil, the skills, and the intelligence of black people.

In an essay first published in Gerald Early's *Lure and Loathing: Essays on Race, Identity, and the Ambivalence of Assimilation*, Giovanni argues that, for her, when the categories of race and national identity are brought together, "the noun is Black" while "american is the adjective."[9] Not only is race central to Giovanni's identity, but it seems always to have been a source of pride. Undoubtedly because of her parents and maternal grandparents, Giovanni recognized from the time she was quite young that privilege and value or merit have no necessary relation to each other. In lectures, she frequently speaks of the many ways her father found to counteract the forces of racism by helping his children actually feel superior to apparently privileged white people. For example, he would take them on Sunday drives to some of the wealthy white neighborhoods of Cincinnati, where the large houses made them feel sorry for the inhabitants because, clearly, heating such large spaces would be impossible. In *Gemini*, Giovanni writes of the fact that her mother asked her "to read three books, one of which was *Black Boy*. I took it to school in the seventh grade and the nun called it trash. Which was beautiful. Because I could intellectually isolate all white nuns as being dumb and unworthy of my attention" (141). Clearly, the self-hatred described so definitively by Toni Morrison in *The Bluest Eye* never factored into Giovanni's sense of self. Some of her best-known poems, in fact, inscribe and celebrate black self-love; "Nikki Rosa," for example, asserts that "Black love is Black wealth," while "Ego-Tripping" presents the black woman as being "so hip even my errors are correct" (*Selected*, 42, 93).

As the latter poem exuberantly illustrates, a large measure of Giovanni's pride in her racial identity is due to her perception and experience of it as a female. Gender, however, is a good deal more complicated category than race, at least for students of Giovanni's work, if not for Giovanni herself. Karen Jackson Ford, for example, has recently written of the pivotal role played by the trope of masculinity in the Black Arts movement, which created special problems for women writers. These women writers (including Giovanni), states Ford, "were faced with the impossible task of being revolutionary poets, who were aggressive, irreverent, and menacing, while being supportive black women, who were submissive, reverent to black men, and feminine. The two personae could not comfortably inhabit the same poem, and their contradictions would trouble African-American women's poetry for the next decade."[10] Although Ford goes on to praise "Giovanni's independence of thought and courage of conviction in rejecting the sexism of the Black Arts movement," she concludes by castigating Giovanni for her failure to "dismantle the structures of masculinity and femininity that undergird" the problems afflicting the Black Power movement: "Like many of her contemporaries, Giovanni rejected the excessive masculinity of the black liberation movement but sought refuge in an excessive femininity that left the oppressive categories of gender securely in place."[11]

By reading selectively in Giovanni's early work, by ignoring much of Giovanni's biography, and, most important, by considering gender in isolation from race, Ford offers a reductive analysis that proves less than useful.[12] Even a cursory glance at Giovanni's poetry—early or recent—reveals her refusal to "read" categories like "femininity" and "masculinity" in (white) traditional ways.[13] As Barbara Ellen Smith reminds us, "the social ideology of white supremacy tended to construct two races but four genders."[14] The "contradictions" disturbing to Ford do not necessarily disturb the author of *Gemini*; indeed, to be black in America has always entailed living with contradictions. In her own personal life, Giovanni has consistently challenged traditional gender expectations, both those based on white norms and those based on black ones. Virtually all of the important people in her life have been women. From her grandmother, who is probably the single most important influence in her life, Giovanni learned that women are the leaders for social change, the activists; in part, this was the result of her grandmother's particular personality, but it was also, more importantly, the result of racial history in the South. As Smith points out, during segregation, when violence against blacks was frequent and widespread, "Southern black women of all classes emerged as important voices for social reform" because "outspokenness on the part of black men could result in death."[15]

Until relatively recently, Giovanni's celebrations of blackness have tended to be highly inflected by gender, so that "black" seems to become almost synonymous with "female" (though "female" is not synonymous with "black"). In her last two volumes of poetry, however, she has begun to reassess and celebrate black men in such poems as "And Yeah . . . This Is a Love Poem" (for the Million Man March) and "Train Rides." In these more recent poems, Giovanni develops a greater awareness not only of the burdens imposed on black men by their socially denied access to (white) gender definitions but also of their efforts to be men notwithstanding; as she states toward the end of "Train Rides," for example, "even when the Black men can't protect them [little girls] they wish they could which has to be respected since it's the best they can do" (*Blues*, 63). Giovanni has been, as she frequently states on stage, a "chauvinist" when it comes to being a black woman, but she has started to regard black men with greater awareness and empathy than she perhaps did when she was younger.

Three

Race and gender are, then, both closely intertwined and highly central components of Nikki Giovanni's sense of identity. To use her own figure, they are both nouns, not adjectives. As we have seen, "black" and "southern" are in some important ways identical to her, but ultimately "southern" and "Appalachian" would have to be regarded as adjectives, not nouns; they are, however, extremely important adjectives for they imbue both "black" and "woman" with historicity. Giovanni recently commented that the "most Southern" thing about her is her love of storytelling, while the most "Appa-lachian" thing is her sense of independence and individuality.[16] Trying to differentiate for me between her sense of these two regions and what charac-terizes them respectively, she emphasized that she sees the southern mental-ity as a herd mentality. She herself has always believed that she could think what she wanted to think, take actions based on that thinking, and stand up for her opinions; she has never thought that she needed other people to think for her. This concept of freedom and independence is, she stated, uniquely Appalachian. Giovanni concluded with the observation that, beyond her love of storytelling and her concept of freedom, she sees herself as an urban writer who has lately been "accessing" her rural roots; this latter statement seemed to refer to the fact that some of her recent poetry has focused on the destruction of rural settings by unethical real estate developers.

Although Giovanni certainly is an urban writer in many important ways, her distinction between urban and rural suggests an opposition which may be somewhat misleading. Giovanni, like many black Americans, was for much of her life a transplanted southerner. But the urban culture created by black migrants from the South contains remnants of the South. In her study of black migration narratives, Farah Jasmine Griffin demonstrates the ways in which, in migration narratives, the migrant incorporates something from southern culture into the northern cityscape for nurturance and strength. Expanding Toni Morrison's concept of the ancestor, Griffin argues that "the ancestor is present in ritual, religion, music, food, and performance. His or her legacy is evident in discursive formations like the oral tradition."[17]

In Giovanni's poetry, both early and recent, the ancestor (always female) is an important presence often represented in food and always associated, like the quilt, with comfort, warmth, and safety. Consider, for example, the early and justly famous poem, "Knoxville, Tennessee." The poem details "corn," "okra," "greens," "cabbage," "barbecue," "buttermilk," and "homemade ice-cream" as important reasons the child speaker of the poem "always" likes "summer / best" (*Selected*, 48). Complementing these foods, which are eaten "at the church picnic," are the various other activities associated with summer: listening to gospel music, going "to the mountains with your grandmother," and being barefooted. These foods, the love with which they are served, and the presence of the grandmother combine to create the warmth which the final lines of the poem celebrate: "and be warm / all the time / not only when you go to bed / and sleep" (*Selected*, 48). The warmth attributed by the speaker to summer, like the warmth associated with quilts, is quite clearly a figurative warmth generated by the presence of her grandmother; when she is with her grandmother, she can be warm—safe, secure, peaceful—"all the time," not just when she is in bed asleep. Significantly, although the poem ostensibly focuses on the reasons summer is the best time of the year, it is not entitled "Summer Poem," but rather, "Knoxville, Tennessee." Even lacking biographical information about Giovanni, the reader of the poem would eventually recognize that if summer is somehow equated with Knoxville, then Knoxville is probably not the child's home. But knowing something of Giovanni's personal history as well as of American history allows us to see the ways in which this poem speaks of what was lost by African Americans in their migration to the North and the necessity somehow to retain connection to it. The ancestor, present here in the food as well as in the actual grandmother, provides the warmth and safety lacking in the everyday world of the North.

After the death of her grandfather, Giovanni realized that her grandmother would find life difficult. Indeed, her grandmother's desire to live was diminished not only by her husband's death but also, and perhaps more greatly, by "urban renewal" and "progress," which destroyed her home at 400 Mulvaney. The new home which the family found for Grandmother Louvenia was, Giovanni writes, "pretty but it had no life" (*Gemini*, 10). The reason it had no life is that it had no memories, no living past, no ancestral whispers. Giovanni describes her own desperate efforts to somehow be her grandfather, and recreate 400 Mulvaney: "And I made ice cream the way Grandpapa used to do almost every Sunday. And I churned butter in the hand churner. And I knew and she knew there was nothing I could do. 'I just want to see you graduate,' she said, and I didn't know she meant it. I graduated [from Fisk] February 4. She died March 8" (*Gemini*, 10–11). Significantly, when Giovanni and her mother, sister, and nephew drove to Knoxville after they received news of Louvenia's death, Giovanni could not get warm: "And I ran the heat the entire trip despite the sun coming directly down on us. I couldn't get warm" (*Gemini*, 11).

The need to preserve her grandmother and all she represented is apparent in another early poem, "Legacies," where, again, food plays a central role. The opening poem of the pivotal volume, *My House*, "Legacies" describes the effort of the grandmother to teach her grandchild "how to make rolls" (*Selected*, 113); that the rolls are one of the grandmother's specialties is reflected in the pride in the grandmother's voice: "'i want chu to learn how to make rolls,' said the old / woman proudly.'" The granddaughter, however, says, "'i don't want to know how to make no rolls' / with her lips poked out." What is important in the poem is the reason the little girl refuses to learn how to make the rolls:

"but the little girl didn't want / to learn how because she knew / even if she couldn't say it that / that would mean when the old one died she would be less / dependent on her spirit" (*Selected*, 113).

Other ancestral figures also appear throughout Giovanni's work, and they are consistently associated with the South or Southern Appalachia. In early humorous poems such as "Alabama Poem" and "Conversation," the speaker is a young, northern urbanite who thinks she is somehow superior to the old, southern country people she encounters. She discovers, however, that she really has little sense of her own racial identity; as the old woman in "Conversation" tells her, "you better get back to the city cause you one of them / technical niggers and you'll have problems here" (*Selected*, 118).

"A Theory of Pole Beans (for Ethel and Rice)," which is dedicated to an elderly couple in Southwest Virginia, celebrates the courage and determination of the ancestors through using the trope of pole beans. The "segregation and hatred and fear" experienced by the black couple were unable to destroy them, just as the "small towns and small minded people" failed "to bend [their] taller spirits down" (*Love*, 67). The title metaphor is presented in these lines:

> pole beans are not everyone's favorite
> they make you think of pieces of fat back
> cornbread
> and maybe a piece of fried chicken
> they are the staples of things unquestioned
> they are broken and boiled
> (*Love*, 67–68)

The ancestors celebrated in this poem are, like pole beans, plain, simple, and unsophisticated; the conditions in which they have lived have been difficult and yet, just as pole beans are "staples" that nourish, this elderly couple "bought a home reared a family / supported a church and kept a mighty faith / in your God and each other" (*Love*, 68). They possessed, in other words, the qualities that enabled black people not simply to survive racism but to resist and survive it whole, and the seed they planted will continue to be fruitful: "your garden remains in full bloom" (*Love*, 68).

Thus, although Giovanni is without question an urban poet (especially in the rhythms of her poetry), she is also without question an urban poet for whom the (rural) South—meaning the various values that cluster around it in her imagination—has enormous significance. The South of slavery, of segregation, of racism exists in her poetry, where it is the source of the anger that suffuses much of her work. John Oliver Killens, with whom Giovanni studied at Fisk, describes the black southern literary voice as one "distinguished by the quality of its anger, its righteous indignation, its reality, its truthfulness."[18] With clear ties to the oral tradition of the black preacher, the black southern literary voice described by Killens clearly and accurately describes one of Giovanni's literary voices. Certainly her conception of the poet and poetry is consistent with this description, for throughout her career she has stated that the poet speaks the truth as she sees it in an effort to change the way people look at the world and situations in it; the writer writes, in fact, out of anger at the way things are: "I have been considered a writer who writes from rage and it confuses me. What else do writers write from?" (*Sacred*, 31).[19]

The South, then, is not an idealized place in Giovanni's poetic imagination. As we have seen, the "herd mentality" of the South is antithetical to her own "Appalachian" sense of independence and freedom. But the racism of the South is not, for Giovanni, limited to the South; it can be found everywhere in America. The ties to family, love, and safety, however, which are among the values most important in Giovanni's life and work, are exclusively associated with the South. And as we have seen these are values associated in her imagination with black people, especially black women. Again, Killens's comments have clear application to Giovanni: "The people of the black South are much closer to their African roots, in its culture, its humanity, the beat and rhythm of its music, its concept of family ... and its spirituality."[20] In Giovanni's work, what Killens identifies as African qualities in southern culture rarely are brought together with the ugliness of southern racism.

The food imagery that recurs frequently in Giovanni's poetry is her primary trope for the ancestor and the South. In "My House," for example, the speaker says, "I want to fry pork chops / and bake sweet potatoes / and call them yams / cause I run the kitchen / and I can stand the heat" (*Selected*, 149); notice here the insistence on using the African "yam." When food images occur, then, they are generally images of what are traditionally southern foods: cornbread, ham, biscuits, fried green tomatoes, blackberries, chitterlings, barbeque, bread pudding, greens, pinto beans, fried chicken—these are typical of the specific food references found in Giovanni's poetry. A recent poem makes explicit the connections between food, women, and the ancestral figure, while it also delineates the symbolic values of food. Written in celebration of the birthday of the famous country cook, the poem is entitled "The Only True Lovers Are Chefs or Happy Birthday, Edna Lewis," and the title's meaning is revealed in the third stanza:

> but this is about love and there can be no better loving than bread
> pudding oh sure I know some people who think bread pudding
> is just food but some people also think creamed corn comes in a
> can and they have never known the pure ecstasy of slicing down

the thicker end of an ear of silver queen that was just picked at
five or six this very same morning then having sliced it down so
very neatly you take the back of the knife and pull it all back up
releasing the wonderful milk to the bowl to which you add a pinch
of garlic and some fresh ground pepper which you then turn into
a gently lit skillet and you shimmer it all like eggs then put a piece
of aluminum foil over it and let it rest while you put your hands
at the small of your back and go "Whew" and ain't that love that
soaks cold chicken wings in buttermilk and gets the heavy iron pot
out and puts just the right pat of lard in it at a high temperature so
that when you dust the wings with a little seasoned flour the lard
sizzles and cracks while the wings turn all golden on the outside
and juicy on the inside and yes I'd say that's love all right cause that
other stuff anybody can do and if you do it long enough you can
do it either well or adequately but cooking / now that is something
you learn from your heart then make your hands do what your
grandmother's hands did and I still don't trust anyone who makes
meatloaf with instruments cause the meat is to be turned with your
hands and while this may not be a traditional love poem let me just
say one small thing for castor oil and Vicks VapoRub and "How
is my little baby feeling today?" after a hard day's work so yes this
is a love poem of the highest order because the next best cook in
the world, my grandmother being the best, just had a birthday and
all the asparagus and wild greens and quail and tomatoes on the
vines and little peas in spring and half runners in early summer and
all the wonderful things that come from the ground said EDNA
LEWIS is having a birthday and all of us who love all of you who
love food wish her a happy birthday because we who are really
smart know that chefs make the best lovers ... especially when
they serve it with oysters on the half shell. . . .
   (*Love*, 39–41)

I have quoted extensively from this poem in order to allow the reader to
hear its rhythms and its colloquial, spoken-language patterns. The poem is
at once a celebration of this particular black woman, who happens to be a
famous chef, and a celebration of all the black female ancestors who showed
their love through the food they prepared, food intended to nurture not
simply the body but the spirit. That is why the heart is the instrument of
knowledge of cooking, and that is why imitating the actions of grandmoth-
ers is the real education one needs.

Four

How strong and effective are the values associated with the South and with black women? Will their quilts always suffice to keep us warm? In her most recent volume, *Blues: For All the Changes*, Giovanni seems to find those values increasingly fragile and inadequate. This collection contains many powerful poems, but it is perhaps Giovanni's darkest and angriest to date. In poem after poem, the love, courage, and strength found in the female ancestor of her earlier work are threatened or destroyed by or found insufficient to protect the speaker from the horrors of her world. It is difficult to ignore the likely autobiographical roots of the tone and mood of this collection of poems. Written during the first few years following Giovanni's encounter with lung cancer in 1995, *Blues* illustrates the way such an experience can often lead to a reassessment of one's world and those who have been a part of it, as well as of one's past and the stories one has created about it.

The initial poem of the volume, "The Wrong Kitchen," explicitly finds "Grandmother" inadequate to protect the speaker from the frightening spectacle of domestic violence. Because of its pun on "kitchen," the poem is perhaps Giovanni's most exclusively "black" poem; that is, unless or until the reader/ listener knows that "kitchen" is the term used by African Americans to describe the hair at the nape of the neck, much of the poem's meaning will be lost. This is a poem Giovanni has read frequently on stage over the last year or so, and she uses her introduction of it to highlight the ways in which white people are oblivious to and ignorant about black culture. Usually to a good deal of knowing laughter from the black members of her audience, and nervous laughter from white ones, Giovanni explains the time, energy, and pain black women experience in order to straighten their hair and make it seem more "white." Because of perspiration, the hair at the back of the neck, the "kitchen," is what "goes back" most quickly; when she was a little girl, Giovanni recounts, every adult woman in the community felt free to offer to "touch up" her kitchen for her. Giovanni's comments make explicit the poem's implicit meaning, that is, that people have worried about "nappy" hair when what they should have worried about is "nappy" lives.

This short yet powerful poem juxtaposes the speaker's grandmother's values to the brutal realities of the speaker's life; those values, the poem suggests, were inadequate to help or protect the speaker:

Grandmother would sit me
between her legs
to scratch my dandruff
and unravel my plaits

We didn't know then
dandruff was a sign of nervousness
hives tough emotional decisions
things seen that were better
unseen

We thought love could cure
anything a doll here a favorite
caramel cake there

The arguments the slaps the chairs
banging against the wall
the pleas to please stop
would disappear under quilts aired
in fresh air
would be forgotten after Sunday School
teas and presentations for the Book Club
We didn't know then why I played
my radio all night
and why I kept a light burning
We thought back then it was my hair
that was nappy

So we—trying to make it all right—
straightened the wrong kitchen
   (*Blues*, 3–4)

One only has to think back to "Knoxville, Tennessee" and recall the power of the grandmother to keep the speaker "warm / all the time / not only when you go to bed / and sleep" to realize how much the perspective on childhood has shifted. The grandmother in "The Wrong Kitchen" misapprehends the causes of the behaviors she sees in her granddaughter. Moreover, the grandmother's solutions to life's problems are, in retrospect, childish in their irrelevance and ineffectiveness. All of the things that in earlier poems Giovanni has found a defense against the treacheries of the world are inefficacious here: "love," "a doll," "a caramel cake," "quilts aired in fresh air," church, reading.

Perhaps more devastating than these failures is the inability of the "we" of the poem to understand correctly the reality that the "I" was experiencing. Because the poem concludes with the statement that "we—trying to make it all right" were the ones who "straightened the wrong kitchen," I am inclined to identify the "we" as all the black women with whom the speaker came in contact when she was a child, including the grandmother. The poem thus suggests that because these women were blind to the realities of the child's life, the child has had to construct her own defenses (the radio and the burning light) against the violence in her home.

The powerlessness of the grandmother in "The Wrong Kitchen" becomes the speaker's own powerlessness in some of the subsequent poems in *Blues*. When Giovanni stated that she thinks of herself as an urban poet who is "currently accessing her rural roots," she probably had in mind the dominant presence of the natural world in this volume. Although nature or the natural world is invoked infrequently in Giovanni's earlier work, when it does appear, it is generally seen as southern. The lovely poem "Walking Down Park," for example, which was first published in *Re: Creation* in 1970, equates urbanization with white capitalist hegemony, and inquires, "ever look south / on a clear day and not see / time's squares but see / tall Birch trees with sycamores / touching hands / and see gazelles running playfully / after the lions" (*Selected*, 81). Looking back past the genocide of Native Americans and the enslavement of Africans to the continent of Africa, the poem insists on the parallels between the destruction of the natural world and the enslavement / oppression of African Americans.

Many of the poems in *Blues* revisit these themes from a rural vantage point; whereas "Walking Down Park" is set in the city, which allows the speaker to envision places where urbanization has not stripped the world of green, these recent poems present particular rural spaces which she is viewing as the last green on earth—and they are in the process of being destroyed. These green spaces are both gendered and racialized; repeatedly, the speaker identifies with nature or creatures in the natural world, especially birds. The speaker, like the birds, is trying to maintain life in a world governed by white men whose greed supersedes all other considerations. "Me and Mrs. Robin," for example, makes explicit the link between the poet's cancer experience and a handicapped baby robin whose mother insists that it should fly, but whose handicap results in its falling to the ground. Watching the drama from her living room window, the speaker of the poem acknowledges that "for the first time in my life I was angry with God" (*Blues*, 75). The speaker of many of the poems in this volume sees herself, like she sees the robin, as vulnerable and powerless, a condition that generates her anger; as the speaker states in "Road Rage," "what is really happening is that no one is listening to you and no one cares about your concerns and you have no rights that anyone is bound to respect and you are finally made to realize that you are just a small colored woman trying to protect her home and that will not be allowed" (*Blues*, 46). The systematic destruction of the natural world is also the systematic destruction of black people, black women in particular; not surprisingly, it is also the destruction of art. The final poem in *Blues* is entitled "The Last Poem," in which Giovanni asserts that "The Last Poem on the last day will be a love poem"; it will be, however, a love poem that will "scream" and ultimately kill "to try to make it right" (*Blues*, 99, 100). Destruction of the white men who are "developing" the land is, the poem asserts, the only solution to the evil they represent. The speaker has seen a mother bird fly out of her tree to get some worms for her nestlings, and has watched in dismay as excavators take down the hill on which the tree stands, turning the tree with its nest and nestlings under a huge mound of earth. How else does one respond to the ultimate horror of watching the mother bird peck at the dirt which has buried her babies?[21]

Five

Several poems in *Blues* strike a more optimistic note. Of these, the finest is without question "Train Rides." This poem also provides an appropriate conclusion to some of the ideas about Nikki Giovanni's poetry that I have been exploring in this essay. As we have seen, Giovanni frequently uses the quilt as a metaphor for her own writing, but there are few of her poems which so perfectly resemble the quilt in terms of structure as "Train Rides." The rhythms of the poem, its title, and the title of the whole volume suggest, however, musical metaphors. Although I have not addressed the connections between Giovanni's poetry and music in this essay, certainly those connections have been extremely important. Indeed, her reading of her poetry in juxtaposition to gospel music on the award-winning album, *Truth Is on Its Way*, helped bring Giovanni national attention and fame.[22] Her later work has taken on qualities often associated with jazz: the apparent formlessness, the fragmentation, the improvisation. Yet the ease with which one could describe a poem like "Train Rides" as either a quilt or a jazz composition allows us to see just how closely related these two art forms can be. In many ways, a quilt—especially, for example, a crazy quilt—is the visual equivalent of a jazz piece by someone like Charles Mingus or Thelonius Monk. As Houston A. Baker Jr. and Charlotte Pierce-Baker point out in their discussion of Alice Walker's "Everyday Use," "the crafted fabric of Walker's story is the very weave of blues and jazz traditions in the Afro-American community, daringly improvisational modes that confront breaks in the continuity of melody (or theme) by riffing. The asymmetrical quilts of southern black women are like the off-centered stomping of the jazz solo or the innovative musical showmanship of the blues interlude."[23] The structure of "Train Rides" similarly invites us both to envision a quilt and to hear a jazz solo.

"Train Rides" is divided into four sections of unequal length, each of which is followed by the one-line refrain, "and this poem recognizes that" (*Blues*, 60). The first section of the poem begins with the outrageous idea that the speaker fears being "shamed" for wearing a linen blouse as late in the season as "early October." This allusion to the violation of a fashion "rule" allows the poet to segue into an improvisational interlude about jails and prisons, about what our society builds and why, about the guaranteed obsolescence of new roads, and about the fact that "we could have had a wonderful rail system if we hadn't been more interested in Ferguson winning instead of Plessy and the entire system collapsed under the weight of racism" (*Blues*, 59). Here we receive the first hint of the title's meanings. The allusion to the 1896 Supreme Court decision in *Plessy vs. Ferguson* is central to the poem's themes. This case, in which the Supreme Court ruled that Tennessee's policy of "separate but equal" facilities for whites and blacks on trains was constitutional, heralded the official beginning of Jim Crow segregation in the United States. *Plessy* was the law of the land until the 1954 *Brown vs. Board of Education* decision set the 1896 ruling aside by stating that separate was inherently unequal.

For the benefit of live audiences, when Giovanni reads this poem on stage she generally provides another piece of historical information often unknown to people unfamiliar with the history of the Civil Rights movement. *Brown vs. Board of Education* was pivotal in many ways, but most especially because it provoked a backlash of white violence in the South. The violent episode that proved to be the most historically significant was the murder of fourteen-year-old Emmett Till, whose mother sent him from Chicago to Mississippi to spend his 1955 summer holidays with his great-uncle, Mose Wright. The story of what happened just a few days after young Emmett arrived in Mississippi is not entirely clear. He apparently had in his billfold a photograph of a white girl, and he may have claimed to his cousins that she was his girlfriend. "Up North," he may have bragged, black boys can date white girls. His cousins apparently dared Emmett to speak to a white woman in Mississippi. Whether he whistled at Carolyn Bryant, who was working in the country store she owned with her husband, Roy Bryant, or said something to her like "Bye, baby," is not clear; in her remarks, Giovanni generally emphasizes the fact that Emmett stuttered and had a gimpy leg. What is known is that Roy Bryant and his brother-in-law, J. W. Milam, came during the night to Mose Wright's home, and took young Emmett away. They brutally beat, stripped, and then shot him, weighted his body down with a fan from a cotton gin, and put him in the Tallahatchie River.[24]

What was done to Emmett Till was not significantly different from what had been done to hundreds of black boys and men across the South since the end of the Civil War, although it is only recently that the full truth and complete documentation of lynching in America has begun to be published (see, for example, *Without Sanctuary: Lynching Photography in America*, published in 2000). What was unique about the Emmett Till case was that his mother, against the express orders of the Mississippi sheriff in charge, and therefore at great personal risk, had his body brought back to Chicago, opened the casket, and invited the world to see what had been done to her boy—whose face and body had been so badly battered and mangled that he could be identified only by the ring he wore on his finger. Photographs of Till's body, published by *Jet* magazine, drew the world's attention to the scene of the crime, Money, Mississippi, where Bryant and Milam actually stood trial for the murder, though, of course, the all-white jury found them not guilty.

In recounting this history for her audiences, Giovanni emphasizes the several aspects of the case that she considers most relevant to her poem, which is itself a celebration of the Pullman porters. First, Pullman porters were responsible for helping Mrs. Bradley defy the sheriff's orders by shipping her son's body back to Chicago. Second, one of the results of the publicity the Till case generated was that black people across the South were emboldened by Till's own courage. Till was murdered in August 1955, and that December, just a few short months later, Rosa Parks refused to move to the back of the bus, and the Montgomery Improvement Association was launched as an umbrella association to organize the Montgomery bus boycott. Because he was relatively young and new to town, Reverend Martin Luther King Jr. was named president of the new Association. Giovanni emphasizes the fact that one of the key civil rights workers in Montgomery, who in fact posted bail for Mrs. Parks, was E. D. Nixon, a former chairman of the Alabama NAACP, and a Pullman porter. Nixon was the one who conceived of the boycott and the best strategy for making it successful, but he of necessity had to find others—clergymen—to carry out the boycott since he, as a Pullman porter, had to make train runs.

The presence of the Pullman porters in these beginnings of the Civil Rights movement is the principal historical context for "Train Rides." The key parallel between the Emmett Till case and the central memory articulated in the poem is also, of course, the Pullman porters. Till was not unique in traveling from a northern city to the South for summer vacation; as we have seen, this movement is crucially important both to Nikki Giovanni's early poem, "Knoxville, Tennessee," and to the childhoods of countless African Americans. Giovanni likes to emphasize to her audiences that Emmett Till was safe as long as he stayed on the train, because there were Pullman porters all along the way who looked out for him—just as they did for Giovanni and her sister on their journeys from Cincinnati to Knoxville.

If we return to the first and longest section of the poem, we can see that, following the initial allusion to *Plessy vs. Ferguson*, the poem goes off on what initially seems an irrelevant tangent about finding a mother mouse and her babies in a tissue box on Giovanni's screened-in back porch. The second, thematically central, section of the poem recounts the speaker's memories of traveling on the train with her sister to Knoxville. The third section addresses the anti-progressive ideology of black conservatives. And the final, and shortest, section brings the earlier elements of the poem together in a celebration of black men. In addition to the history of civil rights in America, there are several other recurring, unifying motifs in the poem. One of the most important is the relationship between parents and children, in particular, the desire and determination of parents—both human and non-human—to protect their children. For black Americans, however, this desire to protect their young is often thwarted by the racism which has systematically attempted to destroy black men. Societal power and societal institutions (such as racism) can and will overpower individual desires and individual goals. The failure to recognize that no one can be free until all are free is presented in the poem as a major impediment to progress. Thus, for example, white America's determination to maintain a visible white privilege through segregation—even after segregation was made illegal—has meant that America has no effective public transportation system: "we could have had a wonderful rail system if we hadn't been more interested in Ferguson winning instead of Plessy and the entire system collapsed under the weight of racism" (*Blues*, 59). Similarly, those privileged black Americans who argue against affirmative action *after* they have benefited from it (Clarence Thomas, whom the poem references as a "poster boy for lawn jockeys") are merely the pawns of white people; "the only usefulness" of such black conservatives "is to stand in opposition to progress" (*Blues*, 62).

The central theme of the poem, however, is the beauty and wonder of black men like the Pullman porters. What makes them worthy of celebration is not simply the physical safety and protection they provided the Emmett Tills and Nikki Giovannis of America; more importantly, they allowed these children "to grow up thinking people are kind so even though we lived in a segregated world and even though everybody knows that was wrong that band of brothers put their arms around us and got us from our mother to our grandmother seamlessly" (*Blues*, 61). The real threat of segregation to black children is to their apprehension of the world in which they live and the people who inhabit it. We as a society want all of our children to believe that the world is essentially a good, kind, and safe place, for if the world's terrors are experienced by children at too early an age, they erect barriers and defenses to protect themselves from the good as well as the bad. One thinks of Toni

Morrison's character, Nel Wright, in *Sula*, and of the way in which watching her mother be insulted by a white train conductor forever alters Nel's sense of her mother and of herself. The Pullman porters protected many black children from that kind of devastating experience.

The temporal context of the poem reinforces these meanings. The poem begins in early October, with the speaker's putting away the outdoor furniture and flower pots in preparation for winter. Because she is doing these activities, she is inclined to think of it as "the first day of fall" even though "it's still early October." But her memory of childhood is triggered by the fact that this early October day bespeaks a different season altogether: "because it has been such a dry hot summer the leaves aren't really turning so it looks enough like late spring to make you think back to when you and your sister used to catch the train from Cincinnati to Knoxville" (*Blues*, 61). The poem celebrates the Pullman porters because they did all they could to preserve the innocence and safety and security of childhood for little girls like the speaker and her sister; their "fall" into a realization of life's horrors was delayed until adulthood.

Thus, as the final section of the poem makes very clear, the Pullman porters not only preserved and protected the speaker's childhood, but by doing so, they ensured her power to retain/create positive memories of that childhood past: "and somehow you want to pop popcorn and make pig feet and fried chicken and blueberry muffins and some sort of baked apple and you will sit near your fire and tell tales of growing up in segregated America and the tales will be so loving even the white people will feel short-changed by being privileged" (*Blues*, 63). In much the same way that Giovanni has spoken of her father's efforts, the Pullman porters allowed her to grow up celebrating the world she inhabited, which provided her the necessary armor as an adult to confront that world, and all the injustice in it, without succumbing to the racist ideology underpinning it. Notice the echoes in these lines of earlier poems like "Knoxville, Tennessee"; food, warmth, safety, and happiness have been made available to the speaker by those loving and graceful black men, the Pullman porters. But the final section of the poem expands to include not just those specific Pullman porters who encountered the speaker, but all black men: "no matter what else is wrong with winter ... little girls travel back and forth with the love of Black men protecting them from the cold and even when the Black men can't protect them they wish they could which has to be respected since it's the best they can do" (*Blues*, 63). The desires of black men to "protect" children from the "cold" of "winter" are as important to acknowledge and celebrate as the actual protection. Although "Sound in Space," the second poem in *Blues*, addresses the "distance between want and able" (*Blues*, 5), "Train Rides" also acknowledges that such a gap exists, especially for black people, but argues that it should never prevent one from loving or from recognizing love. Giovanni is certainly not alone in her implicit suggestion that the psychological attack on black Americans—and particularly black men—has been fueled by their lack of power to fulfill desire. Stated more simply, the poem suggests that all black men would be like the Pullman porters who protected the speaker—if they could; but the fact that they continue to *want* to protect even when they cannot is also deserving of recognition, respect, celebration.

The final lines of this final section of the poem invoke the late Tupac Shakur, to whom Giovanni's *Love Poems* was dedicated, as the ultimate symbol of the indestructibility of the black male spirit confronting the many facets of white racism:

> and we call it the blues with rhythm and they want it to be rock
> and roll and all the thump thump thump coming from cars is not
> Black boys listening to rap but all boys wishing they could be that
> beautiful boy who was a seed planted in stone who grew to witness
> the truth and who always kept it real and lots of times there is
> nothing we can do through our pain and through our tears but
> continue to love
>
> and this poem recognizes that
> (*Blues*, 63)

Unlike many of the poems in *Blues*, "Train Rides" expresses a belief that somehow even seeds planted in stone can and will find a way to bloom. And it is this spirit, which is embodied by black men, that *all* men wish they could possess. Thus, even though white men steal and then rename black music, that action is motivated by their recognition of the beauty of and their desire to themselves be black men. The unifying riff in the poem—"and this poem recognizes that"—emphasizes the speaker's ability to acknowledge all of these complicated truths about being black in America. If whites have "taken my blues and gone," it is because my "blues" are so beautiful and wonderful; that fact does not mitigate the crime, but it does allow me to celebrate myself.

Notes

1. Quotations from Nikki Giovanni's work are cited in the text with abbreviations: *Blues for All the Changes* (New York: William Morrow, 1999); *Gemini: An Extended Autobiographical Statement on My First Twenty-Five Years of Being a Black Poet* (1971; reprint, New York: Penguin, 1985); *Love Poems* (New York: William Morrow, 1997); *Racism 101* (New York: William Morrow, 1994); *Sacred Cows*

. . . *and Other Edibles* (New York: William Morrow, 1988); *Selected Poems of Nikki Giovanni* (New York: William Morrow, 1996).

2. Cheryl B. Torsney and Judy Elsley, introd. to *Quilt Culture: Tracing the Pattern*, ed. Torsney and Elsley (Columbia: Univ. of Missouri Press, 1994).

3. Elaine Showalter, *Sister's Choice: Tradition and Change in American Women's Writing* (New York: Oxford Univ. Press, Clarendon Press, 1991), 169.

4. Angela Dodson, "Patches: Quilts as Black Literary Icons," *Black Issues Book Review* 1, no. 3 (May–June 1999): 42. In Africa, weaving and textiles were the provenance of men.

5. Alice Walker, "Everyday Use," in *Love and Trouble: Stories of Black Women* (New York: Harcourt Brace Jovanovich, 1973).

6. Roland Freeman, *A Communion of the Spirits: African-American Quilters, Preservers, and Their Stories* (Nashville: Rutledge Hill Press, 1996).

7. Langston Hughes, *The Collected Poems of Langston Hughes*, ed. Arnold Rampersad (New York: Random House, Vintage Books, 1994), 215–16.

8. One of the dominant features of much southern cooking is the long, slow process by which food is prepared. Clearly, this feature is related to the slaves' long workdays, "from sunup to sundown."

9. Nikki Giovanni, "Racism, Consciousness, and Afrocentricity," in *Lure and Loathing: Essays on Race, Identity, and the Ambivalence of Assimilation*, ed. Gerald Early (New York: Allen Lane, Penguin Press, 1993), 54.

10. Karen Jackson Ford, *Gender and the Poetics of Excess* (Jackson: Univ. Press of Mississippi, 1997), 192.

11. Ibid., 196, 196, and 199.

12. Barbara Ellen Smith reminds us of the necessity of seeing race and gender in relation to each other. She points out, for example, that "the social, symbolic, and literal emasculation of black men meant that their power as men was exercised primarily in relation to black women and children; it also lent a masculinist character to their counterassertions of power and integrity." See her essay "The Social Relations of Southern Women," in *Neither Separate nor Equal: Women, Race, and Class in the South*, ed. Smith (Philadelphia: Temple Univ. Press, 1999), 15.

13. See, for example, "Poem (For Anna Hedgeman and Alfreda Duster)":

> thinning hair
> estee laudered
> deliberate sentences
> chubby hands
> glasses resting atop ample softness
> dresses too long
> beaded down
> elbow length gloves funny hats
> ready smiles
> diamond rings
> hopeful questions
> needing to be needed
> my ladies over fifty
> who birthed and nursed
> my Blackness
> (*Selected*, 145)

This poem presents a series of images that many traditional white feminists of the early 1970s would have deplored because of the apparent restrictions they placed on the women. But the outward appearance of these women—a cultivated middle-class appearance—indicates nothing about their inner strengths. From such women, the poet asserts, came her own sense of and pride in her racial identity.

14. Smith, 22.

15. Ibid.

16. Giovanni made this statement in a private conversation on April 9, 2000, and she later reiterated it in a lecture at Longwood College in Farmville, Virginia, on April 20, 2000.

17. See Morrison's "Rootedness: The Ancestor in Afro-American Fiction," in *Black Women Writers at Work: A Critical Evaluation*, ed. Mari Evans (Garden City, N.Y.: Anchor Press, 1984), 339–45. See also Farah Jasmine Griffin, *"Who set you flowin'?": The African-American Migration Narrative* (New York: Oxford Univ. Press, 1995), 5.

18. John Oliver Killens, introd. to *Black Southern Voices: An Anthology of Fiction, Poetry, Drama, Nonfiction, and Critical Essays*, ed. Killens and Jerry W. Ward Jr. (New York: Meridian, Penguin, 1992), 1.

19. For a full discussion of Giovanni's theory of poetry and the poet, see my volume *Nikki Giovanni* (New York: Twayne, 1992), 125–34.

20. Killens, 3.

21. Space does not allow me to do full justice to Giovanni's poems about the environment in *Blues*; the volume should be of considerable interest to scholars engaged in ecofeminist studies.

22. Giovanni, *Truth Is on Its Way* (Philadelphia: Collectibles Records, 1993). Audio CD.

23. Houston A. Baker Jr. and Charlotte Pierce-Baker, "Patches: Quilts and Community in Alice Walker's 'Everyday Use,'" in *"Everyday Use" / Alice Walker*, ed. Barbara T. Christian (New Brunswick, N.J.: Rutgers Univ. Press, 1994), 163.

24. For a full account of the Till case, see Stephen J. Whitfield's *A Death in the Delta: The Story of Emmett Till* (New York: Free Press, 1988).

ZOFIA BURR

Maya Angelou on the Inaugural Stage

Whether one is dealing with Emily Dickinson's letter-poems to Susan Gilbert Dickinson, Josephine Miles's anti-Vietnam War poetry, Gwendolyn Brooks's black power poetry, or Audre Lorde's poetry about the politics of difference, there's a consistent tendency to devalue the poetry as prosaic, propagandistic, or journalistic or to interpret it as narrowly autobiographical, expressive of personal experience and sensibility rather than engaged with the poet's—and the reader's—world. By focusing on the dynamics of address, we have seen how Miles, Brooks, and Lorde elaborate poetic practices that escape the confines of the personal and how each of them articulates, in her own way, a "women's poetry" that engages with the politics of the public world. As she works out an idiom that can make of poetry a genre interested in communicative utterance, each of these poets contends with the powerful prescriptions about what constitutes poetic merit and with pervasive expectations about the character of poetry by women. Miles, Brooks, and Lorde have been regularly misunderstood and marginalized as poets; they do not figure in any of the larger narratives about twentieth-century American poetry. In examining their careers and reading their poems, I have offered some ways of rethinking our commonplace assumptions about women, poetry, and politics. But by attending extensively to the actual reception of poetry by women across this century in the United

From *Of Women, Poetry, and Power: Strategies of Address in Dickinson, Miles, Brooks, Lorde, and Angelou*, pp. 180–94, 219–21. Copyright © 2002 by the Board of Trustees of the University of Illinois.

117

States, I have found little evidence to encourage optimism about the state of our thinking about these issues. Maya Angelou's poem for the presidential inauguration in 1993 can serve as a kind of coda to my argument.

First known in the literary world for her best-selling autobiographies, Angelou (b. 1928) has become probably the most widely recognized poet in contemporary U.S. culture. She is found on television, in the movies, on the radio, in print, on the lecture circuit, on the Internet, at the 1993 presidential inauguration, and at the Million Man March. Given this extraordinary career, she also serves as an exemplary figure, the reception of whose work allows us to discern some of the complications and impasses that attend us when we seek to examine a poetry that is unabashedly public in its ambitions.

The role of inaugural poet, positioning the poet as a nationally representative public voice, conflicts fundamentally with dominant conceptions of poetry, its purposes, and its character as a linguistic practice. This concluding discussion serves to underline some of the concerns this project has raised about the possible uses of poetry and about avenues for critical response opened up by attention to poetry as utterance and performance, to the poet's person and persona, and to audience and poetic address.

Poet and Public

Angelou's failure to impress professional poetry critics has always been linked to her success with a larger public audience. For instance, in a review of Angelou's 1976 collection, *Oh Pray My Wings Are Gonna Fit Me Well*, James Finn Cotter describes the book as an "unfortunate example" of the "dangers of success."[1] He argues that Angelou's access and responsiveness to the public have muted the private and personal quality that he takes to be essential to poetry. In Angelou's poetry, he argues, "the public voice drowns out the private emotion" (103). Cotter suggests that when Angelou writes with an ear to the oral presentation of the poem, she is writing for a public audience; by contrast, when she writes for its reception by a solitary reader, she is able to be true to the "private emotion" that is the source of good poetry. "Too many public readings may prove the undoing of the *personal* voice," Cotter suggests. "What wows an audience may offend on the printed page" (104; my emphasis). There is a striking difference between the sensibilities attributed to the auditor and to the reader of poetry in this assertion. The remark speaks to that most modern and western of our poetic prejudices, construing poetry as a written genre, the difficulties and interests of which respond to the attentions of the private reader rather than the face-to-face public auditor. The audience member who responds to the oral presentation of poetry is criticized for not knowing (or not caring) that he or she is responding to a poetry in which what is valuable is "drowned" or submerged. And Angelou's critics do nothing more energetically than dismiss the people who value her poetry.

In 1971, John Alfred Avant, for instance, deliberately insults the taste of those readers who like the poetry in *Just Give Me a Cool Drink of Water 'fore I Diiie*: "there will be an audience for this rather well done schlock poetry, not to be confused with poetry for people who read poetry. . . . This collection isn't accomplished, not by any means; but some readers are going to love it."[2] The point of Cotter's and Avant's remarks is clearly not to instruct the audience whose sensibilities are in question. The reviews do not address them; Angelou's readers are presumed, in any case, not to be readers of such reviews. As Joanne Braxton points out, "Angelou's audience, composed largely of women and blacks, isn't really affected by what white and/or male critics of the dominant literary tradition have to say about her work. This audience does not read literary critics; it does read Maya Angelou."[3] Comments critical of Angelou's audience are addressed to readers outside of that audience and designed to confirm us in our sense that Angelou is not an interesting poet and that we are discerning readers.

Even critics who value poetry as an oral tradition have nonetheless found Angelou wanting. Their terms reveal the extent to which they also privilege an intimate poetic "voice" as the essential constituent of good poetry. In an article linked to several Maya Angelou web sites, Bryan D. Bourn attributes her "success as a writer" to her use of the "oral tradition of many African tribes."[4] Bourn argues that "Angelou slips into banality when she abandons [these traditions], which is frequently the case in her poetry." "When she strays from [the African oral tradition], her writing gets flatter, less emotional. To put it simply, we no longer hear Angelou's '*voice*.'" Bourn associates this "voice" with what he identifies as a "conversational tone" and "immediacy of feeling."

Bourn posits a poetic voice whose source of vitality is identical with that which kills the poetic voice by Cotter's definition—the oral context. Nevertheless, Bourn's privileging of the emotional is closely connected to Cotter's sense of the private. In both cases, the expectation is that the poet's voice is an intimate, personal voice. We see this more clearly when Bourn points to those rare "examples in Angelou's poetry where her 'voice' does come through," that is, in the "poems relating *personal* experience" (my emphasis).[5] From the perspective of the critic privileging the written context, the poet must be an individual speaking as if to herself; from the perspective of the critic privileging the oral context, she must be speaking to and for her people.

Like Cotter, Bourn faults Angelou for going public, but not because she has left the garret for the soapbox. Instead, he faults her for turning away from her more immediate community to address a general audience. What neither critic thinks worth exploring is that to do this, she has, in places, taken a stance that is meant to be representative rather than individual, authoritative rather than confessional—most strikingly, of course, in her 1993 inaugural poem, "On the Pulse of Morning." The narrowness of Cotter's and Bourn's conceptions of poetry means that, for them and many other like-minded critics, Angelou's acceptance of the role of inaugural poet was bound to end in failure. Yet the decision to appoint an inaugural poet was only made in light of John F. Kennedy's success with Robert Frost as inaugural poet in 1961. Examining the response to Frost's inaugural performance more closely, however, reveals that his "success" was ambiguous at best and not necessarily that different from Angelou's perceived failure.

Inaugural Poets

When it made the news in late 1992 that Maya Angelou had been asked to read a poem at Clinton's upcoming inauguration, commentators inevitably compared her role as inaugural poet to that of Robert Frost at John F. Kennedy's 1961 inauguration. Frost had been the first poet ever to deliver a poem at an American presidential inauguration, and Angelou was the second.[6] Newspaper and magazine articles that compared the two poets underlined the differences in their racial and gender identities and asserted an ostensibly uncomplicated narrative of social progress in the fact that a "black woman" would be standing in the place of a "white man,"[7] occupying a representative role that, in the earlier era, it would have been hard to imagine anyone other than a white man fulfilling.

Angelou herself made the comparison with Frost. But unlike her contemporaries' accounts of Frost's reading, her account focuses on the identification she felt with Frost as a result of the difficulty he encountered in trying to read his prefatory poem. Although Frost had written a prefatory poem for the occasion to accompany "The Gift Outright," the sun's glare made it too difficult for him to read it, and after struggling with a few lines he decided to forego it and simply recite the poem "The Gift Outright," which he knew by heart. Recalling this scene, Angelou says: "Robert Frost was such a fine poet. . . . He was white and male, but he stood for me, and for Spanish people and Chinese people. . . . He was old and soon to die and couldn't see his own notes. He had the moxie to push on and recite what he knew. That further endeared him to me."[8] Angelou directs us away from the differences between herself and Frost. She doesn't say that she sees Frost's white maleness as an impasse in his capacity to represent her; rather, she focuses on his "moxie" and his mortality as traits that made him dear to her.

That Angelou reads Frost's triumph over his temporary vulnerability on the inaugural stage as a sign of his capacity to represent much more than himself is of a piece with journalistic coverage at the time of the event. Reporting on the Kennedy inauguration, the press in 1961 repeatedly turns Frost's difficulties at the podium, and his overcoming those difficulties, into a figure for the resilience of the nation and, in the context of Kennedy's inaugural address, of the resilience of the nation under the pressures of the cold war. *Life* magazine's coverage of the Kennedy inauguration makes the analogy most explicit by applying what Frost's (unread) dedication says about the nation's struggles to Frost's struggle to read the dedication itself: "In an affecting episode during the inaugural ceremonies, Robert Frost, 86, the patriarchal New England poet, received the undivided sympathy of the distinguished gathering. Frost, who had been asked by Kennedy to render his celebrated poem, 'The Gift Outright,' had thoughtfully written a dedicatory preface to the new President. But as the winter sun flared over his manuscript, Frost muttered, 'I can't see in this light.' Finally he gave up the attempt to read it. Frost was true, however, to two lines in his preface which he never got to: 'The turbulence we're in the middle of / Is something we can hardly help but love.' Dignified in his distress, he recited 'The Gift Outright,' which he knew by heart in a voice that was rich and strong."[9] Here we see how, in a sense, whatever was personal about Frost's struggle accrued a public meaning by virtue of its occurrence in a public (and highly ritualized) setting. Frost may have been trying, hardily, to read a written text, but his performance was rescripted by commentators as a "scene" in a larger narrative of international tensions and rivalry. Or, given its airing on television, it might be described as an "episode" in an unfolding story of politics and public culture. Ultimately, the meaning of Frost's inaugural reading, as reflected in its reception, was focused more on the context in which it occurred than on the poem itself.

Though at the time, Frost's person, poem, and dilemma were accepted as representative, expressive of the various vulnerabilities and struggles faced by Americans since 1942 when "The Gift Outright" was first published, retrospectively, Frost himself has not been considered "representative" of the people, nor has his representation of the nation in "The Gift Outright" been considered honest by later commentators. The poem locates the nation in the relationship between the "land" and the prerevolutionary Anglo settler, eliding the devastation to Native American and African cultures upon which the new nation silently depends and focusing instead on the bond between the land and "us":[10]

> The land was ours before we were the land's.
> She was our land more than a hundred years
> Before we were her people. She was ours
> In Massachusetts, in Virginia,

But we were England's, still colonials,
Possessing what we were still unpossessed by,
Possessed by what we now no more possessed.
Something we were withholding made us weak
Until we found out that it was ourselves
We were withholding from our land of living,
And forthwith found salvation in surrender.
Such as we were we gave ourselves outright
(The deed of gift was many deeds of war)
To the land vaguely realizing westward,
But still unstoried, artless, unenhanced,
Such as she was, such as she would become.[11]

Though the poem is in places ambiguous in tone ("The deed of gift was many deeds of war"), contemporary readers tend to be quick to distance themselves from what is frequently taken as an unambiguous celebration of "expansionism based on violence," to use the words of the *Washington Post* from January 1993.

There has thus been a nearly complete reversal in the perception of Frost's representativeness as inaugural poet, and this transformation marks the changes in cultural perceptions and cultural politics in the last thirty years.[12] The repeated event of a poet reading at a presidential inauguration, however, unearths a tension between the representativeness and the individuality of the poet's voice that has persisted in the reception of modern poetry in the United States. The occasion of the inaugural poem resurrects an ideology about the role of poetry in the public sphere that is as influential now as it was in the early 1960s. Kennedy's views on the value of the poet as the voice of the private individual, the voice of individual integrity over and against all the compromises and distortions of public discourses and institutions—including the state as the prototypical public institution—nicely illuminates the perceived incompatibility of the true poet as individual voice and poetry as a public idiom.

Prompted by Interior Secretary Stewart L. Udall, Kennedy's decision to invite a poet to read at his inauguration underlined his frequently stated belief that the responsible exercise of political power requires the resistance of the arts. In the terms Kennedy used at the dedication of the Robert Frost Library at Amherst College in October 1963 (after Frost's death in January of that year), the politicians are "the men who create power," while the artists are the men "who question power."[13] In this configuration, the artists provide a check on those who hold political power in much the same way political protest and "freedom of speech," in a democracy, are considered a check on elected representatives. Kennedy states: "When power corrupts, poetry cleanses. For art establishes the basic human truths which must serve as the touchstones of our judgement. The artist, however faithful to his personal vision of reality, becomes the last champion of the individual mind and sensibility against an intrusive society and an officious state" (136). But even as Kennedy criticizes the state for being "officious," he makes it clear that a society that allows or encourages the artist to fulfill his function as "champion of the individual mind" is far superior to a society that would require the artist to fulfill some other function. "In free society," Kennedy asserts, "art is not a weapon, and it does not belong to the sphere of polemics and ideology. Artists are not engineers of the soul. It may be different elsewhere. But [in a] democratic society . . . the highest duty of the writer . . . is to remain true to himself and to let the chips fall where they may" (136). By "elsewhere," Kennedy obviously means the Soviet Union and other communist states. And that the American artist is free "to let the chips fall where they may" is an obvious and familiar cold-war assertion of our superiority.

This sense of the independence of the artist in America, however, has a history that extends before the cold war and has also been defined in contrast to the relationship between the British monarch and his or her Poet Laureate.[14] In accord with national sentiment, no president of the United States would want it said that he honored a poet for the sake of having the occasions of his state or his rule praised in return. In fact, about a month after Kennedy's inauguration, a *New York Times* writer took the opportunity to distinguish this president's relationship to his inaugural poet from the English monarch's relationship with the Poet Laureate: "We have not and cannot have a national poet laureate, but we do need poets who without flattering us tell us how to face danger and how to conquer it. It is a good sign that President Kennedy recognizes this function of the poet."[15] Kennedy's perspective acknowledges a public role for poetry, but only insofar as it remains untouched by the public world or public commitments, only insofar as poetry's public is based on its private orientation.

The function of the poet as a check on power is both analogous to that of the press as the Fourth Estate (understood as having a responsibility to scrutinize the actions of the government from the perspective of the people) and also absolutely unlike the press, insofar as the press remains part of the public sphere and its imperatives—the very things that poetry is designed to check and counter in the name of integrity defined in terms of the private, the personal, the individual. Thus, if poetry has a public role to perform it is only by virtue of and on the basis of its ability to remain an idiom apart from all the public discourses of society. By this account, the maker of the poem cannot anticipate a public role for his or her work and have it remain poetry.

In this light, Frost's failure to read the verse he wrote for the occasion of the inauguration preserved his integrity as a poet. (In fact, subsequent critical commentary on the unread "Dedication" tends to refer to it as "a lamentable work.")[16] "The Gift Outright," which he did read, was already an authentic poem; now it was being overheard at the inauguration—a legitimate, because accidental or unanticipated, transition onto the stage of national politics. The poem's status as a genuine poem was never put into question. But Angelou's poem "On the Pulse of Morning," conceived and unveiled as an inaugural poem, is read in the suspicious light of public discourse. And having taken form as a poem designed to grace the inaugural stage, it must subsequently seek an afterlife as a genuine poem—a very different and hugely fraught (perhaps impossible) transition.

When it came time to tell the stories that Angelou's presence at the inauguration licensed us to tell about ourselves as "American" people, no one in the liberal press disputed Angelou's representativeness or the appropriateness of such a gesture of inclusion on the Clinton administration's part.[17] But the response to the poem as a poem uncovered and raised literary anxieties to a fever pitch. At its most politely critical, the evaluation of the poem was phrased as a question of genre. As the poet David Lehman put it: "If you define her task as a theatrical one, she did what was expected. If you define her task as a political one, she did what was expected. But if you ask me as a poet to be as ruthless on this poem as I would be on any other, I would have to say it's not very memorable."[18]

From Lehman's account, "as a poet," what we learn about (what counts as) poetic discourse is that it is not theatrical or political discourse. Instead, it is an ascetic idiom that eschews such forms of popularity and public engagement. But the fact that Lehman applies all three categories to Angelou's presentation suggests that while the political, theatrical, and poetic may be theoretically extricable, in this instance they are intertwined. Perhaps the most important thing about Lehman's response to Angelou's poem as a poem is the distance his poetic purism puts between him and the poem's multivalent function in the context of the inauguration. This distance makes the utterance available for narrowly literary evaluation rather than any other kind of response: the question of the poem's literary quality comes to be divorced from its substantive content and manner and is treated as an autonomous aspect of the poem, separate from its political and performative impact.[19]

The question of whether or not Angelou's poem fulfilled the auditor's expectations or requirements for a good poem became so important for some commentators that it overwhelmed the poem's politics. In Ishmael Reed's response, for instance, the length of the poem becomes more important than its argument: "Frost's poem is the last gasp of the settler sensibility. It says the country was created so it could be occupied by Europeans. "The Gift Out-right" [however] has the advantage of being short—only 16 lines. Angelou took the risk of going more than six times that length. I always taught my students to stick to 12 lines. You just can't win when you write a long poem."[20] It's possible, of course, that coming from Reed—a writer known for irony and parody—these comments represent his parody of an academic poet's perspective as much as (or more than) they represent his own perspective. Nevertheless, sincere or parodic, they are a good representation of narrowly "literary" responses to poetry and the way in which such responses can celebrate a poem that endorses colonialist domination by focusing on its brevity and concision and can damn another poem by invoking a categorical objection to long poems. The separation of literary from ethicopolitical concerns is here subjected to a kind of reductio ad absurdum.

Even as the length of the poem is at issue, so is the fact that it is a poem made on this occasion to be performed and heard rather than to wait silently for its reader. For many commentators, what counts as poetic richness and complexity must be distinguished from any complexity that would be the effect of the context of performance. As Sterling Plumpp puts it, expressing an opinion that was repeatedly articulated, "At the level of a public poem, which is performed, I think it's brilliant. I'm not quite as enthusiastic about it as a text."[21] Among the most diplomatic to make this distinction between "public poem" and poetic "text" was Rita Dove, who said: "I wouldn't compare it to a poem I'll read over and over again in silence. That's not the kind of poem it was meant to be. It's a song, really."[22] Dove's comment taps into that commonplace of critical discourse that if a poem is good, it is worth returning to "over and over again." It draws on the assumption that a poem is meant to be read silently and in private because what counts as poetic richness and complexity must be distinguished, as I have suggested, from any complexity that would be the effect of the context of performance. Indeed, if the performance of a poem is particularly striking, and if a poem seems to depend on its performance for its power, then it is not as highly valued as a poem. So the quality of the speaking voice itself—the instrument for which the poem might be said to be written—can be read as a suggestion of the poem's lack. Louise Erdich offers praise of Angelou's reading that serves to belittle and disregard the poem in just this manner: "I felt that this woman could have read the side of a cereal box," she comments. "Her presence was so powerful and momentous."[23]

This kind of backhanded compliment was not, however, meted out to Frost's recitation of "The Gift Outright." No one took his capacity to recite the poem "in a voice that was rich and strong" as a sign of the inadequacy of the poem itself. Frost's powerful reading served to supplement the poem in the sense of enhancing it, while Angelou's powerful reading of her poem supplemented it in the sense of making evident its inadequacy and lack. A prime reason for the differences between these articulations of the trouble with poetry in the public sphere has to do with the fact that the notion of the "public" is always already gendered and racialized. So the ideology making it difficult for a poet to speak with anything other than a private voice will bear unevenly, sometimes contradictorily, on women and men, nonwhites and whites. With regards to the reception of Angelou's poetry in particular, because our assumptions about the private nature of women's voices heighten our expectation that women poets will speak out of a place that is private and intimate at the same time that our expectations about nonwhite poets suggest that they should speak for "their people," as their representative, the bridge between the work of an African American woman poet and the notion of a general public is especially fragile.

The assumptions about poetic idiom at work in these negative responses to Angelou's poem are not, of course, fully shared by all American poets. Ntozake Shange's response to Angelou's poem clearly has more to do with its performativity and its affective impact than with whether or not it fulfills expectations of the genre of poetry: "I think ['On the Pulse of Morning'] is going to sustain me now. My father just died the other day, and I really needed some sustenance. I got it from her." And Shange goes on to suggest the way in which Angelou's poem, even as it provides personal sustenance in a time of loss, provides sustenance at the more explicitly political or national level. "[F]or the first time since I was on the Mall for an anti-war rally in 1969 have I felt so moved as to actually want to be here now in this country."[24] Shange does not separate the poem from the context in which it functioned and does not separate the poetic from the political or the dramatic. In fact, she compares the presentation of Angelou's poem not to another poem but to another situation in which public utterance functioned as political protest.

What all of the responses to Angelou's poem neglect, however, is the multiplicity of ways in which Angelou's inaugural poem speaks back to Frost's inaugural poems. By focusing on the contrasts between Angelou's and Frost's poems, the intertextual dialogue between the two poems is elided from view, as is the underlying continuity of the conceptions of poetic integrity and literary quality evident in the public discourse about poetry in 1961 and in 1993. Angelou's poem, at one level, rewrites Frost's "The Gift Outright" (and his prefatory poem "For John F. Kennedy His Inauguration"), revisiting some of its commonplaces from another perspective, and in so doing, it also seeks to refashion some of our assumptions about the purposes of public poetry, rearticulating the inflection of national panegyric.

Angelou's poem returns to the scene of the European colonization of America treated by "The Gift Outright." But instead of speaking from the (expected) "human," "American" perspective, Angelou's poem offers as its main speakers "I, the Rock, I, the River, I, the Tree." Through these voices, "the land" of Frost's poem speaks back to colonizer and colonized. Playing as they do on their meanings in black American spirituals, Angelou's animation of the rock of "No hiding place," the river of "Down by the riverside," and the tree of "I shall not be moved" articulates a "land" imbued with a specific history of oppression.[25] While Frost's poem constructs its inaugural moment as the founding of an American identity by instituting a break with the English past, Angelou repeats but transforms this gesture by alluding to the devastation of Native American and African cultures on which the founding of American culture depends and by highlighting the presence of non-Anglo communities in American culture. The history of the relation between the people and the land is still something of a matter of "possessing" and being "possessed," but not in the vaguely psychological sense of Frost's poem; rather, the history is rendered in terms of the stealing, buying, and selling of land and peoples. Unlike Frost's poem, in which the *cost* of the creation of the nation remains abstract and ambiguous, Angelou's poem represents the "Tree" as speaking to all the descendants of these cultures as persons for whom a significant *price* has been paid: "Each of you, descendant of some passed-/ On traveler, has been paid for" (271).

For Angelou as for Frost, a new beginning is to be inaugurated by a break with the past, but the "break" is only possible once the past is faced "with courage": "History, despite its wrenching pain, / Cannot be unlived, but if faced / With courage, need not be lived again" (272). Frost, in his prefatory poem for "The Gift Outright," states that "Heroic deeds were done" in the European conquest of the Americas and suggests that the subsequent rise of the U.S. polity established "a new order of ages"; he identifies this inaugural era of the past as an age of "glory" and the present as presaging "The glory of a next Augustan age / . . . / A golden age of poetry and power." For Frost, the stance of the Kennedy era, confronting the new frontier and the challenges it poses, allows "us" to reconnect with the outlook and ambitions of the era of the founding fathers; it allows "us" to relive that glorious history. Angelou revisits the terrain of Frost's inaugural poems, but only to confront the past, not to relive it. She too speaks of a new day dawning, of "a dream" waiting to be realized, but for her such a new age belongs not to the nation "we" have become but to the nation we have *yet* to become.

Most insistently, however, in a gesture related to the gesture of Lorde's "For Each of You," Angelou's poem places the responsibility for the future in the hands of its auditors by calling upon them specifically. Animating the voices of the Rock, River, and Tree throughout to evoke and call upon specific communities among a diverse and divided United States, Angelou's poem recognizes

> The African, the Native American, the Sioux,
> The Catholic, the Muslim, the French, the Greek,
> The Irish, the Rabbi, the Priest, the Sheik,
> The Gay, the Straight, the Preacher,
> The privileged, the homeless, the Teacher (271)

as they "hear / The speaking of the Tree" (271) as it tells us to "shape" "the dream" (272) in that "space" the "horizon" of a new day offers us "To place new steps of change" (273). That the poem (here and throughout) acknowledges the many "Americans" that Frost's poem elides is certainly an important aspect of its impact. And insofar as that acknowledgment testifies to the changes in our understanding of American culture, it marks a significant development in the complexity of our self-understanding.

Angelou calls on each of her auditors to take the dream that sustains them and to "Mold it into the shape of your most / Private need. Sculpt it into / The image of your most public self" (272). She argues for a world in which "private need" and "public self" enter into a kind of consonance rather than simply celebrating private integrity as a check on the public sphere. Unlike Frost in his prefatory verses for the inauguration, Angelou never directly addresses the president or the politicians in her inaugural poem. Her words carry an admonition to "study war no more" (rejecting the "many deeds of war" that "The Gift Outright" identifies as our primary "deed of gift" to "our" new land), but her poem's address is directed elsewhere and otherwise—from the land itself to the many peoples who have sought harbour there, "Each of you" (271). Angelou's most significant rewriting of Frost is to adopt a stance that eliminates entirely the compact and homogenous, the complacent "we" and "our" of Frost's inaugural poems. And she does this not by abandoning Frost's chosen ground but by reversing the perspective from which it is viewed and relocating her auditors in relation to it.

In addition to Frost's inaugural poems, "On the Pulse of Morning" gathers up strands from such poems as Walt Whitman's "Song of Myself" and Langston Hughes's "The Negro Speaks of Rivers" to construct a poem that was, to judge by its brisk sales as a booklet and audiotape, resonant for many Americans, however much it was lambasted or patronized by professional poets. The response of the poets and critics to Angelou's poem has, however, its own significance in light of my concerns in this study. By comparing some of the public responses to Angelou's performance of "On the Pulse of

Morning" at Bill Clinton's inauguration in 1993 with some of the responses
to Frost's performance of "The Gift Outright" at Kennedy's inauguration in
1961, we have seen how unevenly, but determinedly, we continue to decon-
textualize poetry, defining it as private, personal, individual, and antipublic, or
defining it (which amounts to much the same thing) as "literary," as divorced
from political and performative engagements. Thus, the presence of poetry at
an American president's inauguration is at once an occasion on which poetry
can be said to speak to an audience far broader than the academic and elite
audiences that are often its selected cohorts and, at the same time, an excep-
tional appearance of poetry in public discourse—in response to which critics
insistently reinscribed the generic boundaries separating genuine poetry, a
public idiom, and a mass audience.

Poetic Justice

In John Singleton's film *Poetic Justice*,[26] the title character, Justice (played
by Janet Jackson), is presented as the author of five previously published
poems by Maya Angelou.[27] The presence of Angelou's poetry in this
movie is yet another example of the wide circulation her work has enjoyed
in contemporary American culture, and Singleton's movie seems, on the
face of it, a cultural text in which poetry might be seen to have some kind
of public function in relation to a broad audience. Such expectations are,
however, quickly dispelled. For the most part, the poems enter the movie
as voiceovers, spoken in Justice's voice as if she were composing them and
serving as sound bridges across visual sequences. At only one point in the
movie—when we see Justice reading a poem to her friend, Iesha—does the
voice of the poet come from within the frame of the scene in which it is
heard. Only on this occasion does it constitute diagetic sound, forming part
of the action of the scene, rather than remaining a kind of commentary on
the action that exists at one remove from the intersubjective world of the
filmed scenario.[28]

Throughout the movie, Justice is represented as a private poet, writing
to ease her own pain (after the loss of her murdered boyfriend). One critic
describes her poetry writing as "therapy."[29] Justice is a young hair stylist who
witnesses her boyfriend's murder at the beginning of the movie and has with-
drawn from the world of relationships as a result—at least until Lucky, played
by the rapper Tupac Shakur, draws her out. By casting the popular recording
artists Janet Jackson and Tupac Shakur in the lead roles, Singleton implicitly raises generic questions about who counts as a poet and what counts
as poetry.[30] Jackson, as Justice, writes poetry and Shakur, as Lucky, plays a
young postal worker who aspires to rap. The presence of the rapper and the

expectation that the audience will read his public image onto the movie role is further underlined by the fact that Justice and Lucky listen to and discuss rap recorded by Lucky's cousin. The tension created by the disparity between the status of the discourses of "poetry," "pop song," and "rap" is implicit in the casting and explicit as a struggle between the two main characters. At one point, Lucky asks Justice: "What you write about in that notebook you carry around?" She answers: "Ah, that's my poetry." Somewhat unexpectedly, the word "poetry" makes Lucky defensive. He responds: "You trying to say my cousin's shit ain't poetry?" She says, "Yeah it ain't if he ain't got nothin deep to say; gotta have a voice, and perspective." The exchange between these two characters potentially repositions poetry as one in a series of "spoken word" genres of performance, but the criterion that Justice invokes—it's not poetry if it doesn't have a personal, individual "voice"—returns us to the generic expectations that have accrued to poetry as a private and written art. I'd like to be able to argue that, by virtue of poetry's use as voiceover throughout, Singleton's movie accords poetry a public role—especially in those places where as a result of its juxtaposition with scenes of public strife it serves as a kind of social commentary. But within this movie there is little explicit acknowledgment of the poetry having anything other than a purely private and personal resonance; Justice, in particular, seems unaware even of the possibility that her poetry could have a more public dimension. Thus, even though Singleton's movie links Angelou's poetry with the popular genre of rap, it does so in a way that reinscribes poetry as an essentially private and personal affair. To the extent that a public idiom and intention are attached to "poetic" speech, they are constellated around the genre of rap and the figure of the rapper. In this movie, the public and private personae of the poet are divided between the gangsta rapper (who is decidedly masculinized) and the woman poet (who is equally emphatically feminized), thus confirming the expectations about women's poetry as private, personal, and autobiographical we have seen repeated time and again.

Despite the very different occasions of Angelou's reception that I have touched on—literary critical commentary on her published work, responses to her performance at the 1993 inauguration, and incorporation of her work into the mass medium of movies—there are surprisingly constant assumptions about the nature of poetry and its essential incompatibility with public engagements operating across all of these terrains. If we are dealing with a literary-critical prejudice, fostered by the academy and the poetry establishment, it turns out to be a prejudice that is widely disseminated. So much so, in fact, that even the very visible career of our most public poet at some of its most public moments has served only to reinscribe the assumed incompatibility of poetry and the public sphere.

NOTES

1. James Finn Cotter, review of *Oh Pray My Wings Are Gonna Fit Me Well*, by Maya Angelou, *Angel of Ascent*, by Robert Hayden, and *The Women and the Men*, by Nikki Giovanni, in *America*, 7 Feb. 1976, 103–4. Subsequent references appear parenthetically in the text. Sandra Gilbert also argues that fame has weakened Angelou's poetry. See "A Platoon of Poets," review of *Oh Pray My Wings Are Gonna Fit Me Well*, by Maya Angelou, and of books by Rosemary Daniell, Kenneth Koch, Diane Wakoski, Norman Dubie, and Etta Blum, in *Poetry* 128 (1976): 290–99.

2. John Alfred Avant, review of *Just Give Me a Cool Drink of Water 'fore I Diiie*, by Maya Angelou, in *Library Journal* 96 (1971): 3329

3. Joanne M. Braxton, "Maya Angelou," in *Modern American Women Writers: Profiles of Their Lives and Works, from the 1870s to the Present*, ed. Lea Baechler, Elaine Showalter, and A. Walton Litz (New York: Macmillan, 1993), 7.

4. Bryan D. Bourn, "Maya Angelou and the African-American Tradition" <http://www.usinternet.com/maya.htm>.

5. "There are examples in Angelou's poetry where her 'voice' does come through. Her narrative poems and poems relating personal experience, both tend to be more successful because they allow Maya to use her talent for storytelling that makes her prose work so successful" (ibid.).

6. Miller Williams was the third inaugural poet, reading "Of History and Hope" at the 1997 Clinton inaugural. Roy P. Basler notes, "The only precedent in American history, so far as I know, for a poet's elevation to the inaugural platform was Adlai's [Stevenson's] selection of Carl [Sandburg] to perform the ancient duty of ruler's chosen bard, at his inauguration as Governor of Illinois in 1948" (*The Muse and the Librarian* [Westport, Conn.: Greenwood Press, 1974], 75).

7. See, for example, Janet Cawley, "Poet Aims to Capture Spirit of America," *Chicago Tribune*, 19 Jan. 1993, 6; and Irvin Molotsky, "Poet of the South for the Inauguration," *New York Times*, 5 Dec. 1992, A8+.

8. Molotsky, "Poet of the South for the Inauguration."

9. The lines quoted in *Life* magazine's coverage are from the version of the poem printed in newspapers across the United States the day after Kennedy's inauguration. These lines (and many others) are altered in subsequent printings of the poem. "The turbulence we're in the middle of / Is something we can hardly help but love" becomes, "No one of honest feeling would approve / A ruler who pretended not to love / A turbulence he had the better of." In shifting the subject of the turbulence from the people to the ruler, the revised version of the poem brings out the way in which the "ruler" (Kennedy) is seen to stand for the people, while *Life* magazine uses the lines to set the (president's) poet in the place of the people. For Frost's final version of the poem, see Stewart Udall's "Frost's 'Unique Gift Outright,'" *New York Times*, 26 Mar. 1961, as well as subsequent printings of the poem in Frost's *In the Clearing* (New York: Henry Holt and Company, 1962,), 28–30, and in Edwin A. Glikes and Paul Schwaber, eds., *Of Poetry and Power: Poems Occasioned by the Presidency and by the Death of John F. Kennedy* (New York: Basic Books, 1964), 7–10.

10. Insofar as this elision is in keeping with generic American ideology, critics still sometimes miss the politics of Frost's poem. A. R. Coulthard says, for instance, "'The Gift Outright' transcends politics by catering to no party line" ("Poetry as Politics: Maya Angelou's Inaugural Poem, 'On the Pulse of Morning,'" *Notes on*

Contemporary Literature 28.1 (Jan. 1998]: 2). Coulthard launches a particularly energetic critique of both the poetics and the politics of "On the Pulse of Morning."

11. "The Gift Outright," written around 1935, was published in *A Witness Tree* (New York: Holt and Co., 1942)—a volume that sold over ten thousand copies in two months and won for Frost his fourth Pulitzer Prize for Poetry. The poem was reprinted, with his dedicatory poem for Kennedy's inauguration, in *In the Clearing* (1962), from which I quote (31).

12. Notwithstanding changes in the national discourse on multiculturalism that Angelou's presence on the inaugural stage signifies, for a discussion that emphasizes the continuities between the versions of nationalism conveyed in Frost's and Angelou's inaugural poems, see Minoo Moallem and Iain A. Boal, "Multicultural Nationalism and the Poetics of Inauguration," in *Between Woman and Nation: Nationalisms, Transnational Feminisms, and the State*, ed. Caren Kaplan, Norma Alarcón, and Minoo Moallem (Durham, N.C.: Duke University Press, 1999), 243–63.

13. Kennedy's address at the dedication of the Robert Frost Library is included in Glikes and Schwaber, eds., *Of Poetry and Power*, 135–37. Subsequent references appear parenthetically in the text.

14. For a discussion of the distinction between the role of the poet in the United States and role of the Poet Laureate in England, see Willian McGuire, *Poetry's Catbird Seat: The Consultantship in Poetry in the English Language at the Library of Congress, 1937–1987* (Washington, D.C.: Library of Congress, 1988), 424–32.

15. "Government and Poetry," *New York Times*, 28 Feb. 1961, 32.

16. Michael Folsom, "Poets and Presidents: Frost and Lowell," *New Orleans Review* 5 (1979): 23.

17. See, for example, Colman McCarthy's editorial in the *Washington Post*, 19 Jan. 1993. Outside the liberal press, the tabloids, however, did their best to ruin Angelou's character for the American people by citing the fact that she was raped as an eight-year-old child and was an unwed mother at sixteen. And various explicitly racist publications must have also disparaged the choice.

18. Qtd. in David Streitfeld, "The Power and the Puzzle of the Poem," *Washington Post*, 21 Jan. 1993, D11.

19. For an essay that considers the performance of the poem as integral to its meaning, see Annette D. Sahar, Sebastian M. Benninkmeyer, and Daniel C. O'Connell, "Maya Angelou's Inaugural Poem," *Journal of Psycholinguistic Research* 26.4 (1997): 449–63.

20. Qtd. in Streitfeld, "The Power and the Puzzle of the Poem."

21. Qtd. in Mary Schmich, "Maybe Poetry Has a Chance after All," *Chicago Tribune*, 22 Jan. 1993, sec. 2C, p. 1.

22. Qtd. in Streitfeld, "The Power and the Puzzle of the Poem."

23. Ibid.

24. Ibid.

25. On the Random House audiotape of Angelou's "On the Pulse of Morning," Angelou describes the sources of the three elements in the poem as coming from black American spirituals. Maya Angelou, *On the Pulse of Morning: The Inaugural Poem*, audiocassette (New York: Random House Audio, 1993). Maya Angelou, "On the Pulse of Morning," in *The Complete Collected Poems* (New York: Random House, 1994), 270–73. Subsequent references appear parenthetically in the text.

26. John Singleton, dir., *Poetic Justice: A Street Romance* (Columbia Pictures, 1993).

27. The poems spoken by Jackson come from Angelou's previously published books of poetry: "Alone" and "A Conceit" are in *Oh Pray My Wings Are Gonna Fit Me Well*; "In a Time" is in *Just Give Me a Cool Drink of Water 'fore I Diiie*; "A Kind of Love, Some Say" and "Phenomenal Woman" are from *And Still I Rise*.

28. Justice's boss, Jesse, is also represented as an audience for her poetry. This is signaled early in the movie when she says to Justice: "You got a poem for me? Lord knows I need one."

29. Hal Hinson, "Poetic Justice," *Washington Post*, 23 July 1993. This is contrary to Angelou's own representation of the writing process: "it is not cathartic," she tells Oprah Winfrey (*Oprah Winfrey Show: One on One with Maya Angelou* [Harpo Productions, July 13, 1993]).

30. In an interview Angelou gave just before Clinton's first inauguration, Angelou makes it clear that she understands Jackson's lyrics to be "poetry."

A: We may see, thanks to our new President, a rekindling of interest in poetry and even a rekindling in the courage to call poetry, poetry. A number of people use a form of poetry but wouldn't let it be known that they call it poetry.

Q: For example?

A: Young men and women who know every lyric that Michael Jackson or Janet Jackson sing. . . ."

Gayle Pollard Terry, "Maya Angelou: Creating a Poem to Honor the Nation," *Los Angeles Times*, 17 Jan. 1993, sec. M, p. 3.

HILARY HOLLADAY

Black Names in White Space:
Lucille Clifton's South

As the daughter of a Virginian and a Georgian, the African American poet Lucille Clifton has always had the South in her blood, and the region has naturally found its way into her life and writing. Born in 1936 in Depew, New York, Clifton grew up there and later in Buffalo. Despite these northern credentials, she maintains that her upbringing was southern ("A Music in Language" 74). Her parents had come to the North during the Great Migration, but that did not mean that they had truly left the South behind. It was alive in their memories and in the stories they told their attentive daughter, who retells many of those tales in *Generations: A Memoir* (1976).

In recent years, Clifton—who won the 2000 National Book Award for Poetry for her eleventh volume of verse, *Blessing the Boats: New and Selected Poems* 1988–2000—has frequently read her poetry in the South, and she has held visiting teaching positions at Memphis State University and Duke University. But she has lived most of her adult life in Maryland, which is in or near the South, depending on your perspective and perhaps depending on where you are in Maryland. The poet and her husband, Fred Clifton, moved to Baltimore from Buffalo early in their marriage and brought up their six children there. Clifton became poet-in-residence at Coppin State College in 1974 and served as Maryland's poet laureate for a decade beginning the

From *Southern Literary Journal* 34, no. 2 (Spring 2002): 120–33. Copyright © 2002 by *Southern Literary Journal*.

following year. Widowed in 1984, she took a teaching position at the University of California at Santa Cruz but after several years returned to Maryland, where she now holds the Hilda C. Landers Chair in the Liberal Arts at St. Mary's College of Maryland. From the slight but seemingly strategic remove that Maryland affords her, Clifton is able to contemplate her ancestral South. Although she does not have the intimate knowledge of the region that her father and mother had,[1] her feelings about the region are nevertheless complicated and passionate. The South we encounter in her poems is a conceit enabling her to address two subjects, the first concrete and the second abstract, that have been equally important to her poetry for many years: 1) slavery and its seemingly endless impact on American life, and 2) the all-powerful role of language in determining our knowledge of ourselves and others. In her poems with southern settings, we don't see much of the region's landscape, but we do see how language, especially the language of names, can either obliterate or validate one's identity. While this is true to a certain extent for all, Clifton shows how names are especially germane to our knowledge and understanding of slaves and their descendants.

In "at the cemetery, walnut grove plantation, south carolina, 1989" (*Quilting* 11–12), the silencing of slaves in their time haunts the poet in her own time:

> among the rocks
> at walnut grove
> your silence drumming
> in my bones,
> tell me your names.

The rocks are unmarked slave graves, and the narrator, confronted with this injustice, yearns to make contact with these lost souls and speak on their behalf. The slaves' silence paradoxically "drumming" within her calls to mind African drums and perhaps even the drums played during the Civil War. The drumming silence is, if not a call to arms, at least a call to speech. Significantly, the silence seems to emanate from the poet's own bones; what she doesn't know about the slaves amounts to things that she doesn't know about herself and her own ancestry.

Generations helps illuminate the emotion animating this poem. In this fifty-four-page memoir (which Toni Morrison shepherded into print at Random House), Clifton writes movingly of her great-great-grandmother Caroline, who as a young child was captured in western Africa's Dahomey region and brought to the United States as a slave. Caroline, who outlived slavery and became a prominent midwife in the community of Bedford, Virginia, helped rear Samuel Sayles, Clifton's father. Samuel's memories of the family matriarch, as recounted in *Generations*, focus alternately on her strongly vocalized strength and her mystifying silences. When Samuel asks her to reveal her African name, for instance, Caroline refuses to answer. We don't know whether she keeps the name secret because it means so much to her or because, in the country of her captivity, it means so little. One hardly dares consider the heartbreaking possibility that Caroline has forgotten her African name and hence has no answer for her great-grandson's question.

When Clifton implores the dead slaves at Walnut Grove to offer up their names, it may well be that she has her great-great-grandmother in mind, since Caroline's grave in Bedford is also unmarked. On the first page of *Generations*, Clifton writes, "Who remembers the names of the slaves? Only the children of slaves" (227). She speaks as a slave descendant in "at the cemetery" as well as in her memoir. The fact that the stones at Walnut Grove have no names on them is no surprise, of course. It is perhaps a wonder that they are even recognizable as graves, let alone slave graves. But it is not just the stones that indicate the slaves' presence on the farm:

> nobody mentions slaves
> and yet the curious tools
> shine with your fingerprints.
> nobody mentioned slaves
> but somebody did this work
> who had no guide, no stone,
> who moulders under rock.

The tools are in plain view, yet, as recently as 1989, when Clifton paid her visit, people touring the plantation heard nothing about the slaves or the work they did ("Lucille Clifton" 87). Like the silence drumming in the speaker's bones, the evidence of a hard-working community of black people demands recognition. No matter what the plantation's present-day staff does or does not say, there is no getting around the fact that the life of this farm depended on slave labor for a very long time. During the plantation's productive years, the farm tools, now laid out for tourists' inspection, did not magically cut wood or tan leather all on their own.

Clifton's poem challenges the received version of Walnut Grove's history and implicitly argues that such a challenge is worthy of literary as well as historical consideration. In acknowledging the palpable if invisible presence of the slaves, she responds to a phenomenon that Toni Morrison identifies in "Unspeakable Things Unspoken: The Afro-American Presence in American Literature":

We can agree, I think, that invisible things are not necessarily 'not-there'; that a void may be empty, but is not a vacuum. In addition, certain absences are so stressed, so ornate, so planned, they call attention to themselves; arrest us with intentionality and purpose, like neighborhoods that are defined by the population held away from them. Looking at the scope of American literature, I can't help thinking that the question should never have been "Why am I, an Afro-American, absent from it?" It is not a particularly interesting query anyway. The spectacularly interesting question is "What intellectual feats had to be performed by the author or his critic to erase me from a society seething with my presence, and what effect has that performance had on the work?" What are the strategies of escape from knowledge? Of willful oblivion? (378)

Rather than accept the willful oblivion perpetuated at Walnut Grove, Clifton speaks directly to the slaves whose presence she feels so strongly: "tell me your names, / tell me your bashful names / and i will testify" ("at the cemetery" 11). If the slaves' names are "bashful," it is perhaps because they have been hidden away and denied for so long. The poet will have to coax them into being by listening closely to the message-laden silence. The white space that follows this entreaty, however, symbolizes the slaves' unwillingness or inability to supply the basic information that the poet craves. This, too, conjures the memory of Caroline.

Drawing on the Christian tradition and the democratic legal system, both of which value "testifying," the poet seeks to affirm the value of the slaves' lives and experiences. She regards them with love and charity, as good Christians are supposed to regard their fellow human beings, but she is also determined to fight for their place in history books and in the history lessons taught at museums like Walnut Grove. In short, she would like to see the slaves recognized and restored to a position of dignity in our collective memory. The poem itself functions as her testimony.

In the middle of "at the cemetery," an italicized statement heaps more injustice on a pile that is already pretty high: "*the inventory lists ten slaves / but only men were recognized*" (11). The slave women did not even count as possessions. The white space following the stanza once again memorializes the void. When the poet resumes speaking, she is an angry prophet crying out in the wilderness of Walnut Grove:

among the rocks
at walnut grove
some of these honored dead

were dark
some of these dark
were slaves
some of these slaves
were women
some of them did this
honored work.
tell me your names
foremothers, brothers,
tell me your dishonored names.
here lies
here lies
here lies
here lies
hear (11–12)

The parallel structure evokes both the Bible and the preaching Clifton heard as a girl attending the Macedonia Baptist Church, a Southern Baptist church in Buffalo.[2] But this is Clifton's own message: The women and men buried anonymously at Walnut Grove were not anonymous during their lifetimes. They worked the fields and served the household, and the plantation would not have functioned without them. They made love and bore children, and their descendants, just like those of the white slaveholders, still walk the earth. The poem makes it clear that the sins of omission—the unmarked graves, the incomplete inventories of human chattel—expose a lie even as they obscure the truth. The poem's closing lines initially seem like epigraphs lacking the names of the slaves. But the insistent repetition turns the incomplete statements into a sharp command: *Hear* the lies being told. Now, as Susan Somers-Willet has noted, the white space "not only actively calls attention to the absence of inscription, but also asks the reader to consider the possibilities of what such an inscription could imply" ("lucy and her girls"). It represents both the unknown names and the cover-up manifested in the incomplete and, hence, inaccurate public record. Through the complex interplay between ambiguous words and white space, the poem illustrates Ralph Ellison's observation that "The essence of the word is its ambivalence, and in fiction it is never so effective and revealing as when both potentials are operating simultaneously, as when it mirrors both good and bad, as when it blows both hot and cold in the same breath" (25). Ellison's point is even more apt when applied to poetry, perhaps especially to the brief lyric mode that Clifton prefers.

Something similar to the compelling dynamic at work in "at the cemetery" occurs in "slave cabin, sotterly plantation, maryland, 1989." In this

companion poem, which follows "at the cemetery" in *Quilting*, Clifton visits another historically preserved plantation (this one located in St. Mary's
County, Maryland) and again takes exception to the portrayal of slave life.
This time, a female slave is identified by a name, but the name has little to do
with her. The poem starts off stealthily:

> in this little room
> note carefully
>
> aunt nanny's bench (13)

The white space surrounding "aunt nanny's bench" helps us imagine the
words of a tour guide whose knowledge of slave history begins and ends
with a gesture toward a bench. Alternatively, these words might appear on a
plaque that provides no further information about "aunt nanny." The white
space serves to illustrate the utter lack of context provided for this tiny sliver
of history.

Confronted with this void, Clifton steps into the white space and fills it
with black language, a visual representation of her racial heritage. She decon-
structs "aunt nanny's bench" and then envisions the flesh-and-blood woman
who once sat on the bench in question:

> three words that label
> things
> aunt
> is my parent's sister
> nanny
> my grandmother
> bench
> the board at which
> i stare
> the soft curved polished
> wood
> that held her bottom
> after the long days
> without end
> without beginning
> when she aunt nanny sat
> feet dead against the dirty floor
> humming for herself humming
> her own sweet human name ("slave cabin" 13)

Neither "aunt" nor "nanny" tells us anything about the slave woman's identity. Together, the labels are nonsensical, amounting to "aunt grandmother," an ironic gloss in itself on the thoughtless, racist habit of addressing older black women in familial—and overly familiar—ways. The name "aunt nanny" is a means of co-opting the unidentified woman's identity and subsuming her into the white family that owned her. Like the farm tools in "at the cemetery," it is the well-worn bench that still possesses something of the lost woman's body and spirit. Concentrating on the bench, the poet calls a life into being. The "soft curved polished / wood" is beautiful in an understated way; it hints at the beauty of the unknown woman who sat there. She, too, would have been soft and curved, her body worn down by years of repetitive labor.

The poem thereby shifts from a pointed condemnation of the powers conspiring to force an identity onto the slave to a sympathetic tribute to the woman's private self. Clifton can only imagine that self, and her own long reach into the past is symbolized by the reluctant, ironic use of "aunt nanny" when she feels compelled to call the slave woman by name. White space again functions symbolically, indicating the woman's remove from the name imposed on her as well as the isolation she would inevitably have felt on a slaveholding farm. But the extra white space also invites us to behold this woman in her own space, apart from the trappings of her subjugated circumstances.

Exhausted from her labors, the woman Clifton imagines still has the energy to hum to herself. This small, private music, the most ephemeral of art forms, symbolizes the woman's core self. The wordlessness of humming is important here, for "aunt nanny" is a nameless, essentially wordless entity. Her humming enables her to define herself on her own terms. Without words, her identity eludes everyone but her. Clifton thus honors the woman, while implying that she had a life that the slaveholders knew nothing about. By labeling her "aunt nanny," her owners—and, later, those historians who saw the bench as a winsome artifact of bygone days—did her a fundamental injustice, but they also unwittingly preserved the protective space between her and them.[3]

The last line emphasizes the woman's humanity, her life apart from whatever burdens her owners imposed on her. Her "human name" ends the poem, though there is no period signifying an endpoint. The possibilities of the woman's private life reverberate in the blank space. We can hear the subtle music in "human name," words that sound like "humming" stretched out and polished to a high gleam. This poem thus takes some solace in the belief that, no matter what indignities the slaves suffered at the hands of their masters and mistresses, their souls (signified by their human names) were theirs and theirs alone.

Both "at the cemetery" and "slave cabin" argue that the degradation of slaves continues today. Even in an age that some deride as politically correct to the point of absurdity, the historical record all too often misses the same point that it has missed for hundreds of years: the slaves were human beings who deserve our respect for all that they suffered and for all that they did for this country. As the descendant of slaves, Lucille Clifton has a personal interest in the way slaves lived and in the way their lives are represented in museums, history books, and graveyards. Slavery does not tell the whole story of the South, but the whole story cannot be told without it. A poet as sensitive and as historically aware as Clifton naturally recognizes this. Her poems ask us to imagine the black names in and around and behind the white spaces, and consider questions such as these: Who is writing the history lessons? Whose stories still go untold? Why does this country still fear the truths embodied in the lives of the slaves?

In summoning the names of the slaves, Clifton begins to answer her own implied questions. Sometimes, as in *Generations*, it is obvious that this is a very personal endeavor for her. She has given a great deal of thought to her ancestors, and she takes her place in the family line quite seriously. Because names are the signifiers of that line, they provide a natural starting point for many of her considerations of family and individual identity. She has written about every part of her birth name, Thelma Lucille Sayles, in her poems and memoir. Her first name, Thelma, was the name of her mother, an epileptic who died at forty-four when Clifton was pregnant with her first child. Lucille was the name of her paternal great-grandmother, who, according to Samuel Sayles, was the "first Black woman legally hanged in the state of Virginia" (*Generations* 240). The elder Lucy's crime: killing the white man who fathered her son Gene, who would grow up to be Samuel's father.

As if all of this family history were not sufficient material for poems, the surname Sayles is also notable. Clifton writes in *Generations* that 'Sale' was the name of the white family who owned Caroline's husband, so it became Caroline's surname. After Emancipation, the black Sales added a *y* to distinguish their name from that of their former owners. Clifton writes that Samuel Sayles took this notion even further: "My father had left school in the second or third grade and could barely write more than his name, but he was an avid reader. He loved books. He had changed his name to Sayles (instead of Sayle) after finding a part of a textbook in which the plural was explained. There will be more than one of me, my father thought, and he added the *s* to his name" (*Generations* 243). The changes in spelling are small but meaningful steps toward autonomy, yet the connection with the white Sales of Bedford remains, as Clifton points out at the beginning of her memoir: after an awkward telephone conversation with a white Sale descendant, who shares the poet's interest in genealogy, Clifton writes, "Yet she sends the history she has compiled and in it are her family's names. And our family names are thick in her family like an omen" (*Generations* 228).

In her poems as well as in *Generations*, we see what that omen means to Clifton. An untitled poem first published in *An Ordinary Woman* (1974) provides an interesting contrast to "at the cemetery" and "slave cabin." The poem's opening couplet comes from the spiritual "Tryin' to Cross the Red Sea" (see Work 208).[4] The allusion to the Israelites' journey to the Promised Land is ironic, since the poem ventures into Virginia, Clifton's ancestral homeland in what was once a slaveholding state. The metaphorical freedom that she seeks will involve a direct confrontation with the problematic place her father cherished yet ultimately abandoned:

> i went to the valley
> but i didn't go to stay
>
> i stand on my father's ground
> not breaking.
> it holds me up
> like a hand my father pushes.
> virginia.
> i am in virginia,
> the magic word
> rocked in my father's box
> like heaven,
> the magic line in my hand. but
> where is the afrika in this? ("i went to the valley" 151)

Published five years after her father had died, the poem commemorates Samuel Sayles's nostalgic love for his birthplace and the hold that "virginia" consequently has on Clifton. Given her father's burnished memories, "virginia" is much more to her than the name of a place; it is a verbal talisman, a sign of all that her paternal ancestors experienced long before she was born. Now that she is in Virginia, she can acknowledge the "virginia" in her: just as she feels her father's hand embodied in the Virginia ground, so does she feel her forebears symbolically present in her own hand's life line. Together, they form a "magic line"—a phrase that also puns ingeniously on her lines of verse, which further preserve the Sayles family memory.

The question she poses at the end of the stanza—"but / where is the afrika in this?"—is a plaintive plea which can be usefully read in the context of Clifton's other works. It seems that Clifton is searching for the spirit of her African ancestors in Virginia. In *Generations*, the stories of Caroline's Dahomey heritage are inseparable from Samuel's stories of growing up in Virginia. Samuel's tales thus provide the poet with a mental portal back to Caroline's Africa, a place Clifton has never visited but has long celebrated in her poems. It seems that for Clifton to get to Caroline's Africa, she must go to Samuel's Virginia first:

> except, the grass is green,
> is greener he would say.
> and the sky opens a better blue
> and in the historical museum
> where the slaves
> are still hidden away like knives
> i find a paper with a name i know.
> his name.
> their name.
> sayles.
> the name he loved.
>
> i stand on my father's ground
> not breaking.
> there is an afrikan in this
> and whose ever name it has been,
> the blood is mine.
>
> my soul got happy
> and i stayed all day. (151)

In contrast to the other two poems discussed here, this poem marks the recovery of an African American name. Having come across her own name in the museum's records, Clifton can now speak for herself rather than relying on her father's words and feelings. Sayles is "his" name and "their" name, but, equally important, it is hers, the family name hidden behind her married name, Clifton. If Clifton is "not breaking" now, it is because she is no longer merely propped up by the memory of her father's strength. Instead, she has identified the source of her own strength: the abiding presence of the Sayles family in Virginia. Tellingly, the third stanza's description of Virginia begins in Samuel's voice ("the grass is green, / is greener he would say") but ends in Clifton's own. The poem's "magic line" allows for this seamless transfer of authority.

The poem revisits its beginning as it moves toward resolution. The line confirming the presence of "an afrikan" in the fourth stanza, for instance, responds to the question posed in the second stanza. But Clifton now focuses on an "afrikan" rather than on the vast continent of "afrika." With the name in hand, she is able to be more particular and personal. Because no noun follows the determiner at the end of the line "there is an afrikan in this," however, we are left to fill in the blank on our own. The line implies variously that there is an African presence in Virginia, in the Sayles family, and in the poet and her poem. Clifton now seems able to claim Virginia and honor the state's hold on her—and her hold on it—because it was not only her father's home but also Caroline's. Caroline was "the afrikan" in the Sayles family, and her blood has passed down through several generations to Clifton.[5] Imagining those generations and their overlapping lives in Virginia, Clifton seems to feel that all of the Sayles family members are within her, part of her. As the poem returns to "Tryin' to Cross the Red Sea" in its closing couplet, it is no wonder that her "soul got happy": The poet has transcended time, place, and white space. She has found a way to commune with all of the spirits commingling within her.

Although she may not often experience the soul-lifting satisfaction of plucking her own family's name from the obscurity of a museum's musty file, Clifton reveals that the quest for names, and the identities they carry with them, is essential to her sense of herself and her history. For her, the writing of poems—the skillful deployment of compressed, inherently political language—is integral to that quest. The writing is itself a restorative act. "I think that writing is a way of continuing to hope," Clifton has said. "When things sometimes feel as if they're not going to get any better, writing offers a way of trying to connect with something beyond that obvious feeling . . . because you know, there is hope in connecting, and so perhaps for me it is a way of remembering I am not alone" ("I'd Like Not to Be a Stranger" 311).

In an effort to honor, and connect with, her own ancestors as well as all African American "foremothers" and "brothers," Clifton has continued to write poems set in the South. These are somber poems reflecting her customary candor and precision. *The Terrible Stories* (1996) contains a section titled "A Term in Memphis," which refers to her semester teaching at Memphis State (now the University of Memphis) but also suggests a time of involuntary captivity. In keeping with this impression, the sequence juxtaposes Clifton's ambivalence about the city with the experiences of slaves. In "slave ships," for example, she ponders the astounding irony of slave ships named "Jesus," "Angel," and "Grace of God." Once again, names are a way for her to approach slavery, a subject that continues to mesmerize her even as it fills her with sorrow and dismay. *The Terrible Stories* also contains an unsettling poem titled "lee," about her father's proud insistence that his mother's family had been owned by the family of Robert E. Lee: "i can see him now / chaining his mother to lee" (50). Her collection *Blessing the Boats* contains two new poems set in the South: "jasper texas 1998," about James Byrd, the black man who was dragged to his death, and "alabama 9/15/63," about the young black girls who died in the 1963 bombing of a Birmingham church. Like the titles of the two plantation poems in *Quilting*, these titles consist of specific locations and dates. This factual information underscores the message that the poems make in no uncertain terms: racial oppression is an ongoing part of American life, and we would do well to face the problem head-on rather than pretend it belongs to some era long before our own.

Lucille Clifton's South is a not-Africa that reminds her of Africa. It is also a land of silences and erasures that inspire her to speak and write. The region seems to represent, furthermore, the maddening, mysterious things about American history, human nature, and herself—her own black name— that she will never fully understand. Perched in the liminal space of her home in Maryland, but seemingly always poised to make a journey South, she writes toward that vanishing point on the horizon where her curiosity, outrage, sorrow, and self-doubt converge. Commenting on a poem in *The Terrible Stories* titled "memphis," she says, "I wanted in that poem to try to see what I was doing there. Why would I go to such a place? What would it hold for me?" ("An Interview with Lucille Clifton" 62). In the poem's concluding stanzas, we see her confronting her own silences, her own implacable white spaces:

> some rivers flow back
> toward the beginning
> i never learned to swim
>
> will i float or drown
> in this memphis
> on the mississippi river
>
> what is this southland
> what has this to do with egypt
> or dahomey
> or with me
>
> so many questions
> northern born (42)

NOTES

1. Clifton tells a revealing story about her parents' perceptions of the South in the 1940s: "My father went to Bedford, Virginia, to see his mother when she was dying—I remember it was the only time I ever saw my father kiss my mother. The

only time *ever*. And it scared me, if you want to know the truth. . . . Then she said, 'You behave yourself now, Sam.' She was scared to death, he was going south" ("I'd Like Not to Be a Stranger" 317).

2. Though she does not identify herself as a Christian, Clifton has frequently cited the Bible and the sermons she heard as a child as formative influences on her writing, and biblical stories provide the basis for many of her poems. See "An Interview with Lucille Clifton," *Lucille Clifton*, "A Music in Language," and "No Ordinary Woman."

3. An informative history of the slaves who lived at Sotterley Plantation may be found on the Plantation's website (http://www.sotterley.com).

4. I am indebted to Professor Kay Roberts of the University of Massachusetts Lowell's Music Department for identifying the spiritual "Tryin' to Cross the Red Sea."

5. Asked how she would like to be remembered, Clifton replied, "I would like to be seen as a woman whose roots go back to Africa, who tried to honor being human" ("I'd Like Not to Be a Stranger" 328).

Works Cited

Clifton, Lucille. "at the cemetery, walnut grove plantation, south carolina, 1989." *Quilting*. Brockport, NY: BOA Editions, 1991. 11–12.

———. *Generations: A Memoir*. 1976. *Good Woman: Poems and a Memoir 1969–1980*. Brockport, NY: BOA Editions, 1987. 223–277.

———. "i went to the valley." *An Ordinary Woman*. 1974. *Good Woman: Poems and a Memoir 1969–1980*. Brockport, NY: BOA Editions, 1987. 151.

———. "'I'd Like Not to Be a Stranger in the World: A Conversation/Interview with Lucille Clifton." Interview with Michael S. Glaser. *The Antioch Review* 58.3 (Summer 2000): 310–328.

———. "An Interview with Lucille Clifton." Interview with Charles H. Rowell. *Callaloo* 22.1 (1999): 56–72.

———. "lee." *The Terrible Stories*. Brockport, NY: BOA Editions, 1996. 50.

———. "Lucille Clifton." Interview with Bill Moyers. *Language of Life: A Festival of Poets*. Ed. James Haba. Garden City, NY: Doubleday, 1995. 81–95.

———. "memphis." *The Terrible Stories*. Brockport, NY: BOA Editions, 1996. 41–42.

———. "'A Music in Language': A Conversation with Lucille Clifton." Interview with Susan B.A. Somers-Willet. *The American Voice* 49 (Summer 1999): 73–92.

———. "slave cabin, sotterly plantation, maryland, 1989." *Quilting*. Brockport, NY: BOA Editions, 1991. 13.

Ellison, Ralph. "Twentieth-Century Fiction and the Black Mask of Humanity." 1946. *Shadow and Act*. New York: Vintage Books, 1953. 24–44.

Morrison, Toni. "Unspeakable Things Unspoken: The Afro-American Presence in American Literature." *Within the Circle: An Anthology of African American Literary Criticism from the Harlem Renaissance to the Present*. Ed. Angelyn Mitchell. Durham: Duke UP, 1994. 368–398.

Somers-Willet, Susan. "'Lucy and Her Girls': Form and the Generational Tradition of Lucille Clifton's Poetry." Paper presented at the College Language Association conference. New Orleans, 20 April 2001.

Work, John W., ed. *American Negro Songs and Spirituals*. New York: Bonanza Books, 1940.

GALE SWIONTKOWSKI

Anne Sexton, Sylvia Plath, and the Allure of Incest

Literary criticism has traditionally esteemed Electra to be a heroic character, but psychoanalysis has used Electra, like Oedipus, another of Sophocles' heroic characters, as the symbolic embodiment of potentially serious psychological difficulties. The "Electra complex" has been used as a psychoanalytic term to identify a type of arrested development in an older female child or woman, in which the daughter adulates the father and scorns the mother. This not uncommon scenario can become a more serious complex if the older daughter regresses to a state of infantile dependency on the father; as Carl Jung puts it, "If the sexual libido were to get stuck in this form the . . . Electra conflict would lead to murder and incest" (1980, 4:154–55). To the contrary, Sigmund Freud mentions the Electra complex briefly toward the end of his life as an acceptable norm for women, not as problematic as the Oedipus complex for men:

> [I]n females we find that . . . it is their lack of a penis that forces them into their Oedipus complex. It does little harm to a woman if she remains in her feminine Oedipus attitude. (The term "Electra complex" has been proposed for it.) She will in that case choose her husband for his paternal characteristics and be ready to recognize his authority. Her longing to possess a penis, which

From *Imagining Incest: Sexton, Plath, Rich, and Olds on Life with Daddy*, pp. 31–56. Copyright © 2003 by Rosemont Publishing & Printing.

149

is in fact unappeasable, may find satisfaction if she can succeed in completing her love for the organ by extending it to the bearer of the organ. (1957, 23:51)

Note that Freud does not suggest that a woman might "find satisfaction" by discovering a source of strength within herself, thereby rendering her dependency on the phallic power of the male unnecessary and creating the potential for an equal social relationship between female and male. Freud does not see this possibility because he disregards the symbolic status of the penis as phallus, as embodiment of male access to social power in a patriarchal society. Freud sees desire as focussing on actual anatomical differences and thus concludes that nothing can be done about the differences between men and women, physical or social. Electra must just accept her fate.

Over time, feminists have noted that Freud accepts a condition that is considered pathological for males as being normative for females. Whereas the male must resolve his Oedipus complex to negotiate the tricky power relationship with the fathers he must live with and then replace, the woman is expected to accept the failure to resolve her Electra complex in order to negotiate the equally, if not more, difficult power relationships with the father-figures of her society.

> It is clear that for a woman to be healthy she must "adjust" to and accept behavioral norms for her sex even though these kinds of behavior are generally regarded as less socially desirable [than male behavioral norms].... Although the limited "ego resources," and unlimited "dependence," and fearfulness of most women is pitied, disliked, and "diagnosed," by society and its agent clinicians, any other kind of behavior is unacceptable in women. (Chesler 1972, 68–69)

Phyllis Chesler developed this analysis of women's psycho-social conditioning in the early 1970s, less than a decade after Sylvia Plath's death and just prior to Anne Sexton's. This ambiguous normative-pathological state, as we shall see, forms the social background to many poems by Sexton and Plath, against which they try to understand their identities as women and poets.

Otto Rank, in *The Incest Theme in Literature and Legend*, asserts an additional connection between neurosis and creativity in the "incest complex," arguing that incestuous desire, when frustrated by the strictures of society, under "especially favorable conditions," can lead to "achievements we admire as the highest creations of the human spirit" (1992, 570, 32). But Rank also acknowledges the unfavorable role of the woman in both the experience of incest and the sublimation of that impulse in creative output:

> Just as the man is the active partner in wooing and in procreation, so too the development of myths and religions, as well as artistic activity, is intended to gratify and justify male sexual fantasies. . . . Whereas the man (father) is able to live out his repressed incestuous impulses toward his daughter in violent and satisfying fantasies, in the woman (daughter), for whom such a solution is not available, the repression of attraction to the father, objectionable in our culture, frequently leads to neurosis. (300–301)

A careful reading of the poetry of Sexton and Plath raises the question of whether it is really repressed sexual desire for the father, for his penis as Freud assumed, that leads to neurosis, or rather an incompletely repressed desire for the father's power to actualize himself in creative social acts, which the woman has traditionally been denied. It becomes clear that these female poets desire the father's creative potency, often symbolized in cultural terms by the phallus, and not the actual father in his physical, personal manifestation; in the poetry of these women the father is used as a symbol of his own social powers. Sexton's poetry seeks the father's power to protect and affirm her; much of Plath's poetry seeks the father's power to advance her ambitions, to accept her as an equal. In several poems Plath draws on the story of Electra to explore her own relationship with this potentially enabling father. In fact, the heroine of Sophocles' *Electra* shows the psychological dilemma of the modern woman to be of long standing. Electra, like Sexton and Plath, seeks from an external male agent, her brother or father, protection and affirmation, fulfillment of ambitions and recognition as an equal.

Surely Electra compares well with her mother, Clytemnestra, who has helped to murder Agamemnon, her first husband and Electra's revered father, and who connives with her new husband to maintain Electra in an enslaved condition. But the Chorus (of community women) and Electra's sister Chrysothemis (who has acceded to the unfortunate reality she lives in without condoning it) frequently remind Electra that she facilitates her own enslavement, for Electra's open hatred and defiance of her mother and stepfather fuel their oppression of her. But Electra continues to find solace only in the thought of her brother acting as her savior, and she fantasizes her own rescue from her cruel mother and stepfather so far as to wish for the return of her father from death to aid her. Sophocles' depiction of Electra's fantasies illustrates several modern psychological theories. Otto Rank has noted that the "rescue fantasy" is "significant in human sexual life" and also "plays an immense role in mythical and literary fantasy creations" (1992, 65). Susan Kavaler-Adler has more recently observed that "the internal father will persist as a demonic or bad object within the psyche of the developmentally arrested female. The antidote is then often sought in the form of an idealized male rescuer" (1993, 72). And Judith Lewis Herman has written of the incestuous daughter's yearning for her father to confer "honorary boy" status on her and thus raise her out of the subordinate fate of women in a patriarchal society (Herman and Hirschman 1982, 57).

When Orestes returns and murders Clytemnestra, however, Electra does not join him but rather runs away, with the excuse of watching for the return of her stepfather. In fact, she never lifts a hand to protect or release herself, as much as she complains throughout the play of her subjection. Her open intolerance of her conditions, combined with her failure to act to relieve herself of these conditions, creates a paradoxical situation that cannot be resolved except by the power of an outside agent, an idealized rescuer who affirms the value of the person he labors to rescue. Electra chooses not to resolve her unhappy situation, either by making the best of her fate, like Chrysothemis, or by acting to free herself, like Orestes; she in effect chooses to remain enslaved until a "champion," brother or father, rescues her: "As I wait forever for Orestes to come and put a stop to this, I perish in my misery" (Sophocles 1994, 243, 191–92).

Perhaps Electra needs the implicit moral affirmation of rescue, since her persistent fidelity to her father is tainted by the primary reason for his own murder—the fact that he sacrificed his daughter, Electra's sister Iphigenia, to the gods to obtain their assistance in war. Sophocles' Electra seems unconsciously troubled by her father's morally questionable behavior. Though she defends it as the work of the gods and not his choice (217), she sings this interesting lament at the beginning of the play: "I shall not cease from my dirges and miserable lamentations, . . . like the nightingale, slayer of her young, crying out loud and making loud proclamation to all before my father's doors" (177). In a real sense, Electra does deny life to any future offspring of her own by persisting in grief for her father and not proceeding with her own life. In not being able to separate herself from the memory of her father, she symbolically duplicates his crime of sacrificing offspring. In the light of her father's questionable morality and her own submission to it, her courage looks more like folly. Electra's ambivalent stand between moral courage and passive fantasy haunts the poetry of Anne Sexton and Sylvia Plath, who both also struggle with the allure of morally questionable poetic fathers. Indeed, one might ask of these poets what the Chorus asks Electra in Sophocles' play:

> But you will never raise up your father from the lake of Hades,
> to which all must come, by weeping or by prayers! No, leaving

moderation aside and plunging into grief irresistible you lament ever, to your ruin. In this there is no way of undoing evil; why are you set on misery? (179)

* * *

Anne Sexton was something of a poetic phenomenon in the 1960s and 1970s; even more than Sylvia Plath, Sexton was a challenger of poetic taboos. For this reason among others, Sexton's friend and fellow poet Maxine Kumin portrays Sexton as a progenitor of the modern female voice in poetry:

> Women poets in particular owe a debt to Anne Sexton, who broke new ground, shattered taboos, and endured a barrage of attacks along the way because of the flamboyance of her subject matter, which, twenty years later, seems far less daring. She wrote openly about menstruation, abortion, masturbation, incest, adultery, and drug addiction at a time when the proprieties embraced none of these as proper topics for poetry. . . . Anne delineated the problematic position of women—the neurotic reality of the time—though she was not able to cope in her own life with the personal trouble it created. (Kumin 1981, xxxiii–xxxiv)

Sexton and Plath became revolutionary poets at least in part because they wrote within the poetic movement of confessionalism. Stylistically, confessionalism speeded the acceptance of "free" or unstructured verse. Both Plath and Sexton began their careers writing highly structured and formally intoned poetry, Plath's very clearly in imitation of esteemed male predecessors, such as W. B. Yeats. But both women soon learned to allow the emotional content of the poem to produce the structure, rather than prearranging structure to direct the emotion. As Jacqueline Rose has pointed out, Plath's poetic form "can be called feminine to the precise degree that it flouts the rigidity (the masculinity) of the requisite forms of literary cohesion and control" (1991, 28).

However, confessionalism had an even greater impact on poetic themes, as the internal, emotional life of the poet became the grounds for poetry, in part replacing the previously dominant social-cultural arena. Again, this thematic change, like the stylistic change, favored women writers, for it opened up what is perhaps a more traditionally female realm of experience to poetry: "Men are generally more verbal about 'justice' and 'equality' when it applies to abstract or public, global issues (*their* reference sphere): they do not apply such concepts to their personal or family lives—women's reference sphere" (Chesler 1972, 294 n). Even more seriously, many feminists feel that traditional male-authored literature, in its abstract or absent sense of justice and equality in regards to women, does violence to a woman's psyche. What Christine Froula has said of the woman reader resounds all the more loudly for the woman writer, who must try somehow to fit herself into the masculine tradition:

> Metaphysically, the woman reader of a literary tradition that inscribes violence against women is an abused daughter. Like physical abuse, literary violence against women works to privilege the cultural father's voice and story over those of women, the cultural daughters, and indeed to silence women's voices. (1989, 121)

By contrast, Plath spoke with great excitement of the movement we now call confessionalism as an "intense breakthrough into very serious, very personal, emotional experience which I felt has been partly taboo," with particular reference to the poetry of Anne Sexton (1966, 167–68).

Both Sexton and Plath were also influenced by personal experience in psychotherapy. Plath received therapy following her suicide attempt during her college years and again early on in her marriage. Moreover, Plath was fairly well read in Freud and Jung. During her later course of therapy she read Freud's "Mourning and Melancholia" (Plath 1982, 280), and in 1959 she read Jung's *Symbols of Transformation* (Stevenson 1989, 163), which focuses on the symbolic value of incest. . . . Sexton began writing poetry at the suggestion of her first psychiatrist, while recovering from a breakdown and suicide attempt after the birth of her second child (Middlebrook 1991, 45 ff.), and her first volume, *To Bedlam and Part Way Back*, won acclaim for its many poems on madness. Paradoxically, Plath's and Sexton's disturbed relations to social norms both freed them to speak of such tabooed topics and tied them to personas with great yearnings for the approval of authority figures. In their poetry, Sexton and Plath both challenge and court male authorities, never quite finding an inner authority to speak of their own experiences without an anxious glance toward the supervising paternal figures of society. Kumin says of this regressive tendency in Sexton's poetry,

> It would be simplistic to suggest that the Oedipal theme overrides all other considerations in Sexton's work, but a good case might be made for viewing her poems in terms of their quest for a male authority figure to love and trust. . . . [I]n Sexton's poetry the reader can find the poet again and again identifying herself through her

relationship with the male Other, whether in the person of a lover
or . . . in the person of the patriarchal final arbiter. (1981, xxix–xxx)

Such a "quest" is like Electra's persistent waiting for her brother or father
to rescue her, and reminiscent of Electra's remark to her brother: "your
pleasure shall be mine also, since I got my delight from you and it is not
my own" (Sophocles 1994, 295). Sexton's poetic persona, like Electra, often
seeks affirmation of her own emotions and experiences in an idealized and
externalized male authority.

Sexton's earliest poems cultivate the voice of a psychiatric patient, who
is necessarily dependent on her doctor for certification of her sanity and for
the fundamental needs and desires of all emotionally intimate relationships.
The opening poem of Sexton's first volume is titled in address to her psychiatrist, "You, Doctor Martin" (1981, 3–4). Doctor Martin is a Daddy-god
to the speaker, omniscient and "oracular," while the speaker and her fellow
patients are "large children" who wear smocks, make moccasins, and are forbidden knives at dinner. This childishly dependent speaker has little choice
but to love her doctor: "Of course, I love you; / you lean above the plastic sky,
/ god of our block." In "Music Swims Back to Me" (1981, 6–7), Sexton finds
no directional signs within the mind or within the mental institution, and
the speaker must ask, helplessly and deferentially, "Wait Mister. Which way
is home?" The doctor and the man who knows the way are soon joined by a
young girl's Electral memories of a time of unity with her idealized father in
"The Bells":

> Father, do you remember?
> . . . .
> I remember the color of music
> and how forever
> all the trembling bells of you
> were mine. (1981, 7–8)

"The Bells" portrays an idealized emotional union, a symbolic marriage
between father and daughter, much like the naive trust in the doctor that is
necessary for the "recovery" and release of the psychiatric patient.

Lurking behind such trust and desire for union, however, is the suggestion of incest between the poet and her father-figures, which surfaces in a
number of poetic references to apparent sexual contact: "even my father came
with his white bone"; "my father arching his bone"; "Frog is my father's geni-
tals"; "I have known a crib. I have known the tuck-in of a child / but inside
my hair waits the night I was defiled" (Sexton 1981, 111, 159, 282, 333). Most

disturbing is the long poem "The Death of the Fathers" (1981, 322–32), in which Sexton portrays childhood memories of intimate moments with her father along with her present dismay at a more recent assertion by one of her mother's old friends that *he* is her real, biological, father. This confusion of fathers is partly based on events in Sexton's life (Middlebrook 1991, 342ff.). In the poem, however, Sexton's speaker apparently attempts to resolve the confusion and determine the identity of her "real" father through the right to incest. The incestuous connection between father and daughter is established early in the poem, in a memory from the speaker's nineteenth year, as a "serpent" presses against the daughter as she dances with her father. Later in the poem, Sexton uses this experience of sexualized intimacy with the father as a standard in evaluating the claims of the other man.

> Who was he, Father?
> What right, Father?
> To pick me up like Charlie McCarthy
> and place me on his lap?
> . . . .
> and his tongue, my God, his tongue,
> like a red worm and when he kissed
> it crawled right in.
> . . . .
> dragging me up and pushing me down
> when it was you, Father,
> who had the right
> and ought.
> . . . .
> He was a stranger, Father.
> Oh, God,
> he was a stranger,
> was he not?

It is tempting to read this poem through the object relations theory of the child's internalized good and bad fathers: "the preoedipal female embraces the malevolent form of the father [demon-lover]—which she cannot avoid doing, for he comes in tandem with the idealized father [muse] from whom she seeks rescue" (Kavaler-Adler 1993, 74). In "The Death of the Fathers," Sexton's speaker seeks rescue from the intrusive father-pretender in the form of paternal affirmation from the man she has always accepted as her father. But even within such a psychological framework, it would not be easy to establish that one "father" is the idealized muse and the other a demonic predator because of Sexton's use of the right to incest as her standard of evaluation. Can the ideal muse be an incestuous father? The father-pretender's behavior is presented in the poem as horrifying only because it is more direct and because the child did not believe he was her father, not because of the nature of the behavior itself, in which the "real" father also participates, though more subtly. The daughter-speaker seems to accept the right to sexual intimacies in the father she has always lived with but not in the man who claims to be her biological father. It is as if she decides the issue of fatherhood on the basis of the long-term emotional incest of the adult man and young daughter who have grown together in the same home. To this speaker, fatherhood is predicated on a history of emotional incest; biological fatherhood, like overt sexual contact, does not qualify one as a father. Being a daughter, Sexton seems to say, is not a physical state of connection but a complex emotional experience in relation to the father.

With such poems as "The Death of the Fathers," Sexton's readers must keep in mind her own depictions of the poet's or the sensitive child's somatic experiences of another person's feelings or unrealized intentions, as she has developed them in "The Death Baby." . . . Sexton is always working more with emotions than with facts, and many of her poems emphasize the impossibility of separating emotional experience from historical experience. In "Mother and Jack and the Rain" (1981, 109–11), Sexton suggests that a daughter's normal identification with her mother leads her almost inevitably and naturally to a kind of vicarious incest with her father: "On my damp summer bed I cradled my salty knees / and heard father kiss me through the wall / and heard mother's heart pump like the tides." Two later lines from this poem recall vividly the frustrations of Electra in her subservience to her parents: "I made no voyages, I owned no passport. / I was the daughter." And in "Cripples and Other Stories" (1981, 160–63), the speaker addresses another "father-doctor," calls herself (though thirty-six years old) a "child-woman," and speaks of physical affection between the two of them. But the final two lines again suggest the symbolic nature of the relationship, as the father-doctor is addressed in this manner: "I'm getting born again, Adam, / as you prod me with your rib." The allusions to the stories of Electra and Eve in these poems raise the connotations of the incest imagery above personal experience and into archetypal knowledge. Jungian psychologist Marian Woodman thus writes of the symbolic incestuous tie between a father and creative daughter as a spiritual, not physical, marriage:

> For [the creative woman], the imagination is the real world, and the father-man who can penetrate and impregnate that world brings "light to the sun and music to the wind." He is her beloved.

Here is where her intimate intercourse is. Here is where incest is
permitted. (1985, 48)

The transference of this confusion of love and power in the Electral
daughter's relations with her father to other father-figures in positions of
social power is a movement of abstraction and generalization that is often
better captured in symbols than in histories of actual experience. Anne Sexton reminds us of this in a late, untitled poem about a dream of a "My Lai soldier" who aims his penis at her and says, "*Don't take this personally*" and "*It's my
job*" (1981, 575). Certainly this is a poem about the power relations between
men and women (and their children) in a society that prefers the dominance
of masculine aggressive power over the relatively passive and caring natures
of women; and the last line is certainly ironic, in that the impersonality of the
soldier's intentions allows for atrocity. But Sexton is careful to introduce this
vision as a dream and to conclude it with what might be, a bit out of context, a
sound psychological warning—"Don't take this personally." Joseph Campbell
has similarly warned, concerning psychic experiences of powerful archetypes,
that it is important not to confuse such universal experience with one's personal being (1973, 234)—in effect, to stay deflated rather than risk inflation
(and perhaps explosion) by archetypes much more powerful than the self.
Sexton is, at least in part, depicting father–daughter incest as an archetype,
though she often presents it in immediate and apparently personal terms.
Her speaker is acting out a part within this archetypal experience, and so is
the father-figure. As she has said, "concrete examples give a verisimilitude. . . .
There is a lot of unconscious truth in a poem. In some ways, as you see me
now, I am a lie. The crystal truth is in my poetry" (1985, 103).

Sexton's explorations of archetypal experience within the context of literary allusion help to ensure that the experience is clearly symbolic, universal—not personal. In the volume *Transformations*, Sexton develops modern
reinterpretations of traditional fairy tales that all little girls know. The most
emotionally intense of these poems is probably the last, "Briar Rose (Sleeping
Beauty)" (1981, 290–94). (For an exhaustive coverage of critical response to
incest in this poem, see Skorczewski 1996.) At first, Sexton presents an objective, revised version of the princess's experience:

. . . Little doll child,
come here to Papa.
Sit on my knee.
. . . . . .
Come be my snooky
and I will give you a root.

. . . .
[The prince] kissed Briar Rose
and she woke up crying:
Daddy! Daddy!
Presto! She's out of prison!

Here Sexton is working with the good girl's easy transference of incestuous desires from father to husband—as long as she works within the patriarchal social structure, does not challenge it, and obediently replaces Daddy with husband, she is "free."

In the last stanza of the poem, however, Sexton personalizes Briar Rose's experience, as the speaker reports no longer from outside the story, ironically, but now from within it:

Daddy?
That's another kind of prison.
It's not the prince at all,
but my father
drunkenly bent over my bed,
circling the abyss like a shark,
my father thick upon me
like some sleeping jellyfish.
What voyage this, little girl?
This coming out of prison?
God help—
this life after death?

Sexton, speaking now in the first person, draws in what seems to be the speaker's personal experience to anchor the traditional fairy tale in modern realities. All the poems in *Transformations* are deeply ironic, if not cynical, for all challenge the "happily ever after" (as long as the woman complies) mentality of the past with the observations of a woman speaking from a higher level of awareness in the present. More to the point, the traditional tale of "Sleeping Beauty," like the others Sexton draws upon in this volume, conveys the idealistic expectations of young girls who have heard these stories from their parents. But the last stanza of Sexton's "Briar Rose," and her ironic reworking of the tale throughout the poem to present Briar Rose in an incestuous dilemma, convey the disillusionment of the adult woman who has discovered the world is very much different from what she first learned to expect in hearing those fairy tales. As Sexton suggests, it is the deceptively romantic socialization of little girls that is at fault.

We see another victim of romantic socialization in the poem "'Daddy' Warbucks" (1981, 543–44), spoken by Sexton's version of the popular comic-strip character Little Orphan Annie. This poem satirizes one of the chief allures of incest—the economic reward for an incestuous compliance:

> What's missing is the eyeballs
> in each of us, but it doesn't matter
> because you've got the bucks, the bucks, the bucks.
> You let me touch them, fondle the green faces
> lick at their numbers and it lets you be
> my "Daddy!" "Daddy!"

"Daddy" Warbucks' money, which comes from exploiting a war-obsessed society, is available even to a fatherless daughter who knows how to play the game:

> And I was always brave, wasn't I?
> I never bled?
> I never saw a man expose himself.
> No. No.

But such blind compliance has its internal consequences, as Annie realizes when she confronts the compromise of her own better nature:

> But I died yesterday,
> "Daddy," I died,
> swallowing the Nazi-Jap-animal
> and it won't get out
> it keeps knocking at my eyes,
> my big orphan eyes,
> kicking! Until eyeballs pop out. . . .

The gain of Daddy's bucks is bought with the loss of personal integrity, symbolized in the loss of eyes, the knowing, conscious "I" of the self. Orphan Annie, compliant woman-child dependent on her "Daddy" for survival, becomes a blind cog in the war machine—perhaps wearing an embroidered sweater and pearls, like Eunice.

In light of these archetypal presentations of the incest motif through literary and cultural allusions, it seems clear that Sexton's apparently personal poems on incest are functioning at least partly in the realm of archetypal experience. "Flee on Your Donkey" (1981, 97–105) is an important poem in this regard, for it depicts Sexton's experience of recounting memories of sexual contact with her father to her first analyst (see Middlebrook 1991, 56ff.). There is in this poem another father-doctor conflation of male authority figures. At issue is the question of the memories themselves, whether they are actual or created; thus, this poem anticipates many of the controversies now surrounding the current "plague" of recovered memories of incest among adult women in therapy.

> Years of hints
> strung out—a serialized case history—
> thirty-three years of the same dull incest
> that sustained us both.
> You, my bachelor analyst,
> who sat on Marlborough Street,
> sharing your office with your mother
> . . . .
> were the new God. . . .

The speaker's desperate need for reassurance, approval, affection from a father-figure creates confusion here over the nature of this "case history." If compliance with her father did not work to secure his love and protection, she seems to suggest, then perhaps she can please the father-doctor-god by meeting his expectations, or what she expects of his expectations, and secure the affirmative relationship she craves. The actual historical events in her relationship with her father seem to be less important than the emotional means of her ongoing relations with him and with his social substitutes; she speaks of "thirty-three years" of incest. Incest imagery becomes a kind of transaction between daughter and father-doctor in the daughter's mind, and the hoped-for end of this transaction is an emotional union expressed in allusions to incest, not unlike the young girl's happy union with her father in "The Bells"—a happy-ever-after fairy tale.

Eventually (as we will see in the conclusion to this study), Sexton's father-fixation, her Electra complex, will lead her to seek a kind of incestuous relation with the ultimate father, God himself. Even in "Flee on Your Donkey," a relatively early poem, Sexton makes a transition from her symbolic emotional relationship with the doctor-god to an intimate and symbolic physical union with God, the Father:

> . . . Soon I will raise my face for a white flag,
> and when God enters the fort,
> I won't spit or gag on his finger.
> I will eat it like a white flower.

Sexton's speaker presents these images after she has left her doctor's office
for a mental hospital. The imagery of raising a white flag suggests again, as
Orphan Annie also finds, that the means of being "saved" for a woman in a
patriarchal society is self-surrender to the more powerful father.

*   *   *

The attraction of the symbolically incestuous relations Sexton presents
between her poetic persona and her father and psychiatrist may be clarified
by reference to another modern woman's writings on this theme. In 1992,
in the midst of the recovered memory "plague," previously unpublished
sections of Anaïs Nin's diary were released under the title *Incest*. These
journal entries tell the stories of Nin's sexual seduction of her own father, a
case of actual incest, and her physically intimate relationships with her two
analysts, Rene Allendy and Otto Rank, which might be termed displaced
incest with father-surrogates. Nin writes with a self-conscious control
of tone and sureness of message that suggest these journals are not the
spontaneous recordings of experience but their creative rewrites. However,
whether these accounts are historically accurate or not, what is of interest in *Incest* is the freedom and rightness Nin feels in pursuing incestuous
relationships with her father and her analysts. Possibly these relationships
affirm Nin's sense of femininity, in Phyllis Chesler's definition of the term
as "dependence on a man." Chesler believes that women who have sex with
their therapists have "committed a dramatic version of father–daughter
incest" (1972, 128): "The *sine qua non* of 'feminine' identity in patriarchal
society is the violation of the incest taboo, i.e., the initial and continued
'preference' for Daddy, followed by the approved falling in love with and/
or marrying of powerful father figures" (138). Clearly, Nin finds the feminine self-affirmation in these relations that Sexton searches for in many
of her poems, and Nin does so without the guilt or ethical conflicts which
Sexton never escapes.

    In her relations with important men, such as her analysts, Nin not only
seeks affirmation but also ensures that she is inflated by it, into a grandiosity
that many analysts might find quite alarming. She writes of her first analyst:
"Allendy. And tonight I need him. I need his strength. He is my father, my
god—all in one" (1992, 55). And she reliably secures this strength; she manages to be rescued, as Sexton is unable to do: "I feel tonight that I want to
embrace *all experience*—that I can do so without danger, that I have been
saved by Allendy" (7). Nin leads up to her account of seducing her father
with this heroic rationalization: "Today I am preparing to liberate my Father
of the pain and terror of life" (153). Certainly she seems to have transcended

her self-image as victim of her father's desertion of the family when she was a child, but only to use him and desert him in turn. She "recovers," if that term can be used, by duplicating her father's error and not by transcending it—much like Electra. After her affair with her father, Nin turns to her next analyst for "absolution for my passion for my Father" (221), and so begins an intimate relationship with Otto Rank. Then she cannot resist asking herself, "Should I go to Jung and get another scalp? ... Jung, too, would become human with me" (358).

Incest ends with an account of Nin's choice to abort a child quite late in the pregnancy. She reasons that real motherhood would divert her from her true calling of caring for the men who need her. After the abortion, Nin cleverly redefines the event: "This little girl ... I reabsorbed into myself. It is to remain in me, a part of me. I gathered myself all together again" (382). Voluntary abortion becomes a more passive "reabsorption." A daughter who would, initially at least, demand more than she gave, could not compete with men who compensated an outwardly compliant Nin with the questionable gift of an inflated role. If one definition of incest is "hoarding" ..., then Nin's "reabsorption" of her daughter is, essentially, the final act of incest in *Incest*. Through the abortion, she upholds the right to self-protection she has gained from her service to the important men of her society; she cannot see any separate identity in the daughter she aborts, and she ensures the continuation of her privileged role as the woman who initiates and benefits from incest with the father and the father-surrogates—the special woman who must inevitably subordinate even her daughter to that predominant specialness. The potential daughter-child is sacrificed to ensure the priority in Nin's life of the "fathers" to be treated as her children, in turn reaffirming Nin as the esteemed "mother" of those patriarchs.

Anaïs Nin's story illustrates quite clearly the psychological allures and dangers of incest, symbolic or actual. Both Sexton and Plath eventually step, like Nin, toward symbolically duplicating the psychological process of incest that has victimized them. However, that step leads not to their hoped-for salvations, as it seems to do for Nin, but to their downfalls ... perhaps because of their greater ethical sensitivities, or at least because of their distaste for the kind of groveling compliance with male authorities that Nin displays. Joining the patriarchy by becoming one of the boys, or the idolized mother-lover, is not a viable option for most women, who seek only to be accepted as they are and to express themselves as individuals. Plath and Sexton spent much of their poetic careers exploring the real need to find acceptance in the patriarchal tradition that excluded them from power, and at tunes they seem to find, or at least to anticipate, some positive alternatives to Electra's or Nin's self-enslavement to men.

In "All My Pretty Ones" (1981, 49–51), a poem on the deaths of her parents, Anne Sexton attempts to realign her relationship with them, seeking to create a more realistic and controlled love among equals in place of the compliant love of a victimized daughter for her feared and idolized parents. Here she remarks to her dead father, while leafing through his photos and diary:

> Now I fold you down, my drunkard, my navigator,
> my first lost keeper, to love or look at later.
> . . . .
> Only in this hoarded span will love persevere.
> Whether you are pretty or not, I outlive you,
> bend down my strange face to yours and forgive you.

Those final two lines anticipate the equal acceptance Sharon Olds later extends toward her father, an acceptance based on a recognition of his mortality and thus his equality with her in at least that respect. Sexton seems to recognize here the equality that mortality enforces and to accept a separation, rather than an identification, between herself and her father—hers is a "strange," not a familiar, face. And she offers forgiveness, indeed achieves the state of being able to forgive her father for his sins against her, for his imperfections. But the worrisome words at the end of "All My Pretty Ones" are "keeper" and "hoarded." Even though Sexton achieves some peace and reconciliation with her father after his death in the very fact of her ability to outlive him, she also hoards her relationship with him, keeps it private and separate and special, and preserves her memory of him as her "first lost keeper." Perhaps for this reason, for failing to take the next step of accepting her own equality with all people, preserving instead a privileged, symbolically incestuous relationship with the memory of her father, Sexton, like Electra and Nin, fails to accept herself as she is on her own.

* * *

Anne Sexton had the opportunity, like Adrienne Rich and Sharon Olds, to watch her father age and die, to gain some insight and empathy for him in the process, and to replace him as an adult. Sylvia Plath had no such opportunity. Plath's father died when she was eight, and he remains preserved in her poetry in the extremely idealized Electral images of an eight-year-old daughter. Enough of her life changed after her father's death that Plath spoke of a tangible separation between the time before her father died and the time after:

And this is how it stiffens, my vision of that seaside childhood. My father died, we moved inland. Whereon those nine first years of my life sealed themselves off like a ship in a bottle—beautiful, inaccessible, obsolete, a fine, white flying myth. (1979, 26)

The story of Electra thus intersects with Plath's story in several respects. Plath realized this and did not shrink from developing some of the similarities in her poetry, particularly in "Electra on Azalea Path," the poem she wrote after her first visit to her father's grave, as an adult. If Sexton often shocked her audiences with the subject matter of her poetry and was less daring in her poetic negotiations with male authorities, Sylvia Plath was usually less daring than Sexton in terms of subject matter but more willing to explore the extremes of human relationships. As Rose puts it, "Plath regularly unsettles certainties of language, identity and sexuality, troubling the forms of cohesion on which 'civilised' culture systematically and often oppressively relies" (1991, xii).

"Electra on Azalea Path" (1981, 116–17) relates a small part of Electra's story as parallel to that of Plath's speaker, who says of her father's death, "The day you died I went into the dirt." For Electra, this entombment was a humiliating enslavement; for Plath's speaker, it was her denial of the reality of her father's death, a denial that allowed her to maintain her childishly idealized image of her father:

> It was good for twenty years, that wintering—
> As if you had never existed, as if I came
> God-fathered into the world from my mother's belly.
> . . . .
> Small as a doll in my dress of innocence
> I lay dreaming your epic, image by image.

When Plath's speaker does awake as an adult to the reality of her father's death, she has to negotiate the unresolved emotions of childhood loss and guilt that have been denied and brewing for so long.

> I brought my love to bear, and then you died.
> It was the gangrene ate you to the bone
> My mother said; you died like any man.
> How shall I age into that state of mind?
> I am the ghost of an infamous suicide,
> My own blue razor rusting in my throat.

> O pardon the one who knocks for pardon at
> Your gate, father—your hound-bitch, daughter, friend.
> It was my love that did us both to death.

Plath's use of the Electra story in this poem implies that, like Electra's murdered sister, an earlier self of Plath's speaker has died ("went into the dirt") along with the father—the younger self who knew that beloved father and had to be denied along with the reality of the father's ordinary death. The self that remains is the ghost of the vibrant, love-empowered self who was killed off, but also the heir of her unresolved ideals. The poem thus ends with an uncomfortable truce: both father and early self have died, their deaths implicated in each other, and a near-dead successor survives. Plath's command of her dead father's image is clear here, like Electra's, but later poems show a progressive shift in power from daughter to father.

In earlier poems, Plath protects herself from the growing power of her dead father through the distance imposed by death. "All the Dead Dears" (1981, 70–71), a poem that explores the tenacity of the dead in the lives of the living, at first depicts a "daft father" drowned in a pond. Nevertheless, Plath's image of her dead father persists, becomes "deadlocked," "tak[es] root" in the living daughter, and a "daft father" becomes gradually more deadly in power, more demonic. For an ambitious daughter, who hopes to make her own mark in the realm of literature, the father's death represents a loss—the loss of the one male who might be positively enough disposed toward her to lend a hand in her ambitions, to lend her some of his social power to succeed in her desires. In essence, a dead father is as useless, or as powerful in opposition, as an enemy; the result of his abandonment is loss and disappointment of personal hopes.

> My father died, and when he died
> He willed his books and shell away.
> The books burned up, sea took the shell,
> But I, I keep the voices he
> Set in my ear, and in my eye
> The sight of those blue, unseen waves. . . .
>   ("On the Decline of Oracles," Plath 1981, 78)

A dead father does not assist his living daughter, as even Electra found; to the contrary, his memory is served by her life. Plath's speaker is dispossessed of her father's tools of creative power, though she clings to his words and visions. She tries to carry on his mission without his power.

Eventually, the Electral daughter loses sight of her own ambitions and desires in her preoccupation with her dead father, and he becomes a demon-lover—an all-powerful loved one demanding full, selfless attention and service from the daughter.... In a very early poem, "On Looking into the Eyes of a Demon Lover" (1981, 325), Plath's persona seems to feel dangerously immune to the power of the demon lover, as if she were so unfortunate to begin with that he would take pity and reverse her haggard self to love and beauty. But later, more mature poems show a gradual but sure growth in the dead father's seductive and selfish power. It is as if without a father to help advance her own personal goals, the daughter is depleted of will and power and must live for him, perhaps also hoping that a union with him in death would result, paradoxically, in an empowerment of herself. In "Full Fathom Five" (1981, 92–93), the father-figure, an old god of the sea, already assumes some of the colossal and dangerous proportions of later, more full-blown manifestations. He is only partly known on the surface of the sea, or consciousness, and what is not known below is dangerous.

> ... You defy other godhood.
> I walk dry on your kingdom's border
> Exiled to no good.
>
> Your shelled bed I remember.
> Father, this thick air is murderous.
> I would breathe water.

The attraction of a union with the father is the empowerment that an orphaned daughter lacks. But if the speaker were to join her father in his ocean-home, she would lose her selfhood as surely as Sexton's Orphan Annie loses her eyes in complying with "Daddy" Warbucks to secure her survival.

"Full Fathom Five" is a more sober version of Sexton's "'Daddy' Warbucks." In both poems, the daughter seeks union with the powerful father. Plath's recognition in this poem of the father's dual nature, both demonic and redemptive, illustrates Kavaler-Adler's description of how a woman moves through psychic cycles

> of projecting the demonic part object outward in an attempt to rid herself ... of distress provoked by terror over the bad object's power to annihilate, destroy, or injure the self, while also seeking fantasy union with the idealized part object for self-protection. (1993, 41)

As the poem shows, however, such protection and consummation are won only through death, never in this world of life. In "The Beekeeper's Daughter" (1981, 118), amidst a world of natural fertility, the speaker's heart is kept under her father's foot. Like the queen bee, though unrivalled even by a mother and served by male drones and by the "Father, bridegroom," she must be sequestered in her hive, segregated from life: "The queen bee marries the winter of your [father's] year." Kavaler-Adler explains why the idealized father turns evil:

> Inevitably, an idealized god turns malicious and malignant, for in the state of desire, when merger is sought there is the threat of self-loss that comes with the desired merger. This "bad" object now is felt to be intruding through strangling or to be devouring through some form of primal erotic swallowing and rape. It can also be felt as suffocating, or as abandoning by means of coldness, remoteness, and indifference. (71)

Notably, the paternal god of these poems is addressed with the formal "Father," not the familiar "Daddy"—he is still a frightening and not yet familiar being. The daughter remains distant from and reverent towards her idolized father.

"The Colossus" (1981, 129–30) again draws on the story of Electra, with reference to the *Oresteia*. In this poem, Plath's speaker has managed to raise the remains of her father out of the water—to bring memory-images of him up to consciousness, in effect. But, no longer buoyed by that other element, the father has broken apart into immovable pieces, much larger than life. His great size and power, however, fail to benefit the speaker:

> Perhaps you consider yourself an oracle,
> Mouthpiece of the dead, or of some god or other.
> Thirty years now I have labored
> To dredge the silt from your throat.
> I am none the wiser.

The daughter tends to him subserviently, labors to clean and reassemble his parts, but in the process she loses her own life and fails to revive his.

> The sun rises under the pillar of your tongue.
> My hours are married to shadow.
> No longer do I listen for the scrape of a keel
> On the blank stones of the landing.

This is an Electral daughter so closely bound to her dead father that she never departs from her intimate relationship with his remains and is no longer aware of any other possibilities for her own life in the world beyond. In effect, she has surrendered the world of reality and committed herself to the realm of fantasy.

Kavaler-Adler remarks on such an idealized father assuming an "archaic, grandiose form": "interactions with the father are intrapsychically experienced as sadomasochistic in nature, since grandiose objects impinge rather than engage in dialogue" (36). Plath's speaker is, literally, "married to shadow," at a dead end herself. A slightly later poem, titled "A Life" (1981, 149–50), depicts a female figure inside a glass dome, aging in the trap of her own life, frozen in a similar relationship with a drowned man who crawls up out of the sea toward her. "Good" behavior may court the gratification of personal desires in Plath's poetry, but it always ends up gratifying the father-figure, the powerful male other, and even inviting an attack. Even through the daughter's denial, even in old age, even after his death, he insists on asserting his presence in her life. In "Stopped Dead" (1981, 320), the speaker seems to bargain with another father-figure, not unlike Sexton's "Daddy" Warbucks (the tone also anticipates Sexton's poem). The speaker's compliance takes the form of going along for a ride in a rich uncle's car. But this speaker, like Sexton's Orphan Annie, finds that a loss of self is the end of compliance; the ride ends at the edge of a cliff. The speaker has the choice of clinging to the rich uncle for safety or of getting out of the car and facing a life without foundation in society.

The speaker of "Fever 103°" (1981, 231–32) seeks more defiantly and proudly to purge herself of her whorish, compliant selves. Interestingly, these selves she casts off are referred to as "old whore petticoats," and they are associated with the repetition of masculine pronouns, as if the compliant female is not really a woman but what Herman has called "an honorary boy" (Herman and Hirschman 1982, 57). Again, this process of purgation and purification is greatly desired but also unavoidably delusional and self-destructive, like the experience of a high fever. And the controlled alternative, as presented in another poem, is equally distressing:

I am his.
Even in his

Absence, I
Revolve in my
Sheath of impossibles. . . .
   ("Purdah," Plath 1981, 243)

Plath's persona is nearly always caught between the ambitions that lead her to seek union with the father-figure and the degradation she must suffer in trying to fulfill them, a paradox quite similar to Electra's condition. Eventually, Plath's persona is driven to a kind of madness, to a frenzied parody of her poorly fitting social role, to a defiant exhibitionism running on the conflicted energies of self-hatred and pride. Jacqueline Rose has written of some of the results of frustrated ambition in Plath's writing:

> For if we have come to acknowledge that writing may involve for the woman an enforced male identification, condition of entry for women into a tradition which has only partially allowed them a place, we have perhaps asked ourselves less what type of strange, perverse, semi-licensed pleasures such an identification might release. In this instance, that license, that pleasure, shows the woman rediscovering herself as pure stereotype, as the reduced, reified and fragmented bits and pieces of sex. (1991, 117)

In "Lady Lazarus" (1981, 244–47), the potentially salutary peeling-off of corrupt social selves becomes the more terrifying and degrading peeling away of lives; attempted suicide becomes a striptease designed to titillate the audience that demands compliance from a talented woman unable to develop her skills socially. Where Nin learns to enjoy her own performance because she regards it from the viewpoint of her gratified paternal heroes, Plath suffers the humiliating irony of watching her own degradation in the conflict between her subjective, emotional point of view and the expectations of society.

> . . . Dying
> Is an art, like everything else.
> I do it exceptionally well.
>
> I do it so it feels like hell.
> I do it so it feels real.
> I guess you could say I've a call.
> . . . .
> There is a charge
>
> For the eyeing of my scars, there is a charge
> For the hearing of my heart—
> It really goes. . . .

The society that requires the death of a woman's internal, subjective sense of self in the attempt to gain personal desires, the society that creates this paradox, must enjoy the spectacle of this writhing, exhibitionistic, masturbatory self-torture—a sustained suicide of soul that never ends, since it leaves the body intact. All the frenzied speaker can do is magnify her powers of suffering beyond the punitive powers of her tormentors, who are already themselves magnified beyond the father to the most powerful of patriarchal figures. The result is a potent, predatory self that conquers the enemy by adopting his own practices and then turning them back upon him.

> . . . So, so Herr Doktor.
> So, Herr Enemy.
>
> I am your opus,
> I am your valuable,
> The pure gold baby
>
> That melts to a shriek.
> I turn and burn.
> Do not think I underestimate your great concern.
> . . . .
> Herr God, Herr Lucifer
> Beware
> Beware.
>
> Out of the ash
> I rise with my red hair
> And I eat men like air.

This ending of "Lady Lazarus," which many critics have preferred to read as the strong and affirmative voice of an independent woman, actually shows the speaker's ultimate entrapment. Playing the violent, male part of the patriarchal game, rather than the submissive role usually played by the woman, is not an escape from the limitations of patriarchy. The violence that is committed is just as damaging to the woman's self as the violence that is endured. In reference to the ending of "Lady Lazarus," Rose speaks of the "risk that feminism might find itself reproducing the form of phallocentrism at the very moment when it claims to have detached itself most fully from patriarchal power" (1991, 149). Both Plath and Sexton saw some of the advantages of compliance; they had desires and needs that they believed could be met through their compliance with patriarchal figures. But they both found that the sacrifices entailed were greater than the gains; they both found passive compliance finally unendurable. . . . Plath and Sexton stated the dilemma of all ambitious and aware women in a patriarchal society, but they failed to find a solution. They became locked in confrontation with the very father-figures from whom they sought relief, satisfaction, and acceptance. Rose speaks of victimization as a "pull" as much as a "predicament" (232), and in her discussion of Plath's "The Rabbit Catcher," she comments on Plath's exploration of both experiences:

> The poem seems remarkable for the way it can offer this political analysis of patriarchal power (violence against nature, violence of the Church, and in the home) at the same time as representing, in terms of sexual pleasure and participation, the competing strains of women's relationship to it. . . . Thus Plath sits on the edge of two contrary analyses of women's relationship to patriarchal power. (141)

Some light may be shed on this dilemma by Twitchell's discussion of the vampire novel as a type of "female *Bildungsroman*," in that the woman must fight off the seduction of a demon-lover. If he is to succeed, the vampire must first persuade the woman to remove her crucifix, since he cannot transgress that greater spiritual power. As Twitchell notes, this is an effort to have the woman "renounce a more powerful Father" (1987, 71), a symbolic father with even greater power than the demon-lover physically before her. Whether the woman yields to the immediate sexual pull of the demon-lover or puts her faith in the symbolic Father is key to the survival of the woman, psychologically: whether she will survive in her own right or be seduced into reproducing the activities of her demon-lover. . . .

One must wonder where Plath's great talents might have led her had she heeded the warning and response preserved in one of her earliest poems, "Bluebeard" (1981, 305):

> I am sending back the key
> that let me into bluebeard's study;
> because he would make love to me
> I am sending back the key;
> in his eye's darkroom I can see
> my X-rayed heart, dissected body. . . .

Such an evasive course might well have extended Plath's life, but it would not have endowed her heirs with a poetic statement of the dilemma that still needed a solution. What Adrienne Rich has said of Anne Sexton applies equally to Plath: the achievements of her poetry redeem the loss of her life. Both poets offered the grounds for a new beginning.

> I think of Anne Sexton as a sister whose work tells us what we have to fight, in ourselves and in the images patriarchy has held up to us. Her poetry is a guide to the ruins, from which we learn what women have lived and what we must refuse to live any longer. Her death is an arrest: in its moment we have all been held, momentarily, in the grip of a policeman who tells us we are guilty of being female, and powerless. But because of her work she is still a presence; and as Tillie Olsen has said: "Every woman who writes is a survivor." (Rich 1979, 122–23)

ROSE LUCAS

Drifting in the Weeds of Heaven:
Mary Oliver and the Poetics of the Immeasurable

"If this was lost, let us all be lost always."[1]

To drift is to take a chance, to refuse the direct path of propriety, of common sense or rationality. To drift may always be to risk oblivion, to become so lost that there is no longer even any point of reference that can be adhered to or described: *terra firma* slips from the horizon and the inexorable elements are poised to consume anyone caught on such a trajectory into elsewhereness. However, the movement of drifting can also make possible a different kind of travel altogether, a transitioning that is responsive to chance and to circumstance, one which allows the various cross-pressures of the tide to carry a human subject, bobbing and vulnerable, to somewhere wholly unexpected, perhaps to somewhere that never could be arrived at via the pathways of rational intention. Indeed, to drift may be to relinquish the notion of arrival altogether and instead to privilege the reactivity of journey itself—the paradoxical mindfulness of inhabiting a present tense which is inevitably protracted across the linearity of moments in time.

The poetry of Mary Oliver uses the motif of drifting as her defining aesthetic and conceptual frame. In this context, to drift is not to lose the 'correct' path, to wander in an exilic aporia of shapelessness and uncertainty. Rather, Oliver's poetry suggests, to drift is to take the path of poetry and of reflection, a way which is always in some relation, but also fundamentally other, to

From *Rhizomes: Cultural Studies in Emerging Knowledge* 13 (Fall 2006). Accessed February 7, 2011. ‹http://www.rhizomes.net/issue13/lucas.html›, n.p. Copyright © 2006 by Rose Lucas.

175

what she describes as the "difficult steps in the empire of thought."[2] While we may invariably always long to "know," to fit our relation to the world into some kind of framework of certainty and expectation, it is "what is beyond knowing" which persistently calls to us, in the intoxicating specificity of the surplus of the image, through the heightened awareness of the self in a world of continuity and radical difference and dissolution. To drift is thus to pay attention to different cues—ones which may not register in trajectories of the rational and of the classificatory. It is to read different markers in what Oliver views as the meditative and non-linear journeying of life, thus reconsidering notions of goal and arrival and success. "I climb. I backtrack. / I float. / I ramble my way home" ("Have You Ever Tried to Enter the Long Black Branches," p. 140), the poet writes, foregrounding an idea of movement, yet a drifting movement which resists all but the most basic points of reference— "home"—in its emphasis upon awareness and sensitivity to the potential of otherness.

To pay attention to the possibilities, the language of otherness, is also to find the possibilities for speech, for a dialogue of poesis which contributes and shapes as much as it listens and responds. Oliver's poetic takes us to this sometimes precarious, but always productive, space of exchange; it is a tidal, littoral space where the desires and creativity of the poetic voice ebb and flow with the mutually sustaining world of perception, with the susurrations of a radically alteric sphere. As she notes in the poem "The Swan":

> . . . The path to heaven
>
> doesn't lie down in flat miles.
>   It's in the imagination
>   with which you perceive
>   this world.[3]

This paper will focus upon five key poems from Oliver's most recent collection, some new and some reproduced—"What Is There Beyond Knowing," "Terns," "Little Summer Poem Touching the Subject of Faith," "Bone" and "Have You Ever Tried to Enter the Long Black Branches"—to explore the motif of drifting both as an enabling personal strategy and as a strategy for the production of poetry. In so doing, it will consider questions of knowledge and its beyond, of the possibilities of affirmation and even of faith, a trust in the possibilities of what is "immeasurable" to sustain and enliven, as well as the varying poetic shapes which drifting and meandering might take.

The poem "What Is There Beyond Knowing" (p. 20) focuses key questions which recur throughout Oliver's poetic; not only is poetry seen as an interplay of attention and inscription, but also as a site of productive tension between the persistent desire of rational, human knowledge to encompass the wide horizons of possibility and a concomitant recognition of the limits of such rational endeavor. Poetry is here seen as a confrontation with the limits of rationality as well as with its vital potential; it hovers always on a liminal edge between the visible and invisible worlds, between speech and silence, between knowledge and whatever it is that might be "beyond knowing." However, not only is this a matter of epistemological failure[4]—a recognition that knowledge must fall short in what we want it to do[5]—but also, Oliver suggests, by means of imagery and poetic structure, perhaps this inability is also facilitatory, opening more possibilities than it closes. Rationality falls short—and we are left, freefalling, into a sphere of beyond-ness—yet it is this very sphere which enables the possibilities of the extra-rational, the shimmering worlds of the imagination, the humility of faith as well as the endless elusivity of any object of desire.[6]

Significantly, the poem's title operates ambiguously; it raises the question—albeit without the question mark—of what it is there might be "beyond knowing," while also suggesting an affirmation, an offer to show the reader what it is that might indeed lie beyond the house of the comprehensible. It is the status of beyond-ness which is given the active position of calling, which draws the poet-speaker forward into that dynamic present:

What is there beyond knowing that keeps
calling to me? I can't

turn in any direction
but it's there. I don't mean

the leaves' grip and shine or even the thrush's
silk song, but the far-off

fires, for example,
of the stars, heaven's slowly turning

theater of light, or the wind
playful with its breath;

or time that's always rushing forward,
or standing still

in the same—what shall I say—*moment.*

These lines suggest a delineation between a closeness—"leaves' grip and shine," "the thrush's / silk song"—which may be within spheres of knowing, and that which is more remote or elemental, far less susceptible to human comprehension—"stars," "wind," "time." The gaze of the poet, the point of her concentration, moves here from the study of the particularity of the immediate or natural world which is such a dominant aspect of Oliver's post-romantic and transcendentalist heritage and style,[7] to a catapulting into the always-unassailable. As Laird Christensen describes it, Oliver's poetic "precision of attention leads the reader along a well-worn transcendentalist path from direct observation toward revelation and an enhanced recontextualisation."[8] It may be of course, that this is a logical extension and that all of these elements, both far and near, are equally apparently available to, yet inevitably in excess of, the determined lasso of human knowing. However, it is the "far-off" which emphasizes the asymmetrical relation between human observer and the world of observations, the smallness of knowing which the speaker struggles with—when to accept its limitations, when to seek to extend its boundaries.

> What I know
> I could put into a pack
>
> as if it were bread and cheese, and carry it
> on one shoulder,
>
> important and honorable, but so small!

There is a journey to be undertaken here, one which leads the speaker, solitary and reflective, into the natural world, and rational knowledge is part of what will sustain her. This is not the *hubris* of a knowledge which claims mastery, which seeks to colonize the world beneath its gaze, but a knowledge which recognizes both its limits and its possibilities. "How wonderful it is / to follow a thought quietly / to its logical end. / I have done this a few times," the speaker notes. There is indeed value in what can be known—"important and honorable"—but nevertheless it is "so small," and not where the gravitational desire of the poem leads us. The simple goodness of a small amount of bread and cheese will support the idea of journey or hike only so long, especially "While everything else continues, unexplained / and unexplainable." And while the poem makes a space for such a finite knowing, the final lines lead the speaker out and into the seductive dark fields which lie beyond explicability, suggesting a space and a way of being which is not confined or classified by logic or by creed. Rather, it is one in which the viscerality and particularity of the body is experienced coterminously with the world of objects, of perception, in a human registering of the possibility of its own excess:

> But mostly I just stand in the dark field,
> in the middle of the world, breathing
>
> in and out. Life so far doesn't have any other name
> but breath and light, wind and rain.
>
> If there's a temple, I haven't found it yet.
> I simply go on drifting, in the heaven of the grass and the weeds.

The movement of the "drift" embodies the desire of the poem, the paradox of an open-ended end-point. It is offered in preference even to the preparations of the hike, although the hike might also be seen as an extension of that romantically-inspired journeying of the individual through the natural world. The extended present tense of the drift—"I simply go on drifting"— embodies the meditative, trusting aspect of this movement, predicated upon the movements of the breath of the human body as well as upon the external pulses of "light, wind and rain." In a Whitmanesque, democratizing gesture, the "heaven" which this drifting leads into is not an elevated sphere of alterity; it is the unclassified, easy to miss and modest world beneath our walking feet, a world of cyclic growth, of decay and animation—a world which speaks in a language we never expected and have so very little ability to interpret. As Rich also described in her poem "Transcendental Etude," writing consciously in the legacy of transcendentalism as a form of American romanticism, evoking also its links to a kind of post-pastoral aesthetic—it is what lies below, out of sight, or seemingly inconsequential, which is both subject matter and source of inspiration for the drifting gaze of the poet:

> I've sat on a stone fence above a great-soft, sloping field
> of musing heifers, a farmstead
> slanting its planes calmly in the calm light,
> a dead elm raising bleached arms
> above a green so dense with life,
> minute, momentary life—slugs, moles, pheasants, gnats,
> spiders, moths, hummingbirds, groundhogs, butterflies
> a lifetime is too narrow

to understand it all, beginning with the huge
rockshelves that underlie all life.[9]

Oliver's poem "Bone" (p. 72) revisits these paradoxes of knowing and
not-knowing, and the desire of the human to understand itself in relation to
what might be "immeasurable" and beyond knowing:

> Understand, I am always trying to figure out
>   what the soul is,
>   and where hidden,
>   and what shape—

The speaker here explicitly uses the language of rational enquiry—to understand, figure out, to pin down and classify the extreme elusivity of the soul,
that "part" of human experience which can seem so difficult to quantify and
yet so vital to an experience of the self and its various "beyonds." So, when
the poet finds along the beach "the ear bone / of a pilot whale that may have
died / hundreds of years ago / . . . I thought: the soul / might be like this—/
so hard, so necessary—/ yet almost nothing." The physical object, itself
trailing the possibilities of history, the scientific and imaginative recon-
struction of a life once lived, is first taken as a kind of clue. To understand
the natural world, if we could, in all its specificity, might be to offer us a
metaphoric template for understanding the relation between what we know
or can see, and what is beyond seeing. However, this impulse toward clas-
sification is problematised almost immediately by the poem; looking at the
"gray sea" before her, the speaker turns over the ambivalence of knowledge
like the fossilized bone in her hand:

> . . . don't we all *know*, the golden sand
>   is there at the bottom,
> though our eyes have never seen it,
> nor can our hands ever catch it

> *4.*
> lest we would sift it down
>   into fraction, and facts—
>   certainties—
>   and what the soul is, also

> I believe I will never quite know.

There is a glimpse of knowing, an assumption or faith in the possibility of the golden sand on the ocean floor beneath the "dark-knit glare" of the waves which, the poem suggests, would be contaminated, damaged in some way by the classificatory and dissecting impulses towards "fractions and facts," the impulse to haul it dripping and exposed into the glare of rationality. Although we stand on the edge of knowing, like the speaker on the liminal sphere of the shore, and although she acknowledges that rational knowledge will never cease to tantalize us, the poem returns to a sense of it as a false god, a false construction of life's business as being one of revelation and taxonomy. Once again, Oliver returns to the sense of the drift as an alternative to such trajectories of rationality, reinforcing a philosophy and an aesthetic of paradox, and an acceptance of the questions of self which derive from a visceral, sensuous receptivity to the world of alterity:

> Though I play at the edges of knowing,
>   truly I know
>   our part is not knowing,
>
>   but looking, and touching, and loving,
>   which is the way I walked on,
>   softly,
> through the pale-pink morning light.

The shape of the poem itself embodies and enacts the idea of drift. The tidal pull between the desires both to know and not to know, the overlapping of waters that obscure and reveal, are echoed in the meandering movement of the words on the page. The lines are not justified to the left; instead there is a pulse which reflects the thinking, interior body, its intakes of breath and exhalation, as well as the unregimentable and interchangeable rhythm of ideas. There is, as is often the case throughout Oliver's work, a run-on of ideas from one line to the next, but here this slipping and sliding movement is emphasized in "Bone" as the enjambment crosses the arbitrary lines of the section numbers—no matter how we might try to codify and classify our sense of self and world, the tumbling dance of the poetic line draws us back to a fluidity of paradox, of a beyond of logic.

The poem "Terns" (p. 34) is quite explicit in its dismissal of classificatory knowledge. "Don't think just now of the trudging forward of thought, / but of the wing-drive of unquestioning affirmation," it begins. What these lines exhort us to leave behind is the wearying sterility of a forward linear trajectory of knowledge which seems to get nowhere particularly fast or worthwhile. And while there may be "years to come" in which a questioning mind might "try the difficult steps in the empire of thoughts," the poem claims to offer the reader something preferable to such a hierarchical and ego-driven ascent—the prospect of flying across, down and up, with the "wing-drive" of the terns. In many ways, this poem reformulates the romantic and post-romantic tension between the experience of the self in relation to the world of nature and of otherness: to what extent can the human only colonize, impose upon the natural world, mining it as a source of metaphor, or objective correlative for an interior state or question; and/or to what extent is it possible to listen, to perceive the language of a world which is exterior to the self? As the Australian poet Judith Wright notes, how possible is it ever to listen to the "language of the leaves,"[10] to perceive the natural world, the world of exteriority to the observing self—as anything other than colonized, written over by the desires and the "human patterns" of the poet?[11]

In his essay on Oliver, Laird makes use of Martin Buber's distinction between, on the one hand, an I–It world, in which the self objectifies and classifies the world of other, and on the other hand, an I–You mode of interaction which describes "our unobjectified relation to another *presence*," as a way of understanding Oliver's delineations of knowing and being. The "I–You moments produce the surges of deeply felt, precognitive responses that are poorly translated to specific labels in an I–It world"—yet which are readily evoked in the slippery associativeness of the poetic image, of the fluid interplay of points of perception available within the "drift" of poetic form. As Laird puts it:

> Despite the fact that language necessarily diminishes presences to object, Oliver clearly believes that poetry can call attention to the fact that we dwell in a world of presences ... The question is not how to *know* this world ... although as a fine naturalist she encourages this kind of familiarity as well. Even the most extensive knowledge, however, merely locks the object of study in a more elaborate cage, whereas love suggests the resistance of objectification.[12]

The principle of "love" then, as linked to the fluidity and generosity of the drift, is a way of referring to those movements within Oliver's poetic, between seeing, and closely observing, and the integral links between those moments of closely attuned observation and the glimpses of the immeasurable which they might offer:

> But nothing you ever understand will be sweeter, or more binding
> than this deepest affinity between your eyes and the world.

This concept of a "deepest affinity" between eye and world, among the various organs of perception and the world that it perceives, offers a model of bi-directional exchange and possibility, where both self and world can be registered as distinct as well as overlapped. What is proffered in this poem is the primacy of engagement with the senses of looking and listening which brings the self once again into a meditative continuum with the natural world, a continuum which the analytic questions of rationality would hinder and obscure.

> . . . Listen,
> maybe such devotion, in which one holds the world
> in the clasp of attention, isn't the perfect prayer,
>
> but it must be close, for the sorrow, whose name is doubt,
> is thus subdued, and not through the weaponry of reason,
>
> but of pure submission.

If the idea of the "prayer" isn't limited to the structures of an institutionalized religion or "temple," it is nevertheless used within Oliver's poetic as a trope for this "clasp of attention," the capacity—which poetry delimits for us—to look, to pay attention, to reflect, in a state of heightened awareness of the world around us, and *not* to inductively write ourselves across the specificity of that world. As the short prose poem "The Real Prayers Are Not the Words, but the Attention that Comes First" (p. 15) suggests, Oliver postulates an even more complex relation between the experience of looking, of holding the world for a moment in that clasp of intensity, and the process of finding a language to correlate, enact or evoke that experience. In this sense, "Terns," like "The Real Prayers," points back toward the genre of the prayer—as a pivotal moment of equilibrised perception, of mutual if asymmetrical engagement—yet also could be seen to be operating *as* the prayer, as it draws the reader, via the aesthetic of the image, into its recreation of the moment of looking:

> . . . Tell me, what else
> could beauty be for? And now the tide
> is at its very crown,
> the white birds sprinkle down,

gathering up the loose silver, rising
as if weightless. It isn't instruction, or a parable.

It isn't for any vanity or ambition
except for the one allowed, to stay alive.

It's only a nimble frolic
over the waves. And you find, for hours,

you cannot remember the questions
that weigh so in your mind.

The questions, the desires to know, are still there, they hang in the mind
in the present tense—but the image of looking at the rising and falling
of the terns, the blue of the sky, the silver of the falling water—provides
another way of being, and, crucially, of overcoming the "sorrow" which
arises in the void of not-knowing, or not being able to rationally compre-
hend the nature of the self and its relation to external processes, seeable
and unseeable.

The path of the senses, "this deepest affinity between your eyes and the
world," is however not the only means to this prayer of attention and reflec-
tivity; indeed as "Little Summer Poem Touching the Subject of Faith" (p.
130) suggests, we can easily "fail as a witness" to mark the wondrous movements and specificities of the world:

Every summer
  I listen and look
    under the sun's brass and even
      in the moonlight, but I can't hear

anything, I can't see anything—
  not the pale roots digging down, nor the green stalks muscling up,
    nor the leaves
      deepening their damp pleats,

nor the tassels making,
  nor the shucks, nor the cobs.

The poem is a celebration of precisely what *can't* be seen, and yet which
is nevertheless recognized as being present. Like the golden sand of the
ocean floor in "Bone," the miracle of the corn—its growth, its beauty and

its bounty—confirms the role of faith, of an "unquestioning affirmation" which allows that much occurs *without* the territorializing impulses of rationality—"all of it / happening / beyond all seeable proof, or hearable hum." Faith, in this context, is not the collapsing of reason or subjectivity into the ideologies of dogma or temple, but rather a position of humility, of seeing the world and its ways as beyond the possibilities of our knowing—and of accepting, rather than railing against this limitation of human logic. Indeed as Oliver suggests in this poem, there is cause for thankfulness because it is this precise failure to witness and to know which makes possible a space for what she here describes as "the immeasurable," bringing with it the Hopkins-like voltage of ecstatic vision:

> And therefore, let the immeasurable come.
>   Let the unknowable touch the buckle of my spine.
>   Let the wind turn in the trees,
>   and the mystery hidden in dirt
>
> swing through the air.

The invocatory voice welcomes the mystery, the lightning bolt of what is unknowable and yet also known to be "hidden in dirt"—both somewhere unexpected, and also the stuff of the earth, the heaven of the grass and the weeds. It is a transfiguring sequence of images, sweeping the humble images of a field of growing corn into the possibilities of radical transformation. The final stanza of the poem echoes the ancient Eleusinian mysteries,[13] where, in a ceremony to both accept and to integrate the earth goddess Demeter's enormous loss of her daughter Persephone, the priest holds up, as a final gesture, the ear of corn. The child is lost, and thus there is an irreparable hole in the fabric of being—but the sight of the "honeycomb" of ripe corn signals the possibility of some sort of return. Whatever limit and loss has been endured, and however fundamentally incomprehensible this might be, the growth of the corn is visceral, tangible testimony to the possibilities of faith and continuity:

> One morning
>   in the leafy green ocean
>   the honeycomb of the corn's beautiful body
>   is sure to be there.

In "Have You Ever Tried to Enter the Long Black Branches" (p. 141), Oliver offers another interweaving of images of interiority and the external, natural world in order to draw our attention to those points of overlap and connection. How *is* it possible to think beyond an I–It, territorializing approach—"Do you think this world is only an entertainment for you?" How is it possible to sympathetically, perhaps even actually, participate in the being-ness of that which is other to the self? The fragrant intensity of Oliver's images suggests a way forward:

> Have you ever tried to enter the long black branches
>   of other lives—
> tried to imagine what the crisp fringes, full of honey,
>   hanging
> from the branches of the young locust trees, in early summer,
>   feel like?

Once again, the exhortation is to leave the rational and the known, comfortable paths—"Quickly, then, get up, put on your coat, leave your desk!"—and to move out into the world, to listen and look, to pay attention. In such a state of alertness, of willingness to think beyond a sense of self as sovereign, as a speaker of the language of dominance, one might even hear "a curl or two of music, damp and rouge-red" from the "stubby buds" of the wild roses. Significantly, however, it is not only what can be heard as emanating from elsewhere, but Oliver's vision also entails the interactive empathy of the creative imagination. The poet, the reader, the mystic, who sits listening in the grass may hear not only the voice of the grass but, because of the act of listening, is able to participate in a dance—a dance in which the creative, inscribing imagination listens and speaks, listens and speaks. The poem here echoes Whitman's own use of biblical inventory, the listing of the parts of perception that accrete rather than fragment:

> To put one's foot into the door of the grass, which is
>   the mystery, which is death as well as life, and
>   not be afraid!
>
> To set one's foot in the door of death, and be overcome
>   with amazement!
>
> To sit down in front of the weeds, and imagine
>   god the ten-fingered, sailing out of his houses of straw,
> Nodding this way and that way, to the flowers of the
>   present hour,

to the song falling out of the mockingbird's pink mouth,

to the tiplets of the honeysuckle, that have opened
  in the night.

To sit down, like a weed among weeds, and rustle in the wind!

The poem presents a model of meditative receptivity, where the self is able both to listen to a "You," and to proffer the activity of human desire, with its possibilities of creative agency. It is the desire of the speaker which leads her—and which challenges us to follow—out of the comfortable paths of rationality and explicability, and into the open fields of beauty, specificity, difference and mystery which are to be found there. The images of the poem—as indeed throughout Oliver's poetic—take as their task the recreation of that experience in the field and away from the desk, in order to lead us, with her, to the moments of clarification or even transcendence in which inner and outer find their point, or image, of convergence:

Meanwhile, once in a while, I have chanced, among the quick things
  upon the immutable.
What more could one ask?

And I would touch the faces of the daisies,
and I would bow down
to think about it.

The "immutable," or indeed the Immeasurable, can be found only among the transience of the observable "quick things," the cyclic passages of change and decay. The paradox of perception, like the Eleusinian mysteries, takes us out of time even as we are profoundly and inevitably embedded within the life and death cycles of the temporal. "That was then, which hasn't ended yet," she describes this perpetual present which is linked to the coming upon, or the recognition of, the mystery. It can't be found by determinedly seeking it out; it is not to be found as the goal on any path of intention. But a life spent in humble attention to the world of nature—or indeed in close attention to a poetic such as Oliver's which reproduces in Wordsworthian "tranquility,"[14] the humble and ecstatic engagement of self with world— makes those moments of clarity possible.

Now the sun begins to swing down. Under the peach-light,
  I cross the fields and the dunes, I follow the ocean's edge.

> I climb. I backtrack.
> I float.
> I ramble my way home.

This track of human movement then is never clearly delineated. There may be a path to go or to make—but it is a way which must be felt out, imagined into by each of us in our turn, improvised through the processes of listening and looking, and all the complex interplay of desire and receptivity, passivity and activity, which they contain. In "Have You Ever Tried the Long Black Branches" Oliver evokes the idea of "home," suggesting that all this rambling and drifting will nevertheless return to an anchor point of reference, an evocation of that emotional and perhaps physical site which provides a rationale and a shelter from the all that the winds of drifting's open fields might bring—exposure, dissolution of the fragile balance of the self, perhaps even too much mystery. In an earlier essay/poem "Upstream,"[15] Oliver juxtaposes that notion of a human home—here epitomized by her anxious parents looking for her—with another kind of reference point, "The sense of going toward the source." The essay recalls a following of the connections of the natural world, a day spent as the girl pursues each clue, each metonymic source of "violets, Dutchman's breeches . . . ferns rising so curled," each taking her further away from her changeling life within the human world. "Upstream" might be the wrong way in human terms, but in terms of paying attention to the world, of accepting the challenge of the drift, it may prove to be the right way after all:

> If this was lost, let us all be lost always. The beech leaves were just slipping their copper coats; pale green and quivering they arrived into the year. My heart opened, and opened again. The water pushed against my effort, then its glassy permission to step ahead touched my ankles . . . I do not think that I ever, in fact, returned home.[16]

This delineation between points of pause and rest which the embodied self experiences and the idea of a source of the immeasurable, is reiterated in the essay "Wordsworth's Mountain":

> . . . we might, in our lives, have many thresholds, many houses to walk out from and view the stars, or to turn and go back to for warmth and company. But the real one—the actual house not of beams and nails but of existence itself—is all of earth, with no door, no address separate from oceans or stars, or from pleasure or wretchedness either, or hope, or weakness, or greed.[17]

Oliver's poetry is a prayer for attention to the fecund interrelation between self and world; it is a powerful visceral call to engage with a philosophy and an aesthetic of the drift. We may become lost, we may lose sight of the small light of home on the vastness of the plain or the ocean—but only in the act of losing, of ceding the fantasy of rational control, can we become open to the possibilities of drifting, and the various moments of finding we never expected.

Notes

1. Mary Oliver, "Upstream," *Blue Iris: Poems and Essays*. Boston: Beacon Press, 2004, p. 53.

2. Mary Oliver, "Terns," *New and Selected Poems, Volume Two*, Boston: Beacon Press, 2005, p. 34. All references to Oliver's poetry are taken from this edition unless otherwise specified.

3. Oliver, "The Swan," *Winter Hours: Prose, Prose Poems, and Poems*. Boston: Houghton Mifflin, 1999, p. 27–28.

4. The question of epistemology, of structures and anchor points of knowing, is of course a recurrent and inevitable concern within a wide range of contemporary poetics for the post-pastoral to the post-modern—because it highlights the equivocal and dialectical relation between notions of self and other, and between the self which perceives and articulates and the world which is perceived.

5. As Adrienne Rich has noted, these limits on the possibilities of poetic speech, are "an old theme even for me: / Language cannot do everything—," "Cartographies of Silence," *The Dream of a Common Language: Poems 1974–1977*. New York: W.W. Norton, 1978, p. 19. In this sense, poetic language can always be seen to operate on a cusp between silence and speech, where silence is not only the not-yet articulated, but where it also functions as a marker of excess, and the possibilities of the extra-linguistic.

6. Cf. also Alice Fulton's exploration of this engagement between the world of perception and the world of the poetic imagination in her poem "Shy One," which, like Oliver's poetry, suggests the need to "meet the universe halfway. / Nothing will unfold for us unless we move toward what / looks to us like nothing; faith is a cascade." *Cascade Experiment: Selected Poems*. New York: W.W. Norton, 2004, p. 60.

7. Cf. for example Diane S. Bonds, "The Language of Nature in the Poetry of Mary Oliver," *Women's Studies*, Vol. 21 (1992): 1–15; Mark Johnson, "'Keep Looking': Mary Oliver's Emersonian Project," *The Massachusetts Review*, Vol. 46, 1 (Spring 2005): 78–98; Janet McNew, "Mary Oliver and Tradition of Romantic Nature Poetry," *Contemporary Literature*, Vol. 30, 1 (Spring 1989): 59–77.

8. Laird Christensen, "The Pragmatic Mysticism of Mary Oliver," J. Scott Bryson (ed.) *Ecopoetry: A Critical Introduction*. Salt Lake City: University of Utah Press, 2002, p. 140.

9. Rich, "Transcendental Etude," *Dream of a Common Language*, p. 73.

10. Judith Wright, "Falls Country," *A Human Pattern: Selected Poems*, North Ryde: Angus and Robertson, 1990, p. 176. "What does the earth say? / . . . Listen. Listen. . . . / There is / there was / a country / that spoke in the language of the leaves."

11. Wright, Cf. "The Shadow of Fire: Ghazals": "I've no wish to chisel things into new shapes. / The remnant of the mountain has its own meaning / . . . Human eyes impose a human pattern, / decipher constellations against featureless dark," *A Human Pattern*, pp. 235, 241.

12. Laird, "The Pragmatic Mysticism of Mary Oliver," pp. 139–140.

13. Cf. for example Frazer's description of the Eleusinian mysteries as alluded to in the *Homeric Hymn to Demeter*, J.G. Frazer, *The Golden Bough: A Study in Magic and Religion*, Macmillan: London, 1974, pp. 517–525.

14. Cf. Wordsworth's famous description of "poetry [as] the spontaneous overflow of powerful feelings; it takes its origin from emotion recollected in tranquility." William Wordsworth, "Preface to the Lyrical Ballads" (1800), David Perkins (ed.), *English Romantic Writers*, New York: Harcourt Brace Jovanovich, 1967, p. 328.

15. Mary Oliver, *Blue Iris*, pp. 52–56.

16. Mary Oliver, *Blue Iris*, p. 53

17. Mary Oliver, "Wordsworth's Mountain," *Long Life: Essays and Other Writings*, Cambridge, Mass: Da Capo, 2004, p. 24.

JANE HEDLEY

Adrienne Rich's Anti-Confessional Poetics

Confession is a self-centered exercise. At the same time, however, it presupposes a "significant other": someone to whom the confessant expects his or her story to matter, in whose name it is told—as in St. Augustine's *Confessions*—or to whom it must be told, as Anne Sexton insists in "For John, Who Begs Me Not to Enquire Further." The confessant's relationship to a designated interlocutor is reciprocal: intertwined, indeed, with the confessant's desire to tell her or his own story is the desire to tell the story of the other, or a story that in some sense belongs to them both. In a secular context, this relationship can easily become a power struggle: if "I" am female and "you" are male I may feel myself to be in danger from you, but you might also be in danger from me, or from my story. Cast as the one "who begs me not to enquire further," "John" is invited by Sexton's poem to see himself as an effeminate coward who would call off her quest for self-knowledge because he cannot face the truth about himself. Cast as Jocasta vis-à-vis Sexton's Oedipus, John is not just a figment of the confessional process; he is its hostage, like the three-year-old daughter to whom Sexton addresses her confession of maternal inadequacy in "The Double Image."

I have given Sexton's confessional project a distinctly unfriendly reading in the immediately foregoing paragraph to call attention to how—and how much—Adrienne Rich's stance as a poet has differed from hers. "Making you

From *I Made You to Find Me: The Coming of Age of the Woman Poet and the Politics of Poetic Address*, pp. 48–70, 159–63. Copyright © 2009 by The Ohio State University.

191

to find me" is a strategy Rich has always found troubling, in both its political and its ethical dimension. Her resistance to this strategy is of a piece with her aversion to the confessional mode; in explaining the one, I will also be exploring the other.[1]

Making "you" to find "me" is of course what lyric poets are very often up to: Shakespeare in his sonnets, urging that "My glass shall not persuade me I am old, / As long as youth and thou are of one date";[2] Wordsworth conjuring up his sister to be his alter ego and soulmate in "Tintern Abbey"; Keats in colloquy with a nightingale or a Grecian urn. Indeed, the figure of apostrophe is one of the most obvious ways for a lyric poet to establish his or her orientation or stance, vis-à-vis both an audience of contemporaries and a prior tradition of poetic discourse. Apostrophizing his beloved as "Stella" in a love sonnet sequence at the end of the sixteenth century, Sir Philip Sidney signals to his readers that in spite of his claim to be a thoroughly modern lover, he and the lady will be found to be playing predictable roles. Apostrophizing the "wild west wind," Percy Bysshe Shelley lays claim to the traditional role of poet as prophet, but with a difference that has become a canonical marker of British Romanticism: his designated interlocutor is a force of nature rather than God or a god. Apostrophizing a sea rose, "harsh and with stint of petals," H. D. makes her poetic début early in the twentieth century by speaking as only poets speak while adding an exotic new species to the traditional garden of poetic flowers.

The Confessional poets reinvigorated this quintessentially poetic figure by using it to suture their poems to their own personal lives. By calling on specific real people, dead or living, they abrogated the distinction between poet and speaker that had become a fixed canon of both Modernist poetics and the New Criticism.[3] You would learn from Lowell's *Life Studies* what private endearments he used with his wife; from Sexton's poems, the names of her two young daughters. Throughout her career, Rich has also sought to place herself in dialogue with others, "not somewhere else but here."[4] And yet she has always worried about the potential for misusing the other that this kind of interlocutory setup carries. From Rich's perspective, misuse of the other is a misuse of the power a poet wields in the world, which includes the prerogative of bearing witness for others.[5]

In Sexton's poems an aggressively vulnerable female speaker is ready to disclose more about herself than her interlocutor, often a man, has bargained for or can handle. Rich, from the beginning of her career, has striven for a different kind of interlocutory relationship both to the reader of her poems and to significant others within them. She has avoided the scandalous intimacy of the confessional, trying instead for an interlocutory relationship that is more truly a dialogue, an exercise in "trying to talk with" someone else.[6] If Sexton is a poet of intimacy, Rich has been and remains a poet of reciprocity: instead of making "you" to find "me" in her poems, she has always been interested in making "you" to find "we."

But this too is risky business, both politically and rhetorically. If, for instance, I were to tell "your" story for you, as Rich tried to do in an anti-Confessional poem that notoriously misfired, I might replicate and reinforce your experience of disempowerment. "And so," as Rich would ruefully acknowledge in 1984 in her "Notes toward a Politics of Location," "even ordinary pronouns become a political problem": to assert that the personal is political is not to solve the problem of what your experience has to do with me, or mine with you.[7]

* * *

After Sexton committed suicide in 1974, Rich delivered a memorial tribute at City College in New York whose purpose was only partly to honor a sister poet's memory; the occasion also presented itself as an opportunity for damage control. "I wanted," she explains in the headnote she subsequently published with this piece, "to speak to the question of identification which a suicide always arouses."[8] Sylvia Plath's suicide a decade earlier had produced what Rich describes as "an imaginative obsession with victimization and death" on the part of other young women poets. Sexton, who had been Plath's friend and a fellow student in Robert Lowell's poetry class, could almost be said to have sponsored that obsession. In "Sylvia's Death," her unconventional elegy for Plath, she speaks as a frustrated rival who has experienced, "at the news of your death / a terrible taste for it, like salt."[9] Rich's memorial for Sexton had a twofold purpose: to bear witness, in Sexton's name but in spite of her example, for life against death; and to put Sexton's equivocal legacy into perspective for a women's community she describes in this headnote as having been "still-tenuous" in 1974. Rich had published *Diving into the Wreck* the previous year, and her tribute to Sexton is thematically and rhetorically akin to the poems in that volume. "I think of Anne Sexton," she says to her protofeminist audience, "as a sister whose work tells us what we have to fight, in ourselves and in the images patriarchy has held up to us. Her poetry is a guide to the ruins, from which we learn what women have lived and what we must refuse to live any longer" (*OLSS*, 123).

Would Sexton have agreed with this characterization of her work? Many of her poems suggest that she would have. In "Her Kind," which she often used to begin poetry readings, she takes on the persona of a condemned witch on her way to be tortured and burned at the stake.[10] In a satiric epigram entitled "Housewife" she distills the gist of *The Feminine Mystique*, a book we know she had read and discussed with Tillie Olsen and other women colleagues at the Radcliffe Institute.[11] A more sustained instance of "tell[ing] us what we have to fight" is her 1971 *Transformations* sequence, a volume of poems that recast Grimm's fairy tales with what Maxine Kumin describes as "a society-mocking overlay."[12]

Even in that sequence, however, Sexton's confessional imperative resists assimilation into the agenda of the satirist and social critic. In quasi-autobiographical forewords that frame each tale, the voice of the storyteller, a "middle-aged witch" who is a canny satirist of contemporary social mores, keeps giving way to the vulnerable, self-involved confessional speaker more familiar from Sexton's first published volume, who suffers from reminiscences and can tell us what's on her mind but not what it means. In the last of these "transformed" tales, the distinction between the storyteller and the story's protagonist also breaks down. After her story is officially over and she is supposed to be living happily ever after with a handsome prince, we hear Briar Rose—or is it Anne Sexton—speaking as if from the psychiatrist's couch, confessing that she was sexually molested by her father as a child.[13] The voice of the storyteller as middle-aged witch does not return at that point to close the book she had opened in the first poem of the sequence.[14] The sequence as a whole thus contrives to leave us with the thought that it is the poet's task to "enquire further" without attempting a self-diagnosis. "If we understood ourselves we might stop writing poems and become critics," is how Sexton justified the open-endedness of her confessional strategy for an audience of academic critics in 1962.[15]

Confessional poetry puts the onus on its readers to spell out the larger implications of its autobiographical disclosures. That is one of the ways this poetry draws us in, by inducing us to derive a fuller or at least a different meaning from the poet-speaker's experience than she or he is in a position to do. This was also Robert Lowell's premise, but Lowell contrived to have it both ways, rejoining his readers on the other side of the confessional relationship he himself had crafted. The poems in *Life Studies*, even as they tell us with disarming candor what it is like to be Robert Lowell, are always also contriving to remind us that they are poems. Their language is shot through with subtle allusions to earlier poetry: Lowell will shift into the cadence of a poem by Donne or Marvell or Shakespeare and then back into a contemporary vernacular register within a single sentence or line.[16] As confessant he is thus so apparently also a poet that readers are likely to credit him with having precisely calculated the implications and consequences of "Robert Lowell's" psychic vagaries. For a poet who did not have Lowell's public stature, or who was not as well versed in the canonical tradition of Anglo-American poetry, this sleight of craft was both harder to manage and less certain to be credited. Coming from a woman poet, confessional writing was more likely to be construed as a compulsion to be talking about herself or a simple inability to keep her own psychological house in order. One reason Rich found the confessional mode uncongenial, even at the height of its popularity, is that she was unwilling to put her readers in a position to understand her better than she understood herself.

Rich was also unwilling to cater to readers' voyeuristic avidity for access to unlovely places in her own life and psyche. In projects of intimate self-disclosure such as the Confessional poets had undertaken, you run the risk of having sensationalized the personal instead of politicizing it. If you are a woman, you will scarcely avoid playing into the conventional expectation that this is just what you meant to do. Both Sexton's poetry and her way of performing her poems gave her the reputation of an audience junkie, a woman who exposes herself compulsively to get the public attention she both fears and craves. Sylvia Plath produced an angry parody of "a woman like that" in "Lady Lazarus," whose speaker contemptuously performs the ultimate strip-tease for a "peanut-crunching crowd."[17]

At the City College memorial for Sexton, Rich refers directly to only one of Sexton's poems, and she has chosen it carefully. "Little Girl, My Stringbean, My Lovely Woman" is a poem in which Sexton greets her own daughter's newly emerging womanhood, urging her to embrace her body's capacity for giving and taking sexual pleasure. Sexton had written the poem as a birthday present for her elder daughter on Linda's eleventh birthday, and she often performed it at readings.[18] Rich recalls not only the poem but also the occasion on which she and many other poets heard it first, a "read-in" at Harvard against the Vietnam War. Rich credits Sexton with having precisely calculated the political impact of her own performance on that occasion in 1966. "Famous male poets and novelists were there," she remembers, "reading their diatribes against McNamara, their napalm poems, their ego-poetry. Anne read [her poem] in a very quiet, vulnerable voice . . . setting the image of a mother's affirmation of her daughter against [these] second-hand images of death and violence . . ." (*OLSS*, 121). In an interview with Sexton's biographer Diane Middlebrook several years later, Rich would recall that Sexton's reading "made people rather uncomfortable, but she was completely self-possessed."[19]

We know from Sexton herself that she chose "Little Girl, My String-bean" for the Harvard reading *faute de mieux*: protest poetry, as far as she knew, was beyond her. She was opposed to the Vietnam War, but "caring," as she said to Lois Ames in 1968, was not "the same as good writing."[20] To another interlocutor cited in Middlebrook's biography she observed that she was "not a political poet . . . not even a very social one. I just do my thing and it's very personal."[21] What Rich is suggesting, however, is that she often contrived to make the personal political. In her tribute Rich credits Sexton with having broken the silence concerning much that was difficult and painful in women's experience "long before such themes became validated by a collective consciousness of women, and while writing and publishing under the scrutiny of the male literary establishment" (*OLSS*, 121). What she depicts her doing at Harvard is braving that establishment to assert the power and priority of a woman's words and to insist that even (or perhaps especially) in a time of war, women need to be minding their *own* business, that of helping one another to flourish. By transposing that business from the domestic to the political arena, Sexton created a space for the personal that was within but at odds with the public sphere. Her performance was "so out of kilter with the occasion in one sense," as Rich would recall for Diane Middlebrook, "and in another sense so completely the right thing" (Middlebrook, 296).

The woman who speaks in "Little Girl, My Stringbean" is very conspicuously not "trying to talk with a man."[22] The poem stages an intimate mother-to-daughter conversation about "the facts of life": its "you" is reaching out toward a protofeminist "we." Remembering how it felt to be her daughter's age, the poem's speaker hears, "as in a dream / the conversation of the old wives / speaking of *womanhood*." They are not speaking to her, or including her in their conversation: "I was alone. / I waited like a target" (*The Complete Poems*, 146). As her daughter enters this danger zone, she is committed to helping her cross over into womanhood with greater knowledge and confidence. At "high noon," she tells eleven-year-old Linda, "men bare to the waist, young Romans," will arrive to lay siege to her body; in anticipation of that moment, she asserts the temporal and ontological priority of their relationship to each other:

> But before they enter
> I will have said,
> *Your bones are lovely*,
> and before their strange hands
> there was always this hand that formed. (*CP*, 147)

In this context the power to shape a woman's identity belongs to another woman—specifically, to her *words*. "Women," the poem's speaker tells her daughter, "are born twice": the poem becomes in effect a second womb, where the mother-poet can keep her daughter safe from being manhandled until she has become sufficiently *self*-possessed.

"Little Girl, My Stringbean" is not a confessional poem in the usual sense. Middlebrook does, however, find traces in the poem's rhetoric of erotic feelings for Linda that were a legacy of Sexton's own troubled adolescence. Outside the poem, according to Linda's recollections, her mother had not managed to resolve those feelings: she was still coming to Linda's bed to "cuddle" when she couldn't sleep. Certain "odd emphases" in the poem seem to Middlebrook to be "hold[ing] at bay the shame of incest that occupied neighboring circuitry in the poet's brain...." Middlebrook avers that many readers have nevertheless found the poem "touching and successful, partly because of its theme of a mother's protective pride in her daughter's sexual budding" (Middlebrook, 223). Perhaps the poem is touching and successful precisely insofar as its work of sublimation has not been fully achieved. Its mother-speaker is close kin to the destructively possessive Mother Gothel, a malign but finally pathetic figure in Sexton's tale of Rapunzel, as well as to the wicked queen in her version of "Snow White." Is "Little Girl, My Stringbean" a memorable poem because it betrays the inseparability of maternal protective pride from feelings of rivalry and sexual possessiveness? Such a question is in the spirit of Sexton's insistence in "For John, Who Begs Me Not to Enquire Further" that "this is something I would never find / in a lovelier place, my dear," and that "the worst of anyone / can be, finally, / an accident of hope" (*The Complete Poems*, 34–35).

Rich herself was beginning at the time of the Sexton memorial to explore the "incestuous" bond between mothers and daughters from a self-consciously feminist perspective. Both in poems and in her polemical prose between 1975 and 1985 she would undertake to re-present that bond as the basis of a woman-identified female eroticism. In "Sibling Mysteries" in 1976 she would argue that "the daughters were to begin with / brides of the mother" and would ask her own sister, in a strikingly transgressive apostrophe, to "hold me, remind me / of how her woman's flesh was made taboo to us."[23] But as empathetic as she may have been with Sexton's effort to engage with taboo feelings and make, as it were, a gift of them to her daughter, Rich was acutely conscious in the wake of Sexton's suicide that the traditionally female virtue of empathy could also be a trap. She exhorts her audience of women not to empathize with Sexton's death wish—or at least not to do so uncritically. "Her death is an arrest," she tells them: "in its moment we have all been held, momentarily, in the grip of a policeman who tells us we are guilty of being female, and powerless" (*OLSS*, 123).

* * *

Rich's play on two different meanings of the word "arrest," as well as her invocation of "a policeman who tells us we are guilty of being female," recalls her 1972 poem "Rape," in which "a cop who is both prowler and father" compounds the victimization of the woman who has to "confess" to him that she has been raped. In this poem Rich made an interesting but not wholly successful attempt to construct a stance of identification or of empathy that would represent a feminist alternative to the confessional mode:

> There is a cop you call both prowler and father:
> he comes from your block, grew up with your brothers,
> had certain ideals.
> You hardly know him in his boots and silver badge,
> on horseback, one hand touching his gun.
> You hardly know him but you have to get to know him:
> he has access to machinery that could kill you.
> . . .
> And so, when the time comes, you have to turn to him,
> the maniac's sperm still greasing your thighs,
> your mind whirling like crazy. You have to confess
> to him, you are guilty of the crime
> of having been forced.[24]

This poem achieved a certain notoriety through getting roundly denounced by influential critics. Helen Vendler, in 1980, deplored its "incrimination of all men . . . in the portrait of this rapist supercop." Cary Nelson, in *Our Last First Poets*, was more sympathetic with Rich's feminist project but agreed with Vendler that the poem is "one-dimensionally didactic" and fails to speak to its historical moment in a compelling way.[25] For Nelson, "Rape" became an object lesson in how difficult it is to write successful poems that are politically engaged; his discussion includes an attempt to figure out how a better poem on this subject might have been written.

It would have been more convincing, Nelson suggests, "[h]ad Rich been able imaginatively to enter the experience of her protagonist"; but he doubts "that she really wanted to share the consciousness" of the woman whose experience her poem so unsparingly narrates in second-person voice (*Our Last First Poets*, 152). His most important piece of internal evidence for this is the poem's strategy of address. Third person, he suggests, would have given the poet-speaker room to explore her own thoughts and feelings and make them part of the poem; second-person voice has the effect of "distancing [her] from her subject." "This remains true," Nelson insists, "whether we view the 'you' of the poem as addressed to another woman or to Rich's uncertainty about what her own reactions might be in similar circumstances." The poem ends with what Nelson characterizes as a "harsh interrogation" of its protagonist: "The poet also has access to machinery—" he drily observes, "rhetorical machinery—and she is not willing to abjure its use" (ibid., 151). From this perspective other rhetorical strategies can also be seen to have turned against the woman whose terror and helplessness they were presumably intended to dramatize. Thus, for example, Nelson finds the repetitions deployed in the poem's last two stanzas to convey that "an inexorable fascist bureaucracy [is] closing in on the woman" becoming, ironically enough, its poetic equivalent or counterpart: "He knows, or thinks he knows, how much you imagined; / he knows, or thinks he knows, what you secretly wanted."

The critic thinks he knows what the poet secretly wanted: to think of rape as the kind of thing that happens to *other* women. If that is the case, then her attitude toward the poem's protagonist is more complicated than her rhetorical posture has allowed her to acknowledge. Nelson would like there to be an "I" in the poem who would make "more conscious use of the full range of feelings present in the writing situation"[26] so that her own fears and desires could be acknowledged and figured into her treatment of the other woman's predicament. Uncertainty about what her reactions might be in similar circumstances could then become part of the poem's fabric, unsettling its rhetorical "complacency."

For the author of *Our Last First Poets*—and he is by no means alone in asking for this—good political poetry is thus always to some degree confessional.[27] In his introductory chapter, in which poetry written to protest U.S. involvement in the Vietnam War is his testing ground for the problems and possibilities of American political poetry, Nelson finds that the most successful poems are those whose speakers' relationship to their government's role in Vietnam is one of "ambiguous complicity" (ibid., 30). This, he suggests, is the most authentic relationship that can obtain between the personal and the political, because it enables the poet to bear witness to the present moment "without falsely mastering it"—without, that is, exempting him- or herself from its historical pressures (ibid., 25). But Nelson's reading of this poem underestimates Rich's determination to find alternatives to the kind of empathy that confessional writing both elicits and deploys. A confessional stance would put the poem's speaker at her reader's mercy, authorizing "him" to know her better than she knows herself. In this poem Rich was experimenting with an interlocutory strategy that would instead achieve some of the detachment and inclusiveness of "we"—writing, but in a vernacular register that is often, outside of poems, a marker of both intimacy and solidarity.

Second-person voice implies that you and your conversation partner share a common vantage point. Like the first-person plural, it has the potential to open up a poem's narrative subject-position to the reader—but only to readers who are eligible to be in "your" situation or willing to walk a mile in "your" shoes. It would be difficult for a reader who is male to project himself either into this poem's narrative subject-position or into that of its addressee; second-person voice creates a subjective standpoint that is specifically female for a poem whose subject is the political implications of women's subjective experience. In speeches and polemical essays during the 1970s Rich often spoke about how hard it is for women to put themselves at the center of their own experience, given the history we have learned and the language in which we are immersed, with its pseudogeneric "he" and its supposedly gender-indifferent concepts like "spokesman" and "my fellow Americans."[28] In "Rape" she was using second-person voice to foster unaccustomed habits of group identification among women, so that a feminist "we," a "collective consciousness of women," could begin to be forged.

In the Sexton memorial we find Rich cautioning her female audience against a self-destructive tendency she calls "misplaced compassion," citing "a woman I know [who] was recently raped" and whose "first—and typi-cal—instinct was to feel sorry for the rapist." Only when our first impulse is one of "compassion for ourselves and each other," she admonishes her female audience, will we "begin to be immune to suicide" (*OLSS*, 122). In "Rape" she has ensured that there be no question of feeling sorry for the rapist, who has been kept out of the poem except for its reference to "the maniac's sperm still greasing your thighs." But compassion for ourselves and each other could also be counterproductive: what if it only served to exacerbate our collective sense of helplessness? Rich was trying in "Rape" for a stance of compassion that would not be misplaced in the sense of spending itself in fellow feeling or complicity:

> and if, in the sickening light of the precinct,
> and if, in the sickening light of the precinct,
> your details sound like a portrait of your confessor,
> will you swallow, will you deny them, will you lie your way home?

The rhetorical strategy Nelson thinks is enabling her to talk down to her poem's protagonist is one that aimed to achieve both empathy and detach-ment—empathy with a rape victim's paralyzing terror, detachment enough to draw out its larger political implications. It was a strategy that promised to open up for women a space of identification with one another's experience in which something like consciousness-raising could occur.[29]

The poem's rhetorical strategy is, however, flawed by a crucial miscal-culation, as Rich herself would come to realize. The premise of its use of second-person voice is that every woman's vulnerability to rape affords a common vantage point from which to grasp the social and political rami-fications of having it happen to "you." But would not factors such as class, ethnicity, and sexual orientation also shape a woman's experience of turning to the police for help in such a crisis? Nelson detects, in the condescension toward her protagonist he imputes to the poem's speaker, "a patronizing sense of class difference" (153); the poem has laid itself open to this charge by implying that the "cop" and the woman who has been raped are from the same Boston Irish neighborhood. If the speaker of the poem is Adrienne Rich, she doesn't come from the same part of town; the only thing she has in common with her protagonist is their gender. Perhaps that was precisely her point: a victim of rape could be any one of us. But what are the political implications of speaking for as well as to your exemplary victim, putting yourself in a position to see the predicament she exemplifies more clearly than she can see it for herself?

Rich's involvement with the women's movement during the 1970s brought her up against these very questions, causing her to become aware in a whole new way of her own "location." In her "Foreword" to *Blood, Bread and Poetry*, in 1985, she recalls that in the early 1970s the consciousness-raising session, "with its emphasis on each woman's individual testimony," was what had enabled "the naming as political of women's personal experiences" (*BBP*, viii). But the passage from individual testimony to feminist consensus, from "I" to "we," turned out to be problematic in ways this model could not address. Rich and other white feminists soon found themselves in dialogue with black feminists who challenged their understanding of both women's oppression and the goals of feminist politics. "To believe that it was right to identify with all women, to wish deeply and sincerely to do so, was not enough" (*BBP*, x). In the early 1980s Rich therefore began to dissociate herself from both the radical feminist claim that "patriarchy" is the primary form of human oppression and the corollary claim that false consciousness is the chief obstacle to feminist consensus. The radical feminist obsession with "male evil and female victimization" was itself, she began to think, a characteristically North American form of false consciousness, fostered by the antihistorical bias of the Cold War period.[30] It was also a product of white women's failure to notice their own race and class privilege.

In "Notes toward a Politics of Location," a set of reflections she delivered as a talk several times in Europe and the United States during 1984, Rich faced up to a new set of questions about the bearing of the personal upon the political:

> *The difficulty of saying I*—a phrase from the East German novelist Christa Wolf. But once having said it, as we realize the necessity to go further, isn't there a difficulty of saying "we"? *You cannot speak for me. I cannot speak for us.* Two thoughts: there is no liberation that

only knows how to say "I"; there is no collective movement that speaks for each of us all the way through. (*BBP*, 224)

From this perspective, the mistake she had made in "Rape" was in assuming too easily that she, her female protagonist, and her women readers could share a common vantage point. Her use of second-person voice had entailed a too-simple vision of feminist solidarity.

*   *   *

In a 1980 poem entitled "Frame," Rich did find a way to speak out on another woman's behalf without speaking "for" her in a too-simple way.[31] Once again this poem accuses the Boston police of misusing their powers of law enforcement, but this time the racial status of their victim is at issue along with her gender. The poem was inspired by what actually happened in 1979 to a black student at Boston University who went inside a university building in bad weather to wait for her bus, and ended up in jail.[32] By the end of Rich's poem its protagonist has been "framed" in several senses: by a building custodian who calls the police to arrest her for trespassing; by the police whose harsh treatment goads her into behavior that gets her charged with assault and battery; by the university teachers she is thinking about as the poem begins, who seem unable to see her in the light of her own ambitions and talents; and last but not least, by the poem's camera eye and the poet's act of witness.

This time the police force has not been personified in a single, typical "cop," nor is the poem's central episode an instance of "male evil and female victimization": it is an instance of law enforcement officers behaving as if any black person were a potentially dangerous criminal. The poem's feminist intervention is in the spirit of Rich's reminder in "Blood, Bread and Poetry" that "most women in the world must fight for their lives on many fronts at once" (*BBP*, 218). The issue it raises is not "what are a woman's choices under these circumstances?" or "will you finally acquiesce in your own oppression?" This protagonist's impulse to *resist* oppression is what gets her into trouble, both when a building watchman orders her to "move on" and when she sinks her teeth into the hand of a policeman who has sprayed her in the eyes with Mace.

The poem's narrative is in the third person, but not as a way for Rich to discover and project her own inwardness, the advantage Cary Nelson gave to third-person over second-person writing. Instead, this poem uses third-person voice to tell another woman's story from the other woman's perspective. The narrator filters everything that happens through her protagonist's consciousness: instead of telling us she is black, for example, she identifies everyone else as white. Meanwhile, however, she keeps interrupting her own third-person narrative with italicized first-person passages that call attention to her own location "just outside the frame." "*I don't know her,*" reads the first of these passages; "*I am standing though somewhere just outside the frame / of all this, trying to see*" (*FD* 2002, 188). These "I"-voiced passages serve both to locate the narrative vantage point and to insist on its limitations. In this way the poem's rhetorical strategy is self-problematizing: the poet-narrator acknowledges repeatedly that she is describing events she could not possibly have witnessed.[33] Indeed, her claim is that she is "*not supposed to be present*" when such things happen; for that very reason, however, she needs to be present. "This is Boston 1979": her readers need to know that in a major American city in 1979 it was still not possible for a black woman to go inside a public building for shelter from the weather without getting herself incarcerated.

To underscore the urgency, the imaginative difficulty, and the legally problematic status of this act of witness, the poem's narrator-speaker asserts repeatedly that although she can see what is happening from "*just outside the frame of this action,*" she cannot hear anything:

> . . . . the handcuffs are on her
> wrists he is throwing her down his knee has gone into her breast
> he is
> dragging her down the stairs *I am unable*
> *to hear a sound of all this all that I know is what*
> *I can see from this position there is no soundtrack*
> *to go with this and I understand at once*
> *it is meant to be in silence that this happens* (*FD* 2002, 188–99)

The poem's last three lines play off the past tense of ordinary narrative against the present tense that is a poet's special prerogative, calling attention to a difference that cuts both ways between literal and figurative witness, ordinary watching and poetic vision:

> . . . . . *What I am telling you*
> *is told by a white woman who they will say*
> *was never there. I say I am there.* (*FD* 2002, 189)

Rich deploys the pronoun "you" only once in the entire poem, to emphasize that her readers share her privileged status relative to the events it documents. It is as if we had been watching a soundless newsreel with a super-added soundtrack that calls attention to our collective status as a viewing public. In a revisionary echo of Walt Whitman's "I am the man, I suffered, I was there," the poem associates its project with Whitman's expansive vision of a nation that draws its strength from difference. But the American poet who says "I am there" in 1979 finds it impossible to share her precursor's utopian optimism. Her way of constructing her own poetic location within the poem calls attention to both the impossibility and the necessity of "being there" for one another as fellow Americans, leaving us with a political conundrum and, on another level, a manifesto for political poetry.[34]

*   *   *

In the twenty-five years since this poem was published, Rich has often urged her readers to think about the political status of poems and of the institution of poetry more broadly considered. In the leadoff poem in *Dark Fields of the Republic*, a poem entitled "What Kind of Times Are These," she presumes we think that poetry is not, or should not be, "political." This 1991 poem takes its title from a poem of Bertolt Brecht's that asks, "What kind of times are these / When it's almost a crime to talk about trees / Because it means keeping still about so many evil deeds?"[35] The opening lines of Rich's poem take us to "a place between two stands of trees," a "ghost-ridden crossroads" where "the old revolutionary road breaks off into shadows / near a meeting-house abandoned by the persecuted / who disappeared into those shadows." The poem's speaker hints at evil deeds associated with the place, both past and present, but flatly and repeatedly refuses to "tell you where it is." In the poem's final stanza she poses the question its readers may well have been goaded to ask by her truculence and air of mystery: " . . . so why do I tell you / anything?" and explains that it's "because in times like these / to have you listen at all, it's necessary / to talk about trees" (*FD* 2002, 253). As the first poem in the volume, "What Kind of Times are These" puts us on notice that, as Cary Nelson might have put it, Rich has access to rhetorical machinery whose use she is by no means willing to abjure. She does presume to know what we secretly or not so secretly want from a poem, and has written a poem that won't let us have it; she would rather challenge than flatter us. The relationship this poem constructs with its readers is risky, from the poet's point of view: she is willing to alienate potential readers of the volume, yet makes no secret of her desire to be heard, to be read.

In *What Is Found There* (1993), an interconnected sequence of reflections on the relationship between poetry and politics, Rich deplores the way in which we have been educated "to inspect the poem at arm's length" rather than asking what it wants of us.[36] "What Kind of Times are These" actively refuses to lend itself to such a reading. Its refusal complicates the project of making "you" to find "we," but in a way that is very much in keeping with that project, by provoking a response that unsettles readerly complacency. My immediate response to this strategy is to resent the poet's presumption that she knows who I am and what I want from a poem. On second thought, I recognize that this resentment has made me more aware of my own social and psychic "location" than I was before. Something like this happens again for a reader like me vis-à-vis the final section of "An Atlas of the Difficult World," the section entitled "Dedications."... "I know you are reading this poem," its speaker keeps saying, and she is right, of course, I *am* reading this poem, and yet I do not find myself among the hypothetical readers whose many different locations are mapped by its litany of reader-apostrophes. One of the most important differences between us is that I have more time to read poetry: I do it for a living. By putting readers like me on the defensive, Rich refuses to let the "verbal privilege" we have in common give us an unexamined sense of entitlement to be "the reader" to whom her poem is addressed.[37]

*   *   *

Making "you" to find "we" has been crucial for Rich as a poet ever since she first began to be one. In her "Foreword" to *The Fact of a Doorframe* in 1984 she explains that her "worst fear" in writing poetry has always been "that the walls cannot be broken down, that these words will fail to enter another soul" (*FD* 1984, xv). This formulation evokes a Romantic stereotype of the poet's calling: to have their words enter another soul was also Shelley's desire, and Emerson's. Rich goes on to explain, however, that she "never had much belief" in the notion of the poet as "someone of special sensitivity or spiritual insight, who rightfully lives above and off from the ordinary general life." Instead, her desire to be heard has entailed "hearing and listening to others, taking into myself the language of experience different from my own . . ." (ibid., xv–xvi). And thus she disavows the Romanticist idea of the poet as lonely seer and prophet, in favor of an explicitly social and dialogical conception of poethood.[38] With this conception of the poet's calling comes another set of reasons for avoiding a confessional stance. Like Rich, the Confessional poets were committed to "hearing and listening to others" in their poems and to taking up a vantage point that was not "above and off from" the domain of ordinary domestic and social life. But Rich parted company with Sexton and especially with Lowell over the way in which Confessional poetry seemed bent on trafficking in the personal for its own sake—and in so doing, as Lowell would infamously acknowledge, "not avoiding injury to others."

Rich admired Lowell's poetry in the 1960s, both for its political engagement and for its firm purchase on a particular historical and social location.
From *Life Studies* onward, Lowell's poetic vantage point was unmistakably
local—strongly gendered, redolent of a particular class location, rooted in
the history of the Lowell family of Boston, Massachusetts. As we have seen,
in his poems he put traditional poetic devices to fresh uses; in particular, he
gave the poetic device of apostrophe a new lease on life. Lowell liked to ven-
triloquize significant others, speaking for them in words that vividly captured
their foibles and eccentricities; in a poem of Lowell's the reader was to believe
he was getting not only "the real Robert Lowell" but also the real Hart Crane,
the real Elizabeth Hardwick.[39] But when Lowell published *The Dolphin* in
1973, Rich found that he had purchased this capacity for dialogue at too high
a price. In a sequence of love poems to his third wife, Lowell quoted verbatim
from letters in which his second wife rages and pleads with him to come back
to her. In her review of *The Dolphin*, Rich accused him of "one of the most
vindictive and mean-spirited acts in the history of poetry" and found "the
same unproportioned ego that was capable of this act [to be] damagingly at
work" in his entire body of work since *For the Union Dead*.[40]

Anticipating this kind of reaction from readers of *The Dolphin*, Lowell
acknowledges in the sequence's final poem that he has

> ... plotted perhaps too freely with my life,
> not avoiding injury to others,
> not avoiding injury to myself—
> to ask compassion. . . . [41]

"I have to say," Rich wrote in response to this passage, "that I think this
is bullshit eloquence . . . that it is presumptuous to balance injury done to
others with injury done to oneself—and that the question remains, after
all—to what purpose?"[42] Both at the time and since, other poets and
critics accused her of speaking as a radical feminist rather than as a poet
in passing this judgment. Diane Wakoski pointed out that whenever you
address or quote someone in a poem, you are recreating them as a fictional
character: this is not the real Elizabeth Hardwick, even if we admire the
poet's ability to make us believe that it could be.[43] Richard Tillinghast
argued, in extenuation of Lowell's cruelty to "Lizzie," that it sprang not
from vindictiveness but from the "colossal thoughtlessness" of a poet who
needed to bring other people into his poems to mitigate the solipsism of
the confessional mode.[44]

... Lowell had a different motive for the cross-gender ventriloquism
he began to engage in as early as *The Mills of the Kavanaughs*: I think it

stems from his propensity to envision the domestic arena as a battleground upon which words are weapons and women do most of the talking. But what is most revealing of Rich's orientation, before as well as after she began to be a radical feminist, is that for her "the question remains, after all—to what purpose?" Implicit in this question is the belief that ethical issues cannot be bracketed to arrive at a judgment of the poetry as such. Poets should have a purpose beyond self-disclosure in seeking and claiming our attention: that assumption is a hallmark and also a limitation of Rich's anti-Confessional stance.

When Rich conjures up a significant other to speak to in a poem, her apostrophe is often accompanied by an apology or a self-reflexive critique of the gesture itself on ethical grounds. "The living, writers especially, are terrible projectionists. I hate the way they use the dead," she says to her dead husband in "Sources," explaining that for ten years since his suicide she has avoided "writing to you as if you could hear me."[45] In one of her "Twenty-One Love Poems" she wonders whether in trying to "create [her lover] in words" she is "simply using you, like a river or a war?"[46] In a more recent love poem she has her lover look over her shoulder "at this page and say / *"It's all about you None of this tells my story.*"[47] In the only poem I know of that is addressed to one of her children,[48] her explicit subject is a child's and a mother's reciprocal need to invent the other for the convenience of the self. Looking at a thirteen-year-old snapshot of her son, she confesses that

> I wanted this from you—
> laughter   a child turning
> into a boy   at ease
> in the spring light   with friends
> I wanted this for you

The difference between "for you" and "from you" catches this mother in the act of confusing her own needs with her child's. Speaking to the adult he has by now become, she speculates that his vision of her had been the need-driven obverse of hers:

> Did you think I was all-powerful
> unimpaired   unappalled?
> Yes, you needed that from me
> I wanted this from you

Her confession of maternal narcissism is akin to Sexton's at the end of "The Double Image," especially if the word "this," which is also the poem's title, refers to the poem as well as the carefree childhood its snapshot seems to capture.[49] But the difference between this poem's project and that of a typical domestic poem of Lowell's or Sexton's is even more striking. Rich has waited to speak to her son in a poem until she can engage with him as an equal in dialogue, and the poem is strongly if tacitly protective of the family history they share with one another. If we know that Rich left her marriage shortly after this snapshot was taken and that the boy's father committed suicide, it's not from the poem that we know these things.

Rich has often claimed that her poems teach her things she did not yet know about herself;[50] and yet she has been largely unwilling to publish poems that neither harvest the political implications of their autobiographical disclosures nor instruct their readers in how to do so. A good example of her unwillingness to engage in "purposeless" self-disclosure, even when that is what the poem itself seems to call for, is a 1979 poem entitled "For Memory." This poem's speaker is mentally renewing a long-distance conversation with her lover that broke off angrily some days or hours earlier. Seeking to heal the breach between them, she urges that beyond the anger and recrimination that have temporarily estranged them ("I hear your voice: *disloyalty betrayal* / *stinging the wires*") lies the task of continuing to explain to each other how they have come to see the world differently.

> I fell through a basement railing
> the first day of school and cut my forehead open—
> did I ever tell you? more than forty years
> and I still remember smelling my own blood
> like the smell of a new schoolbook
>
> And did you ever tell me
> how your mother called you in from play
> and from whom? To what?[51]

The ordinariness—triviality, even—of the memories she offers to exchange are what struck me my first time through this poem: for whom but oneself and one's lover would such things count as memorable? "Ah, yes," I said to myself, "what keeps our most intimate relationships going is not our allegiance to abstract ethical notions like 'trust' or 'fidelity' but the sense of a shared past we create for each other by recalling events like these." But the longer I sat with the poem's analogy between the smell of "my own blood" and the smell of a new schoolbook, the more it began to savor of feminist apologetics. In her foreword to *The Fact of a Doorframe* Rich explains that "one task for the nineteen- or twenty-year-old poet who wrote the earliest poems here was to learn that she was . . . a white and also Jewish inheritor of a particular Western consciousness, from the making of which most women have been excluded" (*FD* 1984, xv). Her first day at school would be the day she came into her birthright as an inheritor of that consciousness, a patriarchal inheritance delivered by the "new schoolbook[s]" whose smell she associates with "smelling my own blood." And thus an act of remembering whose ostensible purpose is to summon up her childhood in all of its inconsequent particularity begins to look politically motivated to a degree that undermines that very purpose. For whom but another radical feminist would getting your first schoolbooks be like getting your forehead cut open?

Rich has written a few poems that are confessional in the fullest sense: their process of autobiographical inquiry is inconclusive, attaching a higher priority to self-knowledge than to self-mastery or self-judgment. "A Woman Dead in her Forties," dated 1974–77, is such a poem. It is also a poem that, in making "you" to find "me," risks harm to the interlocutor it summons back from the dead. She died of breast cancer, and the poem's act of mourning is transgressive on several levels: against canons of female beauty but also of female modesty; against giving love and loyalty to another woman via overtly physical expression; against owning up to grief's unlovely complexity, its component of anger toward the one who has died. The reason the poem's speaker gives for bringing her friend back to speak to is that she can't stop dreaming about her: "Of all my dead," she tells her, "it's you / who come to me unfinished" (*FD* 2002, 158). The poem makes an effort to bring their relationship to closure by speaking to her friend of things that went unspoken between them while she was alive: "In plain language: I never told you how I loved you / we never talked at your deathbed of your death" (*FD* 2002, 159). The poem succeeds by failing, since in telling her friend both how much and in what way she loved her, the poet discovers feelings that cannot be summed up in plain language. Their "truth" is complex and many-layered, inextricable from yet irreconcilable with these women's friendship as they actually lived it at a particular moment in the history of same-sex gender relations.

The poem opens with a dream image of "All the women I grew up with" sitting "half-naked on rocks," posed like Sirens with their breasts exposed. Rich "barely glance[s]" at her friend's scarred torso, "as if my look could scald you"; but by averting her eyes she confirms her friend's exclusion from a community of women who "look at each other and / are not ashamed." Her friend then moves to protect her own mutilated body from exposure:

you pull on
your blouse again: stern statement:
There are things I will not share
With everyone (*FD* 2002, 155)

Her friend's wordless statement "send[s] me back to share / my own scars
first of all / with myself." This movement of recoil is emotionally complex,
conveying reproach and self-pity along with acceptance of the imagined
rebuff. It raises questions that go to the heart of the poem's concern with
loyalty and truth-telling: has Rich been loyal or disloyal to her friend in
restraining the impulse "to touch my fingers to where your breasts had
been"; loyal or disloyal in dreaming this dream about her; loyal or disloyal
in publishing it for others to read?

   Jahan Ramazani points out, in discussing this poem as "a radical departure in the history of women's elegies for friends," that the mourner's effort
to "compensate for loving deeds undone and words unspoken" is at the same
time a violation not just of her friend's privacy but of her very selfhood:

   Rich writes poetry for a woman who "never read it much"; she
   speaks to a woman who preferred "mute loyalty"; she presents her
   "passion" to a woman with a "calvinist heritage." "I never told you
   how I loved you," says Rich, but in telling her now, the poet cannot
   help but betray her friend.[52]

The reason Rich was willing to take such a risk is that in this instance her
confession furthers a political project she had already begun to undertake
in speeches and essays during this period—that of gaining visibility for
"lesbian existence." In the feminist journal *Signs*, in 1980, she would urge
feminist scholars to pay more attention to the woman-bonding "that has
run like a continuous though stifled theme" through a historical record
constructed under the aegis of "compulsory heterosexuality." She wanted the
recognition of lesbian existence to become "a politically activating impulse,
not simply a validation of personal lives."[53] One contribution she had already
made to this project was a 1975 essay that rereads the life as well as the
poetry of Emily Dickinson, supplanting the belle of Amherst with a woman
who opted out of marriage for the sake of her writing and whose primary
emotional allegiances were to other women.[54] In the spirit of this commitment to uncovering "lesbian existence," Rich also undertook to revisit relationships of her own that were implicitly or unconsciously sexual.[55] Under
this aegis confession became both an ethically responsible and a politically
necessary activity.

Like "Frame," "A Woman Dead in her Forties" is a politically motivated act of witness. It is also a poem that explores "the full range of feelings present in the writing situation." At all times in this poem its speaker seems aware of her own projectionist tendencies, aware that a dialogue with someone who has died cannot but be an exercise in projection. She transcends the solipsism of such an exercise not through self-conscious critique, as in the poems cited earlier, but through the sheer mnemonic power of sensory experience:

> Wartime. We sit on warm
> weathered, softening grey boards
>
> the ladder glimmers where you told me
> the leeches swim
>
> I smell the flame
> of kerosene   the pine
>
> boards where we sleep side by side
> in narrow cots
>
> the night-meadow exhaling
> its darkness   calling
> child into woman
> child into woman
> woman

These memories are sensually vivid and powerfully specific. Perhaps we could read the "narrow cots" allegorically, but there is a richness and thickness to the language of the entire passage—its pacing slowed by enjambment and internal pauses, its sensory power enhanced through subtle sound—music—that discourages allegorical translation. And indeed, the collective tenor of all these details is what is ineffable in relationships between people and unfathomable in the destiny of each of us: the relationship each of us unconsciously carries in her body to the time and manner of her own death. The poem's final stanza completes its confessional project by making a conscious avowal of feelings that were broached in its opening sequence as a dream-wish: "I would have touched my fingers / to where your breasts had been / but we never did such things." Here again, however, the speaker's motive or purpose in wanting to have touched her friend in this way cannot be fully explicated.[56] The best we can do is to recognize a number of tributaries—sexual longing, sheer physical curiosity, protective tenderness, a desire to share in the other woman's bodily knowledge of her own mortality—that are distinct from and even partly at odds with one another.

Rich's most personal poems often end with the rhetorical gesture of deciding or willing the poem to be as it is.[57] She does this, I think, to affirm that the poem's immersion in personal experience and in relationships with significant others has been purposeful. The last line of her "Twenty-One Love Poems" reads, "I choose to walk here. And to draw this circle" (*FD* 2002, 154). "This circle," a space of allegiance to herself as a woman, is at once her own mind, the city of New York in the late twentieth century, and the poem sequence she has just completed. At the end of "Sources" she commits herself to "knowing the world, and my place in it, not in order to stare with bitterness or detachment, but as a powerful and womanly series of choices."[58] This is reminiscent of Lowell's assertion at the end of *The Dolphin* that his "eyes have seen what my hand did," but Rich's formulation entails the inseparability of eye and hand, existential choice and ethical judgment. The last section of "A Woman Dead in her Forties" also has choice for its theme, but in keeping with its more fully confessional stance the poem ends by transgressing against its own expressed commitments to certainty and closure. Recalling a moment of false epiphany in which "I thought: *I understand / life and death now, the choices*," the speaker finds herself forced to acknowledge that she "didn't know your choice / or how by then you had no choice / how the body tells the truth in its rush of cells" (*FD* 2002, 159). Perhaps she was asking the wrong question in wondering, "How am I true to you?" She has discovered that the truth of a life or a relationship cannot be fully captured in conscious gestures and well-chosen words.

*   *   *

In the opening section of "An Atlas of the Difficult World," Rich salutes the poem's readers with a greeting that emphasizes her commitment to a still-ongoing process of "taking in the language of experience different from my own." "This is no place you ever knew me," she explains: she is living and writing from within two miles of the Pacific Ocean. But if, geographically speaking, "these are not the roads you knew me by," still "the woman driving, walking, watching for life and death, is the same" (*FD* 2002, 234–35). Over a long career spent trying out different strategies of "I–you" engagement Rich has remained a poet for whom poetic challenges are also ethical challenges, for whom the best use of the "verbal privilege" that belongs to poets is to engage with others in figuring out what it means to be living in a particular society at a particular time. In that sense she is engaged in a process of "inquiring further" that cannot come to closure—not because it is typically or essentially a confessional process, but because it is a dialogue with others in which it never will be possible to have the last word.

NOTES

1. *The Fact of a Doorframe: Selected Poems 1950–2001* (New York: W. W. Norton, 2002), hereafter abbreviated *FD* 2002, will be cited where possible for the poems discussed in this chapter. Poems not included in that volume will be cited from *The Fact of a Doorframe: Poems Selected and New 1950–1984* (New York: W. W. Norton, 1984), hereafter abbreviated *FD* 1984, or from *Poems Selected and New, 1950–1974* (New York: W. W. Norton, 1975). Poems not included in any of these collections will be referred to the volume in which they were originally published.

2. These are the first two lines of Shakespeare's sonnet 22.

3. Cf. Stephen Matterson in his essay on *Life Studies* for the Blackwell *Companion to Twentieth-Century Poetry*, ed. Neil Roberts (Oxford: Blackwell, 2001), 482: "Most significantly in terms of the book's immediate influence, these poems came across as naked representations of personal experiences."

4. This is the title Rich gave to the third of the three sections into which *The Dream of a Common Language: Poems 1974–1977* (New York: W. W. Norton, 1978), is divided; it is also the title of the leadoff poem in that section.

5. For a discussion of the issues raised by a feminist stance of witness that is especially attentive to Rich's goals in this regard and to the relationship between witness and consciousness-raising, see Harriet Davidson, "Poetry, Witness, Feminism," in *Witness and Memory: The Discourse of Trauma*, ed. Ana Douglass and Thomas A. Vogler (New York: Routledge, 2003), 153–72.

6. "Trying to Talk with a Man," dated 1971, was published as the leadoff poem in *Diving into the Wreck* in 1973 (*FD* 2002, 93–94).

7. "Notes toward a Politics of Location," *Blood, Bread, and Poetry: Selected Prose 1979–1985* (New York: W. W. Norton, 1986), 224 (hereafter abbreviated *BBP*). In *The Feminist Poetry Movement* (Jackson, Miss.: University Press of Mississippi, 1996), Kim Whitehead thinks through the politics of voice and address in ways I have found helpful, especially in her chapter on Judy Grahn. Other feminist critics who have done valuable work with these issues include Jan Clausen in *A Movement of Poets: Thoughts on Poetry and Feminism* (Brooklyn, N.Y.: Long Haul Press, 1982) and Linda Kinnahan in *Poetics of the Feminine: Authority and Literary Tradition in William Carlos Williams, Mina Loy, Denise Levertov, and Kathleen Fraser* (Cambridge: Cambridge University Press, 1994).

8. Headnote to "Anne Sexton: 1928–1974," in *On Lies, Secrets, and Silence: Selected Prose 1966–1978* (New York: W. W. Norton, 1979), 121 (hereafter cited as *OLSS*).

9. Anne Sexton, *The Complete Poems, with a Foreword by Maxine Kumin* (Boston: Houghton Mifflin, 1981), 127. . . .

10. Sexton, *The Complete Poems*, 15.

11. Sexton, *The Complete Poems*, 77; cf. Diane Wood Middlebrook, *Anne Sexton: A Biography* (Boston: Houghton Mifflin, 1991), 195.

12. Maxine Kumin, "How It Was," in Sexton, *The Complete Poems*, xxviii.

13. *The Complete Poems*, 294–95.

14. Deborah Forbes cites the ending of "Briar Rose" as an example of "the frightening and moving oscillation between poet and persona that makes for [Sexton's] charisma" (149). In *Sincerity's Shadow*, Forbes pairs Sexton and Lord Byron as poets whose "charismatic poetics" refuses to transcend the merely personal, so as to "[imply] that poetry is the irrepressible expression of an unusually intense life" (117).

15. Sexton was the only poet on a panel entitled "The Poet and Extra-literary Criticism" for the New England College English Association in 1962 (cited in Middlebrook, 188).

16. Cf., for example, an apostrophe to Lowell's thirteen-week-old daughter in "Home After Three Months Away" that conjures up the tetrameter couplets of "To His Coy Mistress" to reproach her for "float[ing] my shaving brush / and washcloth in the flush": "Dearest, I cannot loiter here / in lather like a polar bear" (*Collected Poems*, 185).

17. Cf. Plath, "Lady Lazarus," *The Collected Poems*, ed. Ted Hughes (New York: Harper and Row, 1981), 245. "A woman like that" is quoted from "Her Kind" (cf. chapter 1, 35).

18. Middlebrook, 222–23.

19. Interview with Rich, 18 May, 1983, cited in Middlebrook, 296.

20. Letter to Lois Ames dated 30 July, 1968, cited in Middlebrook, 297.

21. A. S. to Joshua Stoller, 25 March, 1970, cited in Middlebrook, 297.

22. Rich's 1971 poem with this title, the leadoff poem in *Diving into the Wreck*, is allegorically situated on a military testing ground (*FD* 2002, 93).

23. Rich, "Sibling Mysteries," *The Dream of a Common Language: Poems 1974–1977* (New York: W. W. Norton, 1978), 52; 49. Cf. "Transcendental Etude," *FD* 1984, 267–68; "Motherhood: The Contemporary Emergency and the Quantum Leap" (1978), *OLSS*, 261; and "Compulsory Heterosexuality and Lesbian Existence" (1980), *BBP*, 32–35.

24. As of the 2002 edition *The Fact of a Doorframe* still includes "Rape" in the selection from *Diving Into the Wreck* that has been chosen to represent this moment in Rich's poetic career. Both Cary Nelson's critique, which I will be citing in some detail, and my own reading of the poem's feminist project can best be weighed by consulting the entire poem at *FD* 2002, 105–6.

25. Helen Vendler, *Part of Nature, Part of Us* (Cambridge, Mass.: Harvard University Press, 1980), 243; Cary Nelson, *Our Last First Poets: Vision and History in Contemporary American Poetry* (Urbana: University of Illinois Press, 1981), 150. Carol Muske recalls in *Women and Poetry: Truth, Autobiography, and the Shape of the Self* (Ann Arbor: University of Michigan Press, 1997) that "Rich was widely attacked by critics" who took the poem to be "an act of linguistic violence against men." Muske argues that "Rich's intent was expository, the revelation of the consciousness of a typical woman, post-sexual trauma" and argues that "statistics bear out [her] portrait of female distrust" (11).

26. Nelson, 153; he is paraphrasing Robert Duncan, whose poetic stance is the subject of *Our Last First Poets'* immediately preceding chapter. The charge of complacency is leveled against Rich's poem on 152.

27. Cf., for example, the study Nelson cites as "an excellent overview of the problems inherent in political poetry" Thomas R. Edwards' *Imagination and Power: A Study of Poetry on Public Themes* (New York: Oxford University Press, 1971) (cf. Nelson 3, n3). Edwards argues that Yeats's most successful political poem, "Easter 1916," "finds its securest note when it confesses insecurity" (197). Praising a 1953

poem of Lowell's in similar terms, Edwards defines "a serious and responsible mind" in this context as "one which takes public actions . . . as imaginative problems demanding a reflective choice of the self one will adopt to meet the public circumstance" (221).

28. Cf. "Toward a Woman-Centered University" (1973–74), in *OLSS*, 125–56, and esp. "Power and Danger: Works of a Common Woman" (1977), which cites "the mere, immense shift from male to female pronouns" as a transformative act that "lets us hear and see our words in a new dimension" (*OLSS*, 248).

29. For an account of consciousness-raising that is attentive both to its importance for second-wave feminism and to its limitations as a strategy for disclosing the political in the personal, see Hester Eisenstein, *Contemporary Feminist Thought* (Boston: G. K. Hall, 1983), 35–44.

30. "Notes Toward a Politics of Location," *BBP*, 221.

31. Roger Gilbert discusses this poem at some length in "Framing Water: Historical Knowledge in Elizabeth Bishop and Adrienne Rich," *Twentieth Century Literature*, 43 (1997): 144–61. He too finds "Frame" succeeding better than "Rape" with its "language of witness," and suggests that Rich may well have written "Frame" "with criticism of poems like 'Rape' in mind" (n5, 160).

32. An article by Joe Stampleman that appeared on Friday, 4 May, 1990 in the MIT student newspaper, *The Tech*, after Rich had given a poetry reading, speaks of "a well-publicized 1979 court case in which a Boston University student filed charges against police who brutally arrested her for trespassing when she sought shelter from driving snow in one of the university's buildings, while waiting for a bus" (http://www.tech.mit.edu/V110/N24/rich.24a.html).

33. In *Sincerity's Shadow* Deborah Forbes cites "Frame" to exemplify how Rich's poetry often "presents an 'I' that is an almost disembodied self-consciousness about the possibilities and limitations of imaginative sympathy" (20).

34. Harriet Davidson also cites the deictic transgressiveness of this assertion in "I Say I Am There: Siting/Citing the Subject of Feminism and Deconstruction," in *Critical Encounters: Reference and Responsibility in Deconstructive Writing*, ed. Cathy Caruth and Deborah Esch (New Brunswick, N.J.: Rutgers, 1995), but reads its implications differently: see esp. 241–45. Davidson valuably unpacks Rich's usage of the word "location" on 255 ff.

35. *FD* 2002, and cf. Rich's *Notes* to this volume, 315.

36. *What Is Found There: Notebooks on Poetry and Politics* (New York: W. W. Norton, 1993), 33.

37. The first phrase in quotation marks in this sentence is from "North American Time" (dated 1983), a poem whose bitter theme is that the "verbal privilege" accruing to a poet's words can lead to their being (mis)read in the context of subsequent events they had no intention of addressing: "We move but our words stand / become responsible / for more than we intended // and this is verbal privilege" (*FD* 2002, 198).

38. Nick Halpern points out, however, that because Rich has an explicitly prophetic vocation, "too often . . . she seems not like someone who is leading an everyday life but someone who is walking the earth, and the question of the balance between isolation and community will not go away." *Everyday and Prophetic: The Poetry of Lowell, Ammons, Merrill, and Rich* (Madison: University of Wisconsin Press, 2003), 185.

39. Cf. chapter 1 above, n48.

40. Rich, "Caryatid: A Column," *American Poetry Review*, 2 (September–October 1973): 42; repr. as "On *History, For Lizzie and Harriet*, and *The Dolphin*" in *The Critical Response to Robert Lowell*, ed. Steven Gould Axelrod (Westport, Conn.: Greenwood Press, 1999), 185–87.

41. Lowell, "Dolphin," in *The Dolphin* (1973), *Collected Poems*, ed. Frank Bidart and David Gewanter (New York: Farrar, Straus and Giroux, 2003), 708.

42. Rich, "On *History, For Lizzie and Harriet*, and *The Dolphin*," 186.

43. Wakoski, "The Craft of Carpenters, Plumbers and Mechanics: Column," *American Poetry Review*, 3 (January–February, 1974): 46; repr. as "Reply to Adrienne Rich," in Axelrod, *The Critical Response to Robert Lowell*, 187–88.

44. Tillinghast, *Robert Lowell's Life and Work: Damaged Grandeur* (Ann Arbor: University of Michigan Press, 1995), 54–55. Access to an unpublished earlier manuscript of *The Dolphin* brought David Gewanter to the antithetical conclusion that Lowell cut back on the verbatim use of conversations and letters in order to cause both of his wives "less pain." In "Child of Collaboration: Robert Lowell's *Dolphin*," *Modern Philology* 93, no. 2 (November 1995): 178–203, Gewanter argues that *The Dolphin* was originally conceived as "a postmodernist poetry of multiple voices and authors in the tradition of William Carlos Williams's *Paterson*"; he finds the published version treating Hardwick "more kindly—at the expense of . . . its art" (179).

45. "Sources," *Your Native Land, Your Life: Poems* (New York: W. W. Norton, 1986), 25.

46. "Twenty-One Love Poems," *FD* 2002, 146–47.

47. "Sleepwalking Next to Death," *Time's Power: Poems 1985–88* (New York: W. W. Norton, 1989), 19.

48. In *Of Woman Born: Motherhood as Experience and Institution* (New York: W. W. Norton, 1976), Rich recalls that "once in a while someone used to ask me, 'Don't you ever write poems about your children?'" The reason she gives in 1976 for not doing so is that she experienced poetry writing and caring for young children as activities that were in conflict: "for me, poetry was where I lived as no-one's mother, where I existed as myself" (12).

49. "This" [dated 1985], *Time's Power*; 6.

50. Cf. esp. "When We Dead Awaken: Writing as Re-Vision," in *OLSS*, 40: "But poems are like dreams: in them you put what you don't know you know."

51. "For Memory," *A Wild Patience Has Taken Me This Far: Poems 1978–1981* (New York: W. W. Norton, 1981), 21–22.

52. Jahan Ramazani, *Poetry of Mourning: The Modern Elegy from Hardy to Heaney* (Chicago: University of Chicago Press, 1994), 321.

53. Rich, "Compulsory Heterosexuality and Lesbian Existence," *BBP*, 23. Rich explains in a footnote that the essay was originally written for the "Sexuality" issue of *Signs* in 1978; the Foreword from which my quotations are drawn was added in 1982 when the essay was reprinted in a feminist pamphlet series.

54. Rich, "Vesuvius at Home: The Power of Emily Dickinson," *OLSS*, 157–83.

55. In an interview with Elly Bulkin in 1977, cited by Deborah Pope in *A Separate Vision: Isolation in Contemporary Women's Poetry* (Baton Rouge: Louisiana State University Press, 1984), Rich explains that "Stepping Backward," one of the poems in her first published volume, "is addressed to a woman whom I was close to in my late teens, and whom I really fled from—I fled from my feelings about her" (130, n15). "To Judith, Taking Leave," a 1962 poem that looks from within an ostensibly heterosexual framework ("two women / in love to the nerves' limit / with two

men—") toward a time when they "can meet . . . as two eyes in one brow / receiving at one moment / the rainbow of the world," went unpublished until *FD* 1984.

56. In *Stein, Bishop, and Rich: Lyrics of Love, War, and Place* (Chapel Hill: University of North Carolina Press, 1997), Margaret Dickie suggests in her valuable, brief discussion of this poem that "among its multiple meanings" is a necrophilic "nostalgia for all the dead and maimed women she might have loved." Necrophilia "associates the woman's desire with what is transgressive in desire and unassuageable" (156). Dickie points out that Rich's "most recent poetry has grown out of an appreciation for those mysteries in her own life that she cannot fully fathom" (199).

57. In *The Regenerate Lyric: Theology and Innovation in American Poetry* (Cambridge: Cambridge University Press, 1993), Elisa New argues that "many of the classic American poems are made not of linguistic possibility but of linguistic decision. Honed things, things that end, these poems are vessels of choice" (231).

58. Rich, "Sources," in *Your Native Land, Your Life*, 27.

Chronology

1917	Gwendolyn Brooks is born on June 7 in Topeka, Kansas.
1928	Maya Angelou (Marguerite Johnson) is born on April 4 in St. Louis, Missouri. Anne Sexton is born on November 9 in Newton, Massachusetts.
1929	Adrienne Rich is born on May 16 in Baltimore.
1932	Sylvia Plath is born on October 27 in Boston, Massachusetts.
1934	Brooks begins contributing to *Chicago Defender;* 75 of her poems appear in the publication within two years.
1935	Mary Oliver is born on September 10 in Cleveland, Ohio.
1936	Lucille Clifton is born on June 27 in Depew, New York.
1942	Sharon Olds is born on November 19 in San Francisco.
1943	Louise Glück is born on April 22 in New York, New York. Nikki (Yolande Cornelia) Giovanni is born on June 7 in Knoxville, Tennessee.
1945	Brooks's first collection of poetry, *A Street in Bronzeville,* is published.
1946	Brooks becomes a Fellow of the American Academy of Arts and Letters.
1948	Wendy Rose is born on May 7 in Oakland, California. Leslie Marmon Silko is born on March 5 in Albuquerque, New Mexico.

1949	Brooks' second book of poetry, *Annie Allen*, is published.
1950	Brooks becomes the first black American to win the Pulitzer Prize (for *Annie Allen*).
1951	Rich publishes *A Change of World* (foreword by W. H. Auden), for which she wins the Yale Series of Younger Poets award. Jorie Graham is born on May 9 in New York, New York. Joy Harjo is born on May 9 in Tulsa, Oklahoma.
1952	Rich publishes *Poems*. Rita Dove is born on August 28 in Akron, Ohio.
1953	Brooks publishes *Maud Martha* (novel). Plath serves as guest editor with *Mademoiselle* during the summer.
1955	Rich publishes *The Diamond Cutters and Other Poems*.
1956	Brooks publishes *Bronzeville Boys and Girls* (children's poetry).
1960	Brooks publishes her third book of poetry, *The Bean Eaters*. Sexton publishes *To Bedlam and Part Way Back*, her first collection of poems.
1961	Rich receives National Institute of Arts and Letters award for poetry.
1962	Plath publishes *The Colossus and Other Poems*; her *Three Women: A Monologue for Three Voices*, a radio play, is broadcast by the British Broadcasting Corporation. Sexton publishes *All My Pretty Ones*. Oliver wins first prize from the Poetry Society of America for "No Voyage."
1963	Brooks publishes *Selected Poems*. Plath's *The Bell Jar* is published under a pseudonym (Victoria Lucas); Plath commits suicide on February 11 in London. Sexton and Maxine Kumin together publish *Eggs of Things*, a children's book. Rich publishes *Snapshots of a Daughter-in-Law: Poems, 1954–1962*.
1964	Sexton publishes *Selected Poems*.
1965	Ted Hughes, Plath's estranged husband, publishes his version of Plath's collection of poems, *Ariel*. *The Bell Jar* is published for the first time under Plath's real name. Oliver publishes *No Voyage, and Other Poems*, her first collection of poetry.
1966	Sexton publishes *Live or Die* (poetry). Glück receives the Academy of American Poets Prize, Columbia University.

1967   Sexton wins the Pulitzer Prize for *Live or Die.*

1968   Brooks publishes *In the Mecca*; she is named poet laureate of Illinois after Carl Sandburg's death. Glück's *Firstborn* is published. Giovanni publishes *Black Feeling, Black Talk* and *Black Judgement,* both books of poetry.

1969   Brooks publishes *Riot.* Sexton publishes *Love Poems;* her play, *45 Mercy Street,* is produced off-Broadway. Rich translates and edits (with Aijaz Ahmad and William Stafford) *Poems by Ghalib.* Clifton publishes *Good Times,* her first book of poems.

1970   Angelou publishes her first autobiography, *I Know Why the Caged Bird Sings.* Clifton publishes the first of eight Everett Anderson books for children, *Some of the Days of Everett Anderson.* Giovanni publishes *Re: Creation* (poetry) and *Poem of Angela Yvonne Davis.*

1971   Brooks publishes *Family Pictures, The World of Gwendolyn Brooks,* and *Aloneness.* Plath's *Crossing the Water: Transitional Poems* and *Winter Trees* are published posthumously. Sexton publishes *Transformations.* Rich publishes *The Will to Change: Poems, 1968–1970.* Angelou publishes her first book of poetry, *Just Give Me a Cool Drink of Water 'fore I Diiie.* Giovanni publishes *Spin a Soft Black Song: Poems for Children.*

1972   Brooks publishes *Report from Part One,* an autobiography. Sexton publishes *The Book of Folly.* Angelou becomes the first black woman to have an original screenplay produced (*Georgia, Georgia*). Clifton publishes *Good News about the Earth: New Poems.* Giovanni publishes *My House* (poetry). Oliver publishes *The River Styx, Ohio, and Other Poems,* her second volume of poetry.

1973   Sexton publishes *O Ye Tongues.* Rich publishes *Diving into the Wreck: Poems, 1971–1972.* Clifton publishes *Good, Says Jerome* and three other children's books. Giovanni publishes *Gemini: An Extended Autobiographical Statement on My First Twenty-five Years of Being a Black Poet* and *Ego-Tripping and Other Poems for Young People.* Rose, under a pseudonym, publishes first book of poetry, *Hopi Roadrunner Dancing.*

1974   Brooks publishes *The Tiger Who Wore White Gloves* (juvenile). Sexton commits suicide on October 4 in Weston, Massachusetts; *The Death Notebooks* is published. Rich wins the National Book Award for *Diving into the Wreck: Poems, 1971–1972.*

Angelou publishes her second autobiography, *Gather Together in My Name*. Clifton is appointed Poet Laureate of the State of Maryland (until 1985); she publishes *An Ordinary Woman* (poetry). Silko publishes *Laguna Woman*.

1975   Brooks publishes *Beckonings* and *A Capsule Course in Black Poetry Writing*. Plath's *Letters Home: Correspondence, 1950–1963*, selected and edited with a commentary by her mother, Aurelia Schober Plath, is published. Sexton's *The Awful Rowing toward God* is published posthumously. Glück publishes *The House on Marshland*. Angelou publishes *O Pray My Wings Are Gonna Fit Me Well* (poetry). Giovanni publishes *The Women and the Men*. Harjo publishes her first book of poetry, *The Last Song*.

1976   Rich publishes *Of Woman Born: Motherhood as Experience and Institution*. Glück publishes *The Garden*. Angelou publishes her third autobiography, *Singin' and Swingin' and Gettin' Merry Like Christmas*. Clifton publishes *Generations: A Memoir*. Harjo wins Academy of American Poetry Award. Rose publishes *Long Division: A Tribal History*.

1977   *Anne Sexton: A Self Portrait in Letters*, edited by Lois Ames and Sexton's daughter, Linda Gray Sexton, is published. Dove publishes *Ten Poems*, her first book of poetry. Rose publishes *Academic Squaw*. Silko wins Pushcart Prize for poetry; she publishes the novel *Ceremony*.

1978   Sexton's *Words for Dr. Y: Uncollected Poems with Three Stories*, edited by her daughter, Linda Gray Sexton, is published posthumously. Angelou publishes *And Still I Rise* (poetry). Giovanni publishes *Cotton Candy on a Rainy Day*. Oliver publishes *The Night Traveler*.

1979   Rich publishes *On Lies, Secrets, and Silence: Selected Prose, 1966–1978*. Rose publishes *Builder Kachina: A Home-Going Cycle*.

1980   Brooks publishes *Primer for Blacks* and *Young Poet's Primer*. Dove publishes *The Only Dark Spot in the Sky* and *The Yellow House on the Corner*. Graham earns the Pushcart Prize for "I Was Taught Three"; she publishes *Hybrids of Plants and of Ghosts*, her first book of poetry. Glück publishes *Descending Figure*. Clifton publishes *Two-Headed Woman*. Giovanni publishes *Vacation Time: Poems for Children*. Olds publishes *Satan Says*, her first book of poems. Harjo publishes *What Moon Drove Me to This?* Rose publishes *Lost Copper*. Silko wins American Book Award.

1981   Brooks publishes *To Disembark.* Plath's *Collected Poems,* edited by Ted Hughes, is published posthumously. Sexton's *Complete Poems, 1981* is published posthumously. Rich publishes *A Wild Patience Has Taken Me This Far: Poems, 1978–1981.* Glück receives the Award in Literature from the American Academy and Institute of Arts and Letters. Angelou publishes her fourth autobiography, *The Heart of a Woman.* Silko publishes *Storyteller,* poetry and short stories.

1982   Plath posthumously wins the Pulitzer Prize in Poetry for *Collected Poems. The Journals of Sylvia Plath,* edited by Ted Hughes and Frances McCullough, is published. Graham wins her second Pushcart Prize, for "My Garden, My Daylight." Rose publishes *What Happened When the Hopi Hit New York.*

1983   Brooks publishes *Very Young Poets.* Dove publishes *Museum.* Graham publishes *Erosion,* her second book of poems. Angelou publishes *Shaker, Why Don't You Sing?* (poems). Giovanni publishes *Those Who Ride the Night Winds.* Oliver wins the American Academy and Institution of Arts and Letters' Award in Literature; she publishes *American Primitive.* Harjo publishes *She Had Some Horses* (poetry).

1984   Rich publishes *The Fact of a Doorframe: Poems Selected and New, 1950–1984.* Oliver wins the Pulitzer Prize for *American Primitive.* Olds publishes *The Dead and the Living,* her second book of poems, which wins a National Book Critics Circle Award. Harjo coauthors the film script *The Beginning* and writes *We Are One, Uhonho* (television play).

1985   Brooks is named Poetry Consultant for the Library of Congress. Dove publishes *Fifth Sunday* (short stories). Glück publishes *The Triumph of Achilles,* for which she receives the National Book Critics Circle Award for poetry. Harjo writes the film script for *Origin of Apache Crown Dance* and the television play *Maiden of Deception Pass.* Rose publishes *The Halfbreed Chronicles and Other Poems.*

1986   Brooks publishes *The Near-Johannesburg Boy and Other Poems.* Rich publishes *Your Native Land, Your Life* and *Blood, Bread and Poetry: Selected Prose, 1979–1986.* Dove earns the Academy of American Poets' Peter I. B. Lavan Younger Poets Award; she publishes *Thomas and Beulah* (poems). Angelou publishes her fifth autobiography, *All God's Children Need Traveling Shoes;* she also publishes *Mrs. Flowers: A Moment of Friendship* and *Poems:*

Maya Angelou. Oliver publishes *Dream Work.* Harjo authors the television plays *I Am Different from My Brother* and *The Runaway.*

1987   Brooks publishes *Blacks* (poetry). Dove wins the Pulitzer Prize in poetry for *Thomas and Beulah.* Graham publishes *The End of Beauty* (poems). Angelou publishes *Now Sheba Sings the Song.* Clifton publishes *Good Woman: Poems and a Memoir, 1969–1980* and *Next: New Poems.* Olds publishes *The Gold Cell* and *The Matter of This World: New and Selected Poems.*

1988   Brooks publishes *Winnie* (poetry) and *Gottschalk and the Grande Tarantelle.* Rich publishes *Time's Power: Poems, 1985–1988.* Dove publishes *The Other Side of the House.* Clifton is the first author to have two books of poetry chosen as finalists for the Pulitzer Prize; she publishes *Ten Oxherding Pictures* (poetry). Giovanni publishes *Sacred Cows . . . and Other Edibles* (essays).

1989   Rich wins the National Poetry Association Award for distinguished service to the art of poetry. Dove publishes *Grace Notes.* Harjo publishes *Secrets from the Center of the World* (poetry).

1990   Glück publishes *Ararat.* Angelou publishes *I Shall Not Be Moved* (poetry collection). Harjo publishes *In Mad Love and War* and wins an American Indian Distinguished Achievement Award.

1991   Brooks publishes *Children Coming Home.* Rich publishes *An Atlas of the Difficult World: Poems, 1988–1991.* Graham wins the Academy of American Poets Lavan Award and publishes *Region of Unlikeness.* Clifton publishes *Quilting: Poems 1987–1990.* Olds publishes *The Sign of Saturn.* Harjo wins American Book Award for *In Mad Love and War.* Silko publishes novel *Almanac of the Dead.*

1992   Rich wins the Poetry Society of America's Robert Frost Silver Medal for Lifetime Achievement in Poetry. Dove publishes a novel, *Through the Ivory Gate.* Glück publishes *The Wild Iris.* Oliver publishes *New and Selected Poems,* for which she wins the National Book Award for Poetry. Olds publishes *The Father* (poems).

1993   Rich publishes *What Is Found There: Notebooks on Poetry and Politics.* Dove becomes the Library of Congress consultant in poetry (until 1995); she publishes *Selected Poems* and *Lady Freedom Among Us.* Graham publishes *Materialism: Poems.* Glück wins the Pulitzer Prize and the William Carlos Williams Award

(Poetry Society of America), both for *The Wild Iris*. Angelou reads her poem "On the Pulse of Morning" at the inauguration of President Bill Clinton; she also publishes *Wouldn't Take Nothin' for My Journey Now, Soul Looks Back in Wonder,* and *Life Doesn't Frighten Me* (children's book). Clifton publishes *The Book of Light* (poems). Rose publishes *Going to War with All My Relations: New and Selected Poems*.

1994   Glück publishes *Proofs and Theories: Essays on Poetry*. *The Complete Collected Poems of Maya Angelou* is published; Angelou also publishes *My Painted House* and *My Friendly Chicken and Me* (juvenile). Giovanni publishes *Racism 101* (essays). Oliver publishes *White Pine: Poems and Prose Poems* and *A Poetry Handbook*. Harjo publishes *The Woman Who Fell from the Sky;* her band also produces an album by the same name. Rich publishes *Dark Fields of the Republic, 1991–1995*. Rose publishes *Bone Dance: New and Selected Poems, 1965–1993* and *Now Poof She Is Gone*. Silko publishes *Voices Under One Sky*.

1995   Dove publishes *Mother Love: Poems* and *The Poet's World*. Graham publishes *The Dream of the Unified Field: Poems, 1974–1994*. Glück publishes *The First Four Books of Poems*. Angelou publishes *Phenomenal Woman: Four Poems Celebrating Women* and *A Brave and Startling Truth*. Oliver publishes *Blue Pastures*. Harjo is given the Lifetime Achievement Award by the Native Writers Circle of the Americas.

1996   Brooks publishes *Report from Part Two,* a second autobiography. Rich publishes *Selected Poems, 1950–1995*. Graham is awarded the Pulitzer Prize for poetry for *The Dream of the Unified Field: Poems, 1974–1994*. Glück publishes *Meadowlands*. Angelou publishes *Kofi and His Magic* (juvenile). Clifton publishes *The Terrible Stories: Poems*. Giovanni publishes *The Selected Poems of Nikki Giovanni, 1968–1995*. Olds publishes *The Wellspring: Poems*. Silko publishes *Rain*.

1997   Rich wins the National Medal of the Arts but declines it. Graham publishes *The Errancy* (poems). Angelou publishes *Even the Stars Look Lonesome* (essays). Oliver publishes *West Wind: Poems and Prose Poems*.

1998   Angelou directs her first feature film, *Down in the Delta*. Oliver publishes *Rules for the Dance: A Handbook for Writing and Reading Metrical Verse*. Olds is named New York State Poet (until 2000).

1999   Rich publishes *Midnight Salvage: Poems, 1995–1998*. Dove
                becomes a Library of Congress special consultant in poetry
                (until 2000); she publishes *On the Bus with Rosa Parks: Poems*.
                Glück publishes *Vita Nova;* she is named special consultant
                for the Library of Congress. Clifton becomes a fellow of the
                American Academy of Arts and Sciences and wins an Emmy
                Award from the American Academy of Television Arts and
                Sciences. Giovanni publishes *Blues: For All the Changes—New
                Poems*. Oliver publishes *Winter Hours: Prose, Prose Poems, and
                Poems*. Olds publishes *Blood, Tin, Straw*. Silko publishes novel
                Gardens in the Dunes.

2000   Gwendolyn Brooks dies on December 3. *The Unabridged Jour-
                nals of Sylvia Plath, 1950–1962* is published. Graham publishes
                Swarm (poetry). Clifton publishes *Blessing the Boats: New and
                Selected Poems, 1988–2000*, which wins a National Book Award
                for poetry. Oliver publishes *The Leaf and the Cloud*. Harjo pub-
                lishes *A Map to the Next World: Poetry and Tales* and *The Good
                Luck Cat* (juvenile).

2001   Rich publishes *Fox: Poems, 1998–2000* and *Arts of the Possible:
                Essays and Conversations*. Glück wins the Böllingen Prize and
                publishes *The Seven Ages*. Clifton publishes the eighth and last
                of the Everett Anderson children's book series, *One of the Prob-
                lems of Everett Anderson*. Harjo wins the Wordcraft Circle of
                Native Writers and Storytellers Writer of the Year Award for
                The Good Luck Cat.

2002   Graham publishes *Never: Poems*. Angelou publishes her sixth
                autobiography, *A Song Flung up to Heaven*. Giovanni publishes
                Quilting the Black-eyed Pea: Poems and Not Quite Poems. Oli-
                ver publishes *What Do We Know*. Olds publishes *The Unswept
                Room*; she receives an Academy of American Poets Academy
                Fellowship for "distinguished poetic achievement at mid-
                career." Harjo publishes *How We Became Human: New and
                Selected Poems, 1975–2001*. Rose publishes *Itch like Crazy*.

2003   Brooks's *In Montgomery, and Other Poems* is published posthu-
                mously. Glück is named U.S. Poet Laureate Consultant in Poetry.
                The Collected Poetry of Nikki Giovanni: 1968–1998 is published.
                Oliver publishes *Owls and Other Fantasies: Poems and Essays*.

2004   Rich publishes *The School Among the Ruins: Poems, 2000–2004*,
                for which she wins the National Book Critics Circle Award

for poetry. Dove publishes *American Smooth* (poetry). Angelou publishes *I Know Why the Caged Bird Sings: The Collected Autobiographies of Maya Angelou, Hallelujah! The Welcome Table* (essays), and four children's books. Clifton publishes *Mercy: Poems*. Oliver publishes *Why I Wake Early, Boston Iris: Poems and Essays, Long Life: Essays and Other Writings,* and *New and Selected Poems, Volume Two*. Olds publishes *Strike Sparks: Selected Poems, 1980–2002*.

2005   Graham publishes *Overlord*. Angelou publishes *Amazing Peace* (poetry). Giovanni publishes *Rosa* (children's book).

2006   Plath's posthumously published poem "Ennui" debuts in *Blackbird* in November. Rich wins the National Book Foundation's Medal for Distinguished Contribution. Glück publishes *Averno*. Angelou publishes *Mother: A Cradle to Hold Me* (essays). Oliver publishes *Thirst: Poems*.

2007   Clifton wins the Ruth Lilly Poetry Prize. Giovanni publishes *Acolytes* and *On My Journey Now: Looking at African-American History Through the Spirituals*.

2008   Graham publishes *Sea Change*. Angelou publishes *Letter to My Daughter* (essays). Clifton publishes *Voices*. Oliver publishes *The Truro Bear and Other Adventures: Poems and Essays* and *Red Bird*.

2009   Dove publishes *Sonata Mulattica*. Glück publishes *A Village Life*. Giovanni publishes *Bicycles: Love Poems*. Oliver publishes *Evidence*. Harjo publishes *For a Girl Becoming* (young adult); she wins Native American Music Award for Best Female Artist.

2010   Rich wins The Griffin Trust's Lifetime Recognition Award. Clifton dies on February 13; the Poetry Society of America posthumously awards her the Robert Frost Medal for distinguished lifetime achievement in American poetry. Oliver publishes *Swan: Poems and Prose Poems*. Silko publishes *The Turquoise Ledge: A Memoir*.

Contributors

HAROLD BLOOM is Sterling Professor of the Humanities at Yale University. Educated at Cornell and Yale universities, he is the author of more than 30 books, including *Shelley's Mythmaking* (1959), *Blake's Apocalypse* (1963), *Yeats* (1970), *The Anxiety of Influence* (1973), *A Map of Misreading* (1975), *Kabbalah and Criticism* (1975), *Agon: Toward a Theory of Revisionism* (1982), *The American Religion* (1992), *The Western Canon* (1994), *Omens of Millennium: The Gnosis of Angels, Dreams, and Resurrection* (1996), *Shakespeare: The Invention of the Human* (1998), *How to Read and Why* (2000), *Genius: A Mosaic of One Hundred Exemplary Creative Minds* (2002), *Hamlet: Poem Unlimited* (2003), *Where Shall Wisdom Be Found?* (2004), *Jesus and Yahweh: The Names Divine* (2005), and *Till I End My Song: A Gathering of Last Poems* (2010). In addition, he is the author of hundreds of articles, reviews, and editorial introductions. In 1999, Professor Bloom received the American Academy of Arts and Letters' Gold Medal for Criticism. He has also received the International Prize of Catalonia, the Alfonso Reyes Prize of Mexico, and the Hans Christian Andersen Bicentennial Prize of Denmark.

HENRY TAYLOR has been a professor at American University. He has written *Understanding Fiction Poems, 1986–1996* and is a Pulitzer Prize–winning poet.

BRIAN DILLON is a research fellow at the University of Kent. His first book, the memoir *In the Dark Room*, won the 2006 Irish Book Award for nonfiction. He is the U.K. editor of *Cabinet*, a quarterly of art and culture based in New York.

HELEN VENDLER is a professor at Harvard University. Her publications include *Last Looks, Last Books: Stevens, Plath, Lowell, Bishop, Merrill* and *Coming of Age as a Poet: Milton, Keats, Eliot, Plath.*

JEANNE PERREAULT is a professor and associate head (graduate studies) in the English department at the University of Calgary. She is the author of *Writing Selves: Contemporary Feminist Autography* and coeditor of *Tracing the Autobiographical* and *Writing the Circle: Native Women of Western Canada.*

JAMES LONGENBACH is a professor at the University of Rochester. He is a poet and critic whose work includes *The Resistance to Poetry* and *Modern Poetry after Modernism*, among other titles.

VIRGINIA C. FOWLER is a professor at Virginia Polytechnic Institute and State University. She is the author of Twayne's *Nikki Giovanni* and editor of *Conversations with Nikki Giovanni* as well as *The Collected Poetry of Nikki Giovanni 1968–1998.*

ZOFIA BURR is a professor at George Mason University, where she also is dean of the Honors College. She is the editor of *Set in Motion: Essays, Interviews, Dialogues, by A. R. Ammons* and also has published poetry, with some appearing in collaborative installations.

HILARY HOLLADAY has been a professor at the University of Massachusetts at Lowell, where she also has been director of the Jack and Stella Kerouac Center for American Studies. Her work includes *Wild Blessings: The Poetry of Lucille Clifton* and a poetry collection and chapbook.

GALE SWIONTKOWSKI has been an associate professor of English and program director of the Institute of Irish Studies at Fordham University; she also teaches at Western Connecticut State University.

ROSE LUCAS is an adjunct senior lecturer at Monash University in Melbourne, Australia. She is the co-author of *Bridgings: Readings in Australian Women's Poetry* and the author of a wide range of articles and book chapters covering women's poetry and other subjects.

JANE HEDLEY is a professor at Bryn Mawr College. She is the author of *Power in Verse: Metaphor and Metonymy in the Renaissance Lyric* and coeditor of *In the Frame: Women's Ekphrastic Poetry from Marianne Moore to Susan Wheeler.*

Bibliography

"Adrienne Rich: A Symposium." *Field: Contemporary Poetry and Poetics* 77 (Fall 2007): 7–71.

Alford, Jean. "The Poetry of Mary Oliver: Modern Renewal Through Mortal Acceptance." *Pembroke Magazine* 20 (1988): 283–88.

Andrews, Bruce. "Is There, Currently, an American Poetry? A Symposium." *American Poetry* 4, no. 2 (Winter 1987): 2–40.

Andrist, Debra D. "Non-Traditional Concepts of Motherhood: Hispanic Women Poets of the Twentieth Century." *Letras Femeninas* 15, nos. 1–2 (Spring–Fall 1989): 100–14.

Barresi, Dorothy. "Baby Boom Poetry and the New Zeitgeist." *Prairie Schooner* 83, no. 3 (2009): 175–93.

Bennett, Michael, and Vanessa D. Dickerson, ed. *Recovering the Black Female Body: Self-Representations by African American Women.* New Brunswick, N.J.: Rutgers University Press, 2001.

Bonds, Diane S. "Language and Nature in the Poetry of Mary Oliver." *Women's Studies* 21 (April 1992).

Brogan, Jacqueline Vaught, and Cordelia Chávez Candelaria, ed. *Women Poets of the Americas: Toward a Pan-American Gathering.* Notre Dame, Ind.: University of Notre Dame Press, 1999.

Bryson, J. Scott, and Roger Thompson, ed. *Twentieth-Century American Nature Poets.* Detroit, Mich.: Gale, 2008.

Burton-Christie, Douglas. "Nature, Spirit, and Imagination in the Poetry of Mary Oliver." *Cross Currents: The Journal of the Association for Religion and Intellectual Life* 46, no. 1 (March 1, 1996).

Caplan, David. *Questions of Possibility: Contemporary Poetry and Poetic Form.* Oxford; New York: Oxford University Press, 2005.

Cates, Isaac. "Louise Glück: Interstices and Silences." *Literary Imagination: The Review of the Association of Literary Scholars and Critics* 5, no. 3 (Fall 2003): 462–77.

Chiasson, Dan. *One Kind of Everything: Poem and Person in Contemporary America.* Chicago: University of Chicago Press, 2007.

Colón, David. "Other Latino Poetic Method." *Cultural Critique* 47 (Winter 2001): 265–86.

Cook, Barbara J., ed. *Women Writing Nature: A Feminist View.* Lanham, Md.: Lexington, 2008.

Dick, Bruce Allen, ed. *"A Poet's Truth: Conversations with Latino/Latina Poets."* Tucson: Arizona University Press, 2003.

Fowler, Virginia C. *Nikki Giovanni.* New York: Twayne Publishers; Toronto: Maxwell Macmillan Canada; New York: Maxwell Macmillan International, 1992.

Frank, Robert Joseph, and Henry M. Sayre, ed. *The Line in Postmodern Poetry.* Urbana: University of Illinois Press, 1988.

Gabbin, Joanne V., ed. *The Furious Flowering of African American Poetry.* Charlottesville: University Press of Virginia, 1999.

Gardner, Thomas, ed. *Jorie Graham: Essays on the Poetry.* Madison: University of Wisconsin Press, 2005.

Georgoudaki, Ekaterini. *Race, Gender, and Class Perspectives in the Works of Maya Angelou, Gwendolyn Brooks, Rita Dove, Nikki Giovanni, and Audre Lorde.* Thessaloniki: Aristotle University of Thessaloniki, 1991.

———. "Rita Dove: Crossing Boundaries." *Callaloo* 14 (Spring 1991): 419–33.

Gubar, Susan. *Poetry After Auschwitz.* Bloomington: Indiana University Press, 2003.

Gwynn, R. S., ed. *American Poets Since World War II: Third Series.* Detroit, Mich.: Thomson Gale, 1992.

Halpern, Nick. *Everyday and Prophetic: The Poetry of Lowell, Ammons, Merrill, and Rich.* Madison: University of Wisconsin Press, 2003.

Harris, Peter. "Four Salvers Salvaging: New Work by Voigt, Olds, Dove, and McHugh." *Virginia Quarterly Review: A National Journal of Literature and Discussion* 64, no. 2 (Spring 1988): 262–76.

Holladay, Hilary. *Wild Blessings: The Poetry of Lucille Clifton.* Baton Rouge: Louisiana State University Press, 2004.

Keller, Lynn. *Thinking Poetry: Readings in Contemporary Women's Exploratory Poetics.* Iowa City: University of Iowa Press, 2010.

Markey, Janice. *A New Tradition?: The Poetry of Sylvia Plath, Anne Sexton, and Adrienne Rich, a Study of Feminism and Poetry.* Frankfurt am Main; New York: P.eter Lang, 1985.

McNew, Janet. "Mary Oliver and the Tradition of Romantic Nature Poetry." *Contemporary Literature* 30 (1989): 59–77.

Mengert, Christina, and Joshua Marie Wilkinson, ed. *12 x 12: Conversations in 21st-Century Poetry and Poetics.* Iowa City: University of Iowa Press, 2009.

Middlebrook, Diane Wood, and Marilyn Yalom, ed. *Coming to Light: American Women Poets in the Twentieth Century.* Ann Arbor: University of Michigan Press, 1985.

Mitchel, Felicia, ed. *Her Words: Diverse Voices in Contemporary Appalachian Women's Poetry.* Knoxville: University of Tennessee Press, 2002.

Mootry, Maria K., ed. *A Life Distilled: Gwendolyn Brooks, Her Poetry and Fiction.* Urbana: University of Illinois Press, 1987.

Morris, Daniel. *The Poetry of Louise Glück: A Thematic Introduction.* Columbia: University of Missouri Press, 2006.

Neubauer, Alexander, ed. *Poetry in Person: Twenty-five Years of Conversation with America's Poets.* New York: Alfred A. Knopf, 2010.

O'Reilly, Andrea, ed. *From Motherhood to Mothering: The Legacy of Adrienne Rich's Of Woman Born.* Albany: State University of New York, 2004.

Ostriker, Alicia. "Kin and Kin: The Poetry of Lucille Clifton." *The American Poetry Review* 22, no. 6 (November–December 1993): 41–48.

Pereira, Malin. *Rita Dove's Cosmopolitanism.* Urbana: University of Illinois Press, 2003.

Pérez, Janet, ed. "Hispanic Women Poets." *Monographic Review/Revista Monografica* 6 (1990).

Perloff, Marjorie. "Ca(n)non to the Right of Us, Ca(n)non to the Left of Us: A Plea for Difference." *New Literary History: A Journal of Theory and Interpretation* 18, no. 3 (Spring 1987): 633–56.

———. *21st-century Modernism: The "New" Poetics.* Malden, Mass.: Blackwell Publishers, 2002.

———. *Unoriginal Genius: Poetry by Other Means in the New Century.* Chicago: The University of Chicago Press, 2010.

Prins, Yopie, and Maeera Shreiber, ed. *Dwelling in Possibility: Women Poets and Critics on Poetry.* Ithaca, N.Y.: Cornell University Press, 1997.

Rampersad, Arnold. "The Poems of Rita Dove." *Callaloo* 9, no. 1 (Winter 1986): 52–60.

Reid, Margaret Ann. *Black Protest Poetry: Polemics from the Harlem Renaissance and the Sixties.* New York: P. Lang, 2001.

Sadoff, Ira. *History Matters: Contemporary Poetry on the Margins of American Culture.* Iowa City: Iowa University Press, 2009.

Schultz, Susan M. *A Poetics of Impasse in Modern and Contemporary American Poetry.* Tuscaloosa: University of Alabama Press, 2005.

Taylor, Henry. *Compulsory Figures: Essays on Recent American Poets*. Baton Rouge: Louisiana State University Press, 1992.

Vendler, Helen. *The Given and the Made: Strategies of Poetic Definition*. Cambridge, Mass.: Harvard University Press, 1995.

Waddell, William S., ed. *'Catch If You Can Your Country's Moment': Recovery and Regeneration in the Poetry of Adrienne Rich*. Newcastle upon Tyne, England: Cambridge Scholars, 2007.

Wagner, Linda W., ed. *Critical Essays on Sylvia Plath*. Boston: Hall, 1984.

Wilson, Norma C. *The Nature of Native American Poetry*. Albuquerque: University of New Mexico Press, 2001.

Wright, Stephen Caldwell, ed. *On Gwendolyn Brooks: Reliant Contemplation*. Ann Arbor: University of Michigan Press, 1996.

Yu, Timothy. *Race and the Avant-Garde: Experimental and Asian American Poetry Since 1965*. Stanford, Calif.: Stanford University Press, 2009.

Acknowledgments

Henry Taylor, "Gwendolyn Brooks: An Essential Sanity." From *The Kenyon Review* 13, no. 4 (Fall 1991): 115–31. Copyright © 1991 Henry Taylor.

Brian Dillon, "'Never Having Had You, I Cannot Let You Go': Sharon Olds's Poems of a Father-Daughter Relationship." From *Literary Review* 37, no. 1 (Fall 1993): 108–18. Copyright © 1993 *Literary Review*.

Helen Vendler, "Rita Dove: Identity Markers." From *Callaloo* 17, no. 2 (Spring 1994): 381–98. Copyright © 1994 *Callaloo*.

Jeanne Perreault, "New Dreaming: Joy Harjo, Wendy Rose, Leslie Marmon Silko." From *Deferring a Dream: Literary Sub-Versions of the American Columbiad*, edited by Gert Buelens and Ernst Rudin, pp. 120–36. Copyright © 1994 Birkhauser Verlag Basel.

James Longenbach, "Louise Glück's Nine Lives." From *Southwest Review* 84, no. 2 (Spring 1999): 184–98. Copyright © 1999 James Longenbach.

Virginia C. Fowler, "And This Poem Recognizes That: Embracing Contrarieties in the Poetry of Nikki Giovanni." From *Her Words: Diverse Voices in Contemporary Appalachian Women's Poetry*, edited by Felician Mitchell, pp. 107–35. Copyright © 2002 by The University of Tennessee Press.

Zofia Burr, "Maya Angelou on the Inaugural Stage." From *Of Women, Poetry, and Power: Strategies of Address in Dickinson, Miles, Brooks, Lorde, and Angelou*, pp. 180–94, 219–21. Copyright © the Board of Trustees of the University of Illinois.

Index

on sense of independence and
   individuality, 100, 115n16
storytelling and, 100
women as influences on, 99
See also specific titles of works (e.g.,
   "Train Rides")
"Glass, The" (Olds), 34
Glück, Louise
   change as highest value, 79, 82
   compared to Yeats, 83
   "discernible form" and, 80
   mythic quality of work, 81
   repetition and, 89, 90
   See also specific titles of works (e.g.,
      Meadowlands)
Gold Cell, The (Olds), 25
Gottschalk and the Grande Tarantelle
   (Brooks), 22
Grace Notes (Dove), 40, 54, 55, 58,
   60n21
Green, Rayna, 64, 75
Gubar, Susan, 1
"Gwendolyn the Terrible:
   Propositions on Eleven Poems"
   (Spillers), 11–12

Halfbreed Chronicles, The (Rose),
   68–70
"Hands: For Mother's Day"
   (Giovanni), 94–95
Hansell, William H., 3
Harjo, Joy
   "Anchorage," 63–64
   "Heartbeat," 65–66
   paths to survival and, 63
   "She Remembers the Future," 64
"Have You Ever Tried to Enter the
   Long Black Branches" (Oliver)
   echoes Whitman's use of biblical
      inventory, 186–187
   idea of "home" evoked by, 188–189
   key poem, 174
   model of meditative receptivity,
      186–187
   paradox of perception and, 187

reader urged to participate in
   "being-ness," 185–186
Wordsworthian tranquility, 187,
   190n14
"Heartbeat" (Harjo), 65–66
"Here Are My Black Clothes"
   (Glück), 81
"Her Kind" (Sexton), 193
"His Stillness" (Olds), 31
"His Terror" (Olds), 35–36
"History: 13" (Olds), 26–27
hooks, bell, 75
House on Marshland, The (Glück), 81
"Housewife" (Sexton), 193–194
Hughes, Langston, 39–40, 42, 56, 97

"I, Too" (Hughes), 56–57
"Ideal Father, The" (Olds), 33
"I love those little booths at
   Benvenuti's" (Brooks), 7
inaugural poem for Clinton. *See*
   "On the Pulse of Morning"
   (Angelou)
Incest (Nin), 162–163
incest complex, 150–151
*Incest Theme in Literature and Legend,
   The* (Rank), 149–150
In the Mecca (Brooks), 4, 18–20
"In the Time of Detachment, in the
   Time of Cold" (Brooks), 4

Jackson, Janet, 129
Jamaican Edward ("In the Mecca"),
   20
JanMohamed, Abdul, 74
"jasper texas 1998" (Clifton), 146
"Jukebox" (Glück), 82
Julia Pastrana (*Halfbreed Chronicles,
   The*), 68, 69–71
Jung, Carl, 149–150
*Just Give Me a Cool Drink of Water
   'fore I Diiie* (Angelou), 119

Kavaler-Adler, Susan, 151–152, 167,
   168

"Rainy Morning" (Glück), 83, 84
Rampersad, Arnold, 39
Rank, Otto, 149–150, 151, 162, 163
"Rape" (Rich)
 confession of rape to cop, 197–198
 criticisms of, 198–199
 empathy and detachment in, 200
 second-person voice and, 199–200, 201, 202
 text of, 198
Re: Creation (Giovanni), 107
Redding, J. Saunders, race and, 15
Report from Part One (Brooks), 3, 4
Rich, Adrienne
 autobiographical poems few, 209
 aversion to confessional mode, 192, 195, 205
 commentary on Sexton, 173
 desire to be heard, 205
 in dialogue with others, 192, 212–213
 on Emily Dickinson, 210, 216n54
 and "incestuous" bond between mothers and daughters, 197
 on Lowell's The Dolphin, 206
 poet of reciprocity, 193
 purposeless self-disclosure avoided by, 208
 Sexton's memorial tribute by, 193, 197, 200
 women's movement in 1970s and, 201
"Riders to the Blood-Red Wrath" (Brooks), 17
Ringgold, Faith, 93
Riot (Brooks), 4
"Road Rage" (Giovanni), 107
Robert Frost Library, dedication of, 122–123
romanticism, British, 192
Rose, Wendy
 Halfbreed Chronicles, 68–71
 "Poet Haunted," 66–67
 untold stories of, 63

"What My Father Said," 68

Sallie Smith ("In the Mecca"), 18
Satan Says (Olds), 25, 26, 33
Satin-Legs ("Sundays of Satin-Legs Smith, The"), 6–8
Sayles, Samuel (Clifton's father), 137, 142, 143
Sayles, Thelma Lucille (Clifton's birth name), 142
Schad ("Agosta the Winged Man and Rasha the Black Dove"), 49–50
second-person voice in poetry, 199–200
"Second Sermon on the Warpland, The" (Brooks), 21
Selected Poems (Brooks), 3, 17
Senghor, Léopold Sédar, 19
"Sermon on the Warpland, The" (Brooks), 21
Sexton, Anne
 achievements of, 173
 as audience junkie, 195
 confessionalism and, 153–154
 father and, 151, 152–53
 memorial tribute by Rich, 193, 197, 200
 modern female voice of, 153
 not a political poet, 196
 poet of intimacy, 192–193
 regressive tendency in poetry of, 154
 suicide of, 193
 See also specific titles of works (e.g., "Little Girl, My Stringbean")
Shakur, Tupac, 113, 129
Shange, Ntozake, 126
Shelley, Percy Bysshe, 192
"She Remembers the Future" (Harjo), 64–65
"Sibling Mysteries" (Rich), 197
Sidney, Sir Philip, 192
"Sight of the Horizon" (Brooks), 4
"Sign of Saturn, The" (Olds), 36